Where Is the Mango Princess?

WHERE IS THE MANGO PRINCESS?

Cathy Crimmins

 ALFRED A. KNOPF   NEW YORK   2000

This Is a Borzoi Book
Published by Alfred A. Knopf

Copyright © 2000 by Cathy Crimmins
All rights reserved under International and Pan-American Copyright Conventions. Published in the United States by Alfred A. Knopf,
a division of Random House, Inc., New York, and simultaneously
in Canada by Random House of Canada Limited, Toronto.
Distributed by Random House, Inc., New York.

www.aaknopf.com

Knopf, Borzoi Books, and the colophon are registered
trademarks of Random House, Inc.

Library of Congress Cataloging-in-Publication Data
Crimmins, C. E.
Where is the mango princess? / Cathy Crimmins. — 1st ed.
p.   cm.
ISBN 0-375-40491-0 — ISBN 0-375-70442-6 (pbk.)
1. Forman, Alan—Health. 2. Brain damage—Patients—United States—
Biography. 3. Forman, Alan—Marriage. 4. Crimmins, C. E.—Marriage.
5. Personality change—Case studies. I. Title.
RC387.5.F67 C75 2000
362.1'9617481044'092—dc21
[B]   00-020917

Manufactured in the United States of America
First Edition

For Alan—past, present, and future

Where Is the Mango Princess?

Prologue

Accidents divide things into the great Before and After.

"Even before his brain injury, Alan had a hard time remembering names," I'll say. "Since Daddy's accident, I have to work more," I tell our daughter, Kelly. The brain injury community marks time by asking how long someone has been "out of" injury, the same way bereavement counselors ask how long your loved one has been dead. Six months out, two years out, ten years out.

Out of what, exactly?

Out of the giant crevice that has been exploded into the bedrock of your life.

Here's how I see it: One day, you and your family are hiking across a long, solid plain, when out of the sky comes a blazing meteor that just happens to hit one family member on the head. The meteor creates a huge rift in the landscape, dragging the unlucky one down to the bottom of the crevice it has made. You spend the next year on a rescue mission, helping him climb to the top, but when he gets up there, you realize that he has been greatly changed by the hardship. He doesn't know a meteor has hit him. He will never know, really. He only knows that he has spent a lot of time in a dark, confusing place. He left a lot of stuff behind, the stuff he was carrying with him, down in that big hole, and it's impossible to get it all back.

How do you even get him out? Well, you and your family have to jump across the crevice first and then pull him up on the "other" side of your life. Or you have to stay on the side where you were, drag him out, and then all leap together to the other edge of the crater. It's not easy. The chasm between the old life and the new is wider than you think. You could fall into the darkness yourself, trying to jump across.

And the damned crevice is always there, the bad-luck meteor stuck down inside it. You turn your back on it and go on, across that wide plain of life, again. But along the way you have to tell the improbable story of the meteor. You have to describe the big hole in the ground and the little holes it left behind. You dream about the crevice. You dream about the time before the meteor came down without warning. And you can never again hear about anyone getting hit on the head without knowing it is the beginning of a new and bewildering journey.

"Look at what he did with that light," says my husband, Alan, studying a canvas at the Philadelphia Museum of Art. It's the last day of the boffo, much-publicized Cézanne exhibit. Supplied with free last-minute tickets from friends, we jump at the chance to get in under the wire, though we know the gallery will be packed. Stories about the city's Cézanne-crazed summer had reached us in airless hospital rooms, seeming more like reports from another planet than an event we could actually attend.

Alan has a long history of never going through an art exhibit just once. He circles it two or three times or more, returning to study individual paintings in detail. I've usually been cooling my heels in the gift shop for twenty minutes by the time he wanders in.

But today a weak, subdued version of Alan leans forward on a cane, gazing at Cézanne's brushstrokes as he listens to the canned narration clamped onto his head. He has no spare energy to walk around the exhibit more than once—he'll have to drink in each painting in one thirsty gulp.

Right now I don't care how long he spends in front of each painting. He can stay there all day, wearing his dorky headset and listening to the droning narrator a couple of times for each picture. I'll wait.

"He can still analyze art!" I think. A revelation, like the one only a few weeks before: "He can still read!"

The brain is an amazing organ. The three-pound blob keeps lots of great information up there, like the lyrics to the *Beverly Hillbillies* theme song, the sensation of your first kiss, and the digits of your childhood phone numbers. Put your brain through a windshield at seventy miles an hour or bash it with a sledgehammer, and then it's a crapshoot. You might remember something or you might not. You might not even recall who was in the room with you five minutes ago. You might not walk or talk again. You might never wake up from that coma. You might wake up and be nasty and aggressive. You might talk in jargon. You might *only* sing a sitcom theme song, over and over and over.

Alan's brain got run over by a speedboat.

That last sentence reads like a bad country-western song lyric, but it's true. It was a silly, horrible, stupid accident. Only months before touring the Cézanne paintings, Alan was lying in a coma in Kingston, Ontario. A Canadian government helicopter touched down on a highway near the remote lake where we were staying and rushed him to a teaching hospital. In the helicopter Alan began to have seizures and stopped breathing. By the time he was stabilized in the emergency room, doctors and nurses were telling me they didn't know what would happen to him.

"You just love me for my brain," says Alan, smiling in his new affability. I laugh every time he says it, sharp tears stinging the corners of my eyes. We used that phrase all the time when we were work-obsessed graduate students newly in love. Now Alan uses it ironically. His brain has been damaged and will never be the same. His rehabilitation counselor says that the "old" Alan died on July 1, 1996, and a new one arose, created by the rivers and lakes of bruises that coursed over his brain as he lay unconscious in the days after his injury. He is a man with different frontal lobes, and a different personality to match.

Several weeks after his accident, while still in an addled state at a rehabilitation hospital, Alan told a doctor that he felt reborn. "That's a common feeling among our brain injury patients," said Dr. Weinstein.

"I have a question, though," continued Al. "If I had to be reborn, how come I'm still forty-four years old?"

1

Traumatic brain injury (TBI), broadly defined as brain injury from externally inflicted trauma, may result in significant impairment of an individual's physical, cognitive, and psychosocial functioning. In the United States, an estimated 1.5 to 2 million people incur TBI each year, principally as a result of vehicular incidents, falls, acts of violence, and sports accidents. The number of people surviving TBI with impairment has increased significantly in recent years, which is attributed to faster and more effective emergency care, quicker and safer transportation to specialized treatment facilities, and advances in acute medical management.

—"Rehabilitation of Persons with Traumatic Brain Injury," National Institutes of Health Consensus Development Conference Statement

All life is context. We thought we had experienced crummy vacations before the disaster on the lake in Canada. You know that kind of generic Vacation from Hell—evacuation because of a hurricane, car troubles, domestic squabbles, sleazy accommodations.

But these are just minor disasters. They all pale beside the vacation we took in late June 1996 to a little island in the middle of a small lake. How did we end up there?

It was luck, of course. We had "won" this weeklong vacation at a secluded lakeside cabin at Kelly's school auction. We had never before won anything. The pictures showed a gorgeous site with lake views all around, a guest cabin for friends, a canoe, a swimming dock. The owner said the cabin had been featured in a recent woodworking magazine, and we immediately ran out to get the issue. We started buying supplies: flashlights, duffel bags, fishing rods, a backpack for the top of our car, and of course a cell phone so that our friends could reach us when they came to visit us at our fabulous country compound. I look back on those days with wonder—couldn't we see it coming? Wasn't it kind of crazy? Couldn't we feel disaster lurking?

There are definitely some mosquitoes in the ointment from the very beginning. For one thing, the people who donated the place to the school auction suddenly pop up to say that they would be happy to rent us their boat to get to the island, for *only* a thousand bucks for the week. A thousand bucks? If we had that kind of money, we wouldn't be so excited about winning a cheap vacation. Alan calls a local marina, and for about seven hundred dollars less they rent us a small boat with a motor. They'll "drop" us in, towing the boat on a trailer over to the small marina on the shore of Bob's Lake.

We love telling people we're going to "Bob's Lake." It sounds so rural, so Canadian. Al develops a routine, saying it is right next to "Fred's Lake," down the road from "Dick's Lake."

There are problems. Al and I fight bitterly while we're loading the car. By the time we are finished, I'm so exhausted I can't even imagine unpacking all of the stuff into a small boat at the other end. Then, when we get to the island, we discover that the owners never fixed the water filter, so we'll have to haul all of our drinking water in by boat and seventy-eight steps straight up a rock ledge to the cabin. To add insult to injury, they leave notes all around, offering to *sell* us the water already there for four bucks a bottle. We seethe and spend the first few nights dreaming up silly, nasty things to write in their cabin guest book.

Our friends Diane and Craig arrive first, with their daughter, Nikki, who is seven, like Kelly. They're both lawyers from Boston, though we were once all English graduate students together in Philadelphia. Craig called us a week ago to say we wouldn't need that much food—he intended to catch us fish every night. The fish, it turns out, don't like Craig, but the mosquitoes do. He doesn't catch a single bass. Whenever he goes outside, Craig has to wrap his entire body and face and run to his destination. He ends his stay with more than fifty insect bites.

Other friends arrive, overlapping their visit with Craig and Diane. Sarah, from Philadelphia, drives up with Honey, one of her oldest friends, and Honey's son, Benjamin, a six-year-old. Kelly knows Benjamin well because she has visited his family in Oneonta, New York, with Sarah.

It rains. Much too much. For about half of our stay, it pours. Whenever the weather breaks a little, we try to have fun. We swim and Al tries to teach the kids to fish. He spends most of his time untangling lines and rebaiting hooks. He just about gets Kelly's line unknotted when she once again casts into a sapling or snags the hook on a root at the bottom of the shallow shore. Then he has to start all over again.

Kelly's having a great time. She's discovered the exoticism of skinny-dipping. She, Benjamin, and Nikki "adopt" a dog from across the lake who swims all the way over to our dock. Encouraged by a movie she's seen about a lake monster, Kelly leaves Oreos on the dock every night for the Bob's Lake monster to eat, and every night Sarah goes down and picks up the cookies, feeding the fantasy. All the kids become accustomed to the designer outhouse at the end of a short path in the backyard. They collect rocks and sticks. They give talent shows.

One night the stars actually come out as we squat over an outdoor fire roasting hot dogs coated with Bisquick on sticks. The rural charms are wearing thin for me, though, especially the mosquitoes and the steps. It's like living in a tower: you must think carefully before you leave the cabin, because if you forget anything, you're doomed to trudge up the seventy-eight steps again.

One of the chief entertainments on the lake seems to be a postdinner spin in the speedboat. Just before dusk whole families from the island and from the mainland beaches promenade in their spiffy cabin cruisers and svelte motor-boats.

"Hey, let's go, too," says Sarah one night as we watch the parade of speedboats, and we pile into our little metal row-boat with the sewing machine motor. With eight of us aboard, our "speed" is reduced to about two miles per hour. Alan guns the motor outrageously, and we sing "Born to Be Wild" as we putt-putt around the lake.

One rainy evening, Alan and I become desperate for privacy. We're going fishing, we say, and we drive the little boat into the middle of the lake and just sit there in the pouring rain. It's cold and wet, but we linger. We pretty much agree that, all in all, we'd rather be in Paris.

"You know, it wouldn't be that bad if we were just alone here," says Al. "We could just read and swim and screw and eat. It's having to deal with amusing everyone else."

It would be nice, we say, if we could come back to a place like this lake someday, just the two of us, when our lives are less hectic and we can spend some time alone.

Craig and Diane left a few days ago, and now Sarah, Honey, and Benjamin are ready to take off. We're planning to leave for the Toronto area tomorrow ourselves, to visit clients of Alan's, so we've loaded our dirty laundry into the boat, as well as much of the garbage, which we have to take off the island to the mainland. I'm staying behind to relax.

I have a snapshot of the overloaded boat, which looks comical. Alan is singing the *Gilligan's Island* theme song as I snap it. He is surrounded by luggage. He and Honey are sitting in the back next to the outboard motor. In the middle are Sarah and Benjamin. At the last minute Kelly decides to go, so they wedge her into the bow of the boat with big bags of garbage and laundry on either side of her. She doesn't seem to mind the stench.

I wave as they leave the dock and head around the bend of the island. For a moment my freedom stuns me. What to do? I consider going back up the stairs, but I've pulled a muscle in my calf and it hurts.

I sit on the lawn chair down at the dock and begin reading a novel about the angst of Bennington students in the 1970s. I will never finish that book—I don't think I ever could, now, without thinking about the moment that changed our lives forever.

Ten minutes go by, and then I hear a boat coming toward our little dock. Oh great, I think, they're back. They forgot something. I dread the circus of seeing all our house-guests again. This is the first moment of peace I've had in six days. Then I hear Kelly's voice floating across the water, though there is still no sign of our little skiff coming around the bend. Instead, a midsized, pleasant-looking speedboat appears, with Kelly sitting in it. Well, they ran out of gas, or they ran aground. Al has probably sent her back with some folks to get help. I actually start chuckling at what helpless urbanites we are.

But then I see the look on Kelly's face, the white, strained look of fear. A man is steering the boat. A woman, sitting next to my daughter, calls out, "There's been a terrible accident. A man has a concussion."

"It's Daddy!" says Kelly, leaping from the boat to the dock. The man says he'll take me to the scene of the collision, but Kelly refuses to budge. "No! I'm not going back there!" The woman offers to stay with her. I feel that strange light-headedness that comes with sudden shock. What should I do? How can I leave my child with a stranger? But I have to get to Al, and these people seem kind. Kelly watches in a daze of fear as I jump aboard the boat.

When I get to the scene, the full impact of Kelly's bravery hits. I wonder how a seven-year-old was able to get into a stranger's boat and come fetch me all the way across the lake.

Her father lies splayed across the stern of our little metal skiff, strangely motionless except for an occasional rapid jerk of a leg or arm. The boat, twisted and crumpled on the outside like a piece of tinfoil, holds about four inches of water in the bottom. Al's head rests crookedly on the back of the motor—it looks as if he's fallen backward onto the outboard. Sarah sits next to him. "Don't move, Al, don't move, Al, don't move, Al," she says, singing the phrase like some crazed mantra. Al moans and twitches slightly. Honey and Benjamin are watching anxiously from another boat nearby.

"What's his name?" asks a woman in a bathing suit, a nurse who was on the speedboat that collided with ours. She's hopped into the crumpled boat and is now wedged behind Al.

"Now, Alan, stay still. We're getting help. The ambulance is coming." She puts her hands on either side of his head to keep him from moving. Sarah and I both notice that Al says, weakly, "Okay." It is a guttural, moaning "Okay" but definitely a word. Sarah continues to talk to him, and I do, too, feeling helpless, marooned in the strangers' speedboat hovering within a few feet of our battered metal skiff. I keep calling Alan's name across the space between the boats, telling him I am there. Six or seven other boats are idling in the water all around the scene; later I find out that everyone with a cellular phone aboard has called the police and the ambulance. Someone in a fairly large boat attaches a rope to the skiff and begins to tow it slowly to the tiny marina about a quarter of a mile away. The boat I'm in follows alongside, as do others. Our own boat is still filled with huge bags of laundry and garbage, so the whole scene looks like a modern Viking funeral procession.

The next thing I remember is a landing-at-Normandy feeling when the people around pitch in and literally pull our little boat ashore with Alan in it. By tugging hard, they get the skiff onto the silt beach, where the ambulance workers rush over and begin their ministrations. Out come the surgical collar and all the scary paraphernalia—the rigid body board, the straps—that mean he might or might not be paralyzed for life. I step aside, feeling ineffectual, as the ambulance workers swarm around Al's inert form. A teenager in a bikini approaches me: "I am so sorry. I hit your husband. I ran over your husband." I feel nothing. I don't even remember replying, in my fog of anxiety. It seems to take forever for them to get Al into one of the two ambulances.

The paramedics continue to work on Al. They've been in radio contact with a helicopter from Kingston General Hospital and know it won't arrive for another half hour. Sarah accepts a ride with another boatman who helps her pick up Kelly from our dock. Then Honey, Benjamin, Sarah, and Kelly are looked after by the second ambulance crew. (Honey is covered with abrasions from where the boat hit her on the back and rump; Sarah, Kelly, and Benjamin are "merely" traumatized.)

I walk over to our crumpled skiff and fish around in the dirty laundry bag in the bow, finding a loose black dress that I slip over my bathing suit. I'll end up wearing it for three days.

In the ambulance, a paramedic named Dave begins quizzing me. "I know this is a hard question," he says, "but is your husband one of those people who normally has very large pupils?"

Terror engulfs me. Dilated pupils are a bad sign, I know that. I remember my anxious father shining a flashlight into my eyes every time I bumped my head as a kid. I think for a second, and then I say what I want to hear: "Yes. Yes. I think his pupils are naturally big. I think they are."

"Hey, it's hard to tell, isn't it, eh?" Dave says kindly. "I mean, if someone asked me that about my wife, I sure wouldn't know. And, well, I hate to ask this, but is his stomach normally a little—bulgy?"

"Yes," I say, without hesitation. "He gained a little weight this winter."

"Oh, yeah. Didn't we all, eh?" says Dave.

Dave isn't fooling me. I think of brain death. I think of Al's organs giving way, gushing blood into his abdominal cavity.

We're about to set off. Al, strapped onto a stretcher, stopped moaning a while ago.

"Alan, how old are you?" Dave asks Alan. No answer. He puts his mouth right next to Al's ear: *"How old are you, Alan?"*

Pause. My age would be the last thing I could locate under stress, I think. I pretend to laugh and turn to Dave. "Maybe he doesn't want to tell you. Why not ask him the name of his daughter?"

"Kelllly," Al says faintly after Dave asks. Or at least he seems to say our daughter's name. Maybe it's just a gasp or a moan. By now his eyes are shut, and he is very, very still. But he seemed to say it. And he seems to squeeze my hand, a bit, when I squeeze his. Maybe. Or am I imagining it completely?

Right before they shut the ambulance doors, Sarah comes running up to the back and shoves a wad of Canadian bills into my hand. "We'll meet you," she says. I don't have any pockets, and after crumpling the paper money in my left hand for a while as I hold on to Al with my right, I stash it in the bottom of my soggy water shoe.

The ambulance makes its way up the dirt road to the main highway. Al, wet and cold to the touch, doesn't move. They've taken off his T-shirt. After what seems like a long while, we come out onto a paved road. Police are stopping scores of cars on each side, and I can hear a helicopter churning away overhead. Gee, Al would be so angry, getting stuck in a traffic jam in a rural vacation spot, I think. He would be yelling and ranting and raving. "What the hell is going on up there?" he'd be saying if he were in one of the cars. A New Yorker by birth, he takes traffic stoppages personally. This is finally his big chance to be the cause of a traffic jam, to ruin Canada Day for a lot of people just trying to get to lakeside barbecues, and he is . . . missing it.

The land ambulance crew waits for the copter to descend to the highway and then goes out to talk to the air paramedics. People from the few houses alongside the highway appear, drawn by the sound of the siren. An elderly woman walks up to where I stand at the rear of the ambulance. "He'll be fine, honey. They're going to Kingston? Oh, you'll like Kingston General. My nephew had an operation there. It's a good place."

On the way up we'd passed Kingston, a town off the highway more than an hour away by land.

Dave comes back with bad news: I can't go with Alan in the helicopter. They won't allow it. For a moment I'm too stunned to speak. I had never considered staying behind. Dave sees the tears in my eyes. "Why?" I finally ask, my voice cracking.

He turns around and goes back to the helicopter. In the meantime, Al begins twitching and making loud guttural noises. "Don't worry," I say, thinking he somehow senses that I will abandon him. I don't know that his agitation is only a precursor of what is to come.

"Okay," says Dave, returning to the back of the ambulance at a trot. "You can go. I convinced them that you won't be hysterical."

They unload Alan, and as his stretcher sits on the highway, someone takes off his Teva sandals. I am holding them, dangling from my fingertips, as the female air paramedic comes over with the ear protectors I'll need to wear while getting into the helicopter. Images from bad TV medical shows wash over me, the doctors and nurses ducking down and holding their ears as they rush around with stretchers. This isn't really happening, is it? As they're loading Al, Dave comes back and takes the sandals from me. "You don't need these," he says. He does it to be kind, but I find it overly chilling, as if he knows that Al will never be walking anywhere again.

The female paramedic looks at me as I climb aboard. "Something might happen," she says. "That's why we didn't want you to come."

"Yes, I know," I say, trying to sound calm, buckling my seat belt. Exactly what was that "something"? Alan might die, and, if he does, I want to be with him. How can you spend nineteen years with a man and not want to be there when he dies?

The "something" starts happening almost as soon as we are in the air. Al's agitation intensifies, and soon he begins having a grand mal seizure. Seizures are a common after-effect of brain injury. The neurons in the brain go into a frenzy as the swelling begins. Al's back arches. His legs go up and down. He makes terrible clenched sounds, like an animal growling. After about ninety seconds he stops breathing, and the crew "bags" him, sticking a tube down his throat and pushing the air in and out. Alan's arms move up and down from the elbow in a rigid motion as his body ripples with seizures. His knees jerk wildly up toward his waist. Buckled into the seat a few feet across from his stretcher, I can't even touch him. Out of the helicopter window I see a landscape dotted with incredibly blue lakes. Al would go crazy for the view. "Look at all the lakes down there," I think. "Beautiful. But my husband is dying."

My ambivalence scares me. Should I be hoping for life or for death? I begin to concentrate on sending good feelings to him. But then another thought overtakes me: "If it is better

to die, it's okay. We have loved you very much. Let go."
Alan's legs and arms continue to pump up and down, as if he
is trying to march uphill on his back. The animal noises have
given way to a frantic gasping sound at each breath of air the
paramedic pushes into his throat. I wonder what the seizures
are doing to his brain and feel glad that the paramedics will
at least keep oxygen flowing to it until we can get him to the
hospital. If he makes it to the hospital.

I look out the window again, down at where glaciers have
dimpled the landscape and left behind dozens of blue pockets of water, and I think of how one's life is supposed to flash
by while one is dying. Is that happening to Alan? Or maybe it
falls to me, the conscious one, to have the flashbacks. Scenes
from our life together go zipping through my mind: the years
in graduate school, the travels, the parties, the birth of our
daughter. Is this all ending now, in some Canadian government helicopter?

Suppose these are Al's final moments? I think about last
night. A huge blue moon hung over the lake—the second full
moon within the month—and at 3:30 a.m., Alan tried to
wake me up to tell me he was going canoeing in the moon-
light. "Come with me," he said.

I was tired, mumbling. Didn't want to go. Only just this
morning, at breakfast, he told us all about what a beautiful
experience he'd had, paddling through the moonlit water in
complete silence, with no motorboats around, and I felt stupid for not getting up to join him.

Why didn't I go with him in the canoe early this morning?
Why didn't I make love to him last night? Maybe it would
have been the last time.

We land on the pad outside the hospital, where joggers and
passersby gawk as the paramedics unload a still-twitching
Alan from the helicopter. I have no idea that the helicopter

pad is directly in the middle of the walking path around Lake Ontario. I only see that Alan's arrival is the main entertainment, and I am filled with a surprising groundswell of rage. Idiots! What are they looking at? Don't they have anything better to do? I don't want perky athletic couples watching my unconscious husband as his body writhes with seizures.

"The wife has to ride in the front," says a paramedic. I am escorted to the front seat of the ambulance waiting to take Al from the helicopter pad to the emergency room. As soon as we get to the hospital, Alan is whisked away while I am ushered into a private waiting room near the emergency area, another clue that his injury is very serious. All the other people, waiting with sprains and bruises and burns from their barbecues, watch as I squish by in my reef shoes.

Gee, I had no idea that such private waiting rooms existed. The place is about eight feet by eight feet, furnished with a nice little love seat and two chairs. The furniture is much less scuffed up than in the ordinary waiting areas. I stare at the nice print on the wall and the Bible on the table. If rooms could talk, this one would scream "Holy shit, your husband is going to die!"

Meanwhile, they work on Al in the emergency room. Every ten minutes or so I leave my little waiting cell to ask about him at the desk. No, I can't see him. No, they don't know what is happening.

Finally the female paramedic from the helicopter takes pity on me, asking the doctor if I can go in to see Alan for a minute.

About six people are working on him. I stand meekly over in the corner, stunned at how much less human he looks than even an hour before, with wires and tubes everywhere, a ventilator on his face, and a new, large neck brace surrounding his head, making it look tiny, like a child's.

Then I return to my special waiting cell and face the phone. I don't know why, but before I pick up the receiver I imagine it as a kind of "batphone" that will enable me to call anywhere in the world. "Hello, my husband is dying!" Surprisingly, it is just an ordinary phone with no long-distance capability. With no wallet, I dial for an outside line and dredge up my credit card calling number from deep inside my brain. The very action of recalling the digits seems to betray me. How, with my husband comatose, am I still able to dial numbers?

I call my mother, but she isn't home. I call her a few more times, each time getting her answering machine and each time saying nothing. Finally, I leave what I hope sounds like a neutral message, saying I am trying to reach her.

Next come Alan's parents and sister. Whenever we call Alan's parents during the day, we always preface it with "Don't worry! Nothing's the matter!" They're old-fashioned enough to get upset at the thought of full-price long-distance calling, something that should be reserved for life-and-death situations—exactly what we have on our hands now. I'm calling with very bad news, I'll say. Somehow, having to tell someone else about the accident will make it real.

Alan's father answers the phone. "Norman, you know how I always say nothing is wrong? Well, this time it is." It is bad, I tell him, very, very bad. I call Long Island and talk to Alan's sister, too, asking that she stay in touch with his parents. They ask me no questions. They are in shock.

I'm in a haze. There is paperwork to do, of course. I hesitate when I come to the space for religion, and then I check off "Jewish," even though Al hasn't been inside a synagogue for years. We have talked about death on occasion, and I think I remember him saying he would like a Jewish funeral. He's always identified himself culturally as a Jew—he calls me his *shiksa*—and perhaps his parents will feel comforted by the presence of a rabbi, whether Al lives or dies.

By now it is more than two hours after the accident, which happened at about two-thirty. The next hour or so is hazy. I am dazed. Now, since Alan's brain injury, I always think of things in terms of brain function. I was having trouble processing information and acting appropriately. I was just going through the motions.

At some point the emergency room doctor comes in to ask me more about Al's health history. All the answers I give make Al sound healthy. Very healthy. Doesn't smoke. Doesn't drink. Exercises. No history of high blood pressure or heart problems. Of course, there is the matter of a massive head injury. All the good health in the world can't help you if your brain is gone.

"Look, your husband may have many things wrong with him—broken bones, bruises. But our priority right now is *head*," says the doctor, a middle-aged, balding man who looks as if the holiday weekend is wearing him out. He gazes directly into my eyes and repeats his words slowly and loudly, as if we don't speak the same language: "Our priority is *head, head, head*."

Amazingly, the doctors believe that Alan's spinal cord has not been damaged. They have put him into a morphine-induced coma to minimize his movements and enable everyone to concentrate on his brain injury. He is also given mannitol, a diuretic that drains fluid from the cranial cavity to help keep the brain from swelling too much, and Dilantin, a drug often prescribed for epileptics, to prevent any further seizures. The ventilator I saw over his head in the emergency room is keeping his brain as oxygenated as possible. Plus, there is uncertainty about whether he'll be able to breathe on his own because of how his brain "forgot" to breathe during the seizure on the helicopter. Later, says the ER doctor, a neurosurgeon will see me about the prognosis.

Though I don't know it, Alan has already had the first of several CT scans, X rays of his skull that show the doctors just where his brain is swelling and bleeding.

At this point I also don't understand exactly how the blow to Alan's head happened. I tell the emergency doctors the wrong story because I didn't see the accident, only its aftermath. The people who were in the boat with Alan—Sarah, Honey, Kelly, and Benjamin—are still on their way, driving along the back roads of the lake country to get to Kingston. I thought from his position when I first saw him that Al had been thrown down, cracking his skull against the metal of the boat. Later, from Honey and Sarah, I learn that the other boat actually went up and over Alan's head, on the left side. The whole left side of his neck and face was scraped and his ear torn—another few fractions of an inch over, and he would have lost his ear.

"It was like a scene from some James Bond movie," says Honey. "That scene where the speedboat is bearing down on Bond, and you know it has been programmed to kill him? We saw this big boat headed right towards us, and we couldn't believe that it wasn't going to stop. They're supposed to pass us on the left, Al kept saying. Then he started panicking and tried to steer our little boat as far over towards the side as possible, but there were rocks all around."

Sarah and Honey stood up and waved their arms at the oncoming boat; Sarah even waved a bra from her dirty laundry bag.

When it became apparent that the speedboat was on a collision course, Honey threw herself across her son, Benjamin, to try to protect him. Turning her head, she saw the speedboat hitting Al and then felt it graze her back. We think Al might have stood up in one last attempt to wave it off or to jump overboard. All we know for sure is that he ended up on the side where Honey had been sitting. Was he thrown there? Or did he jump over to that side before being hit?

No one mentions the noise. I keep wondering about the *sound* of a speedboat hitting a human skull. After the accident, I dream of missed collisions: I am swimming or in a tube, floating down a whitewater river. Everywhere there are boats about to slam into me, and I wait, in terror, for the sound of my own bones cracking. It never comes. I escape all the possible accidents. I'm told this is a classic survivor's guilt dream.

Everyone winces when they hear that the speedboat actually smacked Al on the head as it crunched over our little skiff. When I tell the story, I know exactly where the wince will come. The reality of the accident is almost too much to bear, and the strangeness. People ask us if he was in the water, on water skis, or on a skibob. How can you be *in* a boat and get hit on the head by another boat? Bad timing and bad luck, as Al would later say. The story of his life, he sometimes thinks when he is feeling down. Later the neurosurgeon estimates that the impact of the boat hitting Al's head was equivalent to going through a car windshield at seventy miles per hour.

Doctors are pretty familiar with head injuries caused by car accidents. You won't find a neurosurgeon or neuropsychologist who would ever drive a car without first buckling his or her seat belt. Automobile accidents are the leading cause of traumatic brain injury in men under twenty-five. Most of the accidents are alcohol-related. Bicycling and in-line skating accidents can also cause massive head injuries, especially when the people involved are not wearing helmets. Yet falling off ladders is another major cause, and I'd never have thought of insisting that Al wear a helmet while changing a lightbulb or cleaning out the gutters on our house. I'd never consider making him wear a helmet while driving a dinky rowboat with an outboard motor, either, just as I'd never suggest a helmet to a relative visiting the Empire State Building, and yet one young man I heard about on the Internet suffered his traumatic brain injury—TBI—at the hands of a gun-toting terrorist who shot him in the head while he was showing the city to a friend. Now, after finding out how difficult it is to get treatment for a brain injury through most HMO insurance plans, I tell everyone I know to wear a helmet *everywhere*, just in case.

That first night, even though I know Alan might die, that he's in a coma, I still have no idea of what is happening inside his head. I don't know that the worst damage happens after impact, in the first few days postinjury, as the brain swells and smashes against the skull, shearing off neurons willy-nilly. Al is very far from being out of danger that first night. Yet I still think that once he is stabilized, he will wake up as in cartoons or the movies. Get bonked on the head, stay down for a while, and then pop up as stars dance around your head. Every time George of the Jungle hits a tree, he just gets up again and staggers for a moment. Then he's fine. Maybe there's a cute bout of amnesia.

I wait in the serene, private room and call people. Finally I reach my mother. She begged us not to go on this vacation, because she hates boats and water. Now I tell her that Al is in the hospital and might not make it. She doesn't say "I told you so." My mother was widowed at forty-four, so she is accustomed to sudden, swift downturns of fortune. In her usual, quiet, practical way, she begins laying plans for getting to Kingston as soon as possible.

Kingston General is a small, friendly hospital in a delightful harbor city filled with geraniums, tree-lined streets, nice restaurants, and picturesque red telephone booths. The hospital has a national reputation as a center of teaching excellence. Queens University is just around the corner. It's a wonderful combination: friendly, personal care and state-of-the-art medicine. From the start, nearly everyone is spookily kind and generous, not at all like in the big-city hospitals I am used to.

A nurse comes by and gives me an egg salad sandwich, a brownie, and a soda. Another mentions a special deal the Holiday Inn gives to people whose relatives are in the hospital.

I gather, from their kindness and suggestions, that we are in for a long siege. At some point Honey and Sarah show up with the kids. It has taken them hours to get there, packed like sardines in Sarah's car. They have left our car back at the marina, where Al was pulled to shore.

They are traumatized, and the kids in particular are tired and hungry. Sarah and Honey decide it would be best for them to go over and get a room at the Holiday Inn—where henceforth we will be known as the "boat people."

At last they find a space for Alan in the intensive care unit. I walk beside him and all his machines, once again feeling like part of a strange funeral procession. He sure doesn't look alive. The drugs have paralyzed him, and the ventilator makes his chest heave up and down, as if he were a monster put together by some two-bit Dr. Frankenstein.

Right before we leave for the ICU, a nurse gives me his "effects" in a plastic bag: his soggy wallet, his keys, and various scraps of paper bearing phone numbers that he had stuffed into the mesh pocket of his swim shorts. The keys dangle from a hokey key ring, a gift from an elderly client. It has his initials, ASF, in big brass letters on a leather medallion. I've always hated the key ring, and now, though I know it is irrational, I feel as if it is all that is left of Alan.

I picture him pulling it out of his overstuffed pocket, its jagged edges making yet another little puncture wound in his pocket lining. Suddenly the key ring becomes a beloved object.

"What did you want to know?" asks the neurosurgeon in a belligerent tone, standing at the door to the ICU cubicle. It is one in the morning, almost eleven hours since the accident, and he's tired. He has just finished a complicated spinal surgery. I know that because I've talked to the family of the man whose operation he was performing. The camaraderie of the intensive care unit has already started taking hold for me. Yet even though the nurses persist in telling me that he is unavailable, I insist that he be paged every hour or so. I don't want him to leave the building without telling me what is going on.

"I just want to know more about my husband's condition," I tell him. "What will happen next?"

The neurosurgeon never comes toward me. He's tall and craggy, with an annoyed, wooden expression on his face. You know the type: Dr. Asshole. Still, I think, maybe we have just gotten off on the wrong foot. I put out my hand and begin introducing myself. He backs away. I feel ridiculous, my hand extended to the air, still in the dirty dress over my bathing suit and reef shoes.

"Don't know what will happen," he says, looking at the floor. "Have to watch and wait."

"But he doesn't need surgery," I say. "That's good, at least, right?"

"Not really. If the pressure builds up in one part of your brain, we can go in and relieve it. But your husband's brain is damaged all over. The swelling is everywhere. The chart said he was talking right after the accident. That's a good sign."

He turns around and leaves.

No wonder people accuse doctors of acting God-like. I waited eight hours to hear what a specialist would say about Alan's condition, and my encounter with Dr. Asshole lasted less than two minutes. I won't be told anything more specific about Alan's brain injury until well into tomorrow, when another neurosurgeon will detail it for me. The first doctor simply swooped down from the great Neurosurgery in the Sky to tell me he had nothing to tell me.

Since neurosurgeons are a macho breed, inoperable brain injuries often frustrate them. They are in charge of tracking such injuries, yet there is little they can do but wait along with the family and check the CT scans to see how the bruising is developing.

So I begin to wait.

Www.waiting.com—that's a site that's now on the Internet for families in our predicament. I wish it had been there during the weeks when Alan was in an unconscious and semiconscious state. Coma is an anticlimax. You've gone through the drama of the accident, the rescue, and then—you wait. And wait. And wait.

In the meantime, though, I scare the cute young ICU nurse with my hostility toward the neurosurgeon. I let her know in no uncertain terms that he is an idiot and I don't want him coming near my husband. She doesn't know what to do. Some time during the incredibly long night the head ICU doctor takes me into a private room and chastises me for being so adamantly negative about Dr. Asshole. She doesn't understand, she says, why I have been plaguing the nurses, insisting that he be removed from Alan's case.

"He's one of the best neurosurgeons in Canada," she says.

"Yeah, but my husband doesn't need surgery, they're telling me, so what difference does it make? It's a closed head injury. This surgeon has *no* people skills. I need a doctor who can tell me what is going on." After that I swear a bit under my breath. I am very upset. I dredge up a phrase from an assertiveness training class I took in 1979, fixing the doctor with a stern look and saying, "Please understand, this neurosurgeon is *unacceptable* to me."

After my anger subsides, the ICU doctor begins to talk about severe brain injury. They gave Alan the Glasgow Coma Scale test as soon as he was admitted, rating his stimulus response, eye opening, motion, and awareness. The highest score, one that indicates normal consciousness and brain function, is a 15. At a score of 1 to 3, it is likely that the patient will remain in a vegetative or semivegetative state for life. Alan is a Glasgow Coma Scale 5, which means that he will probably wake up, but beyond that no one has any idea of what will happen.

After our talk, the ICU doctor seems relieved to find that I am not simply a crank but a crank with a cause. I need information. It is the only way I can survive this wait, and my appetite for it is voracious.

The nurse I scared, the one attending Al that first night, is in her twenties. She has a warm, bubbly personality and a rather false sense of optimism about his condition. "I think he knows what is going on," she says. "I think I saw him move his hand."

I've wondered, since then, if it was true. Maybe, before the worst brain swelling began, Al really was more responsive. I don't see it that first night, even though I stay by his side for hours. Occasionally I go out to the ICU waiting room and stretch out on the couch, but sleep never comes, just a series of panic attacks that will soon become a familiar part of my daily routine. Seeing Al seems to lessen the panic a bit, even if he does look like a strange wax figure. So I sit next to his bed and touch his chest and get through that first night by keeping up a long, rambling monologue about our life together.

My anger at the neurosurgeon and terror about Alan's predicament loosen my tongue, and the young nurse is kind enough to listen as the night stretches on toward morning. I tell her about our trip, the accident, Al's job, my writing. I talk about Kelly, and in the few silences she chimes in with stories about her son, a four-year-old. She is particularly upset that he has befriended a strange little boy in her neighborhood, one who has no sense of caution or safety.

"My husband said to me, I think that kid is brain-damaged! Or maybe he's just brain-dead!" She laughs.

She is busying herself with an IV line. She doesn't seem to have the slightest idea that such a comment might upset the wife of a man in a coma due to a severe brain injury. I fake a laugh. I must, because if she realizes what she has just said, the awkwardness between us will never dissipate. I like this young woman. She thinks my husband is doing well.

You never realize how many silly phrases are related to the brain until someone you love has been whacked in the head. About a week and a half after the accident, Al's supervisor from the bank calls Kingston General and asks if Al can come to the phone. I say he isn't well enough (in fact, he is still barely conscious and totally disoriented).

"Gee, that's too bad," says Murray, "because I wanted to pick his brain about something."

Whoa. Suddenly the phrase strikes me as absurd. "Hey, right now, that would be slim pickings!" I want to say.

In real life, if you can get through a bad night, things seem better in the morning. But the intensive care unit is not real life. Overnight, Alan's brain continues to swell and bleed. He starts to spike a fever. The nurse on the next twelve-hour shift is older and more experienced than the bubbly young thing of the night before. When Alan's second CT scan results show up on the chart in the afternoon, she grabs my arm and holds tight.

Her eastern Ontario brogue sounds almost Scottish: "Oh, Cathy—I'm so afraid you'll not be getting your Alan back. The scans are bad. So much bleeding. Oh, it's bad. He'll be much changed, eh? He might be mean and all nasty-like. He won't be the same man."

2

Level 1—No response. The patient appears to be in a very deep sleep or coma and does not respond to voices, sounds, light, or touch.

—Rancho Los Amigos Hospital Scale
of Cognitive Functioning

Coma, it turns out, is not the worst thing in the world. A person in a coma can be placed on a ventilator, which ensures that the damaged brain gets the oxygen it needs to keep from dying. The emergency room doctors had initially put Alan into a drug coma, they explained, because they wanted to be sure that his spinal cord had not been involved. Keeping Al's body motions to a minimum would help guard against disaster. They also want to regulate everything that goes into and out of his body. The first morning, they pump his stomach and push a feeding tube through his nose and down his esophagus. I panic when the nurses mention the feeding tube. I think vegetable. Does this mean he's approaching Karen Ann Quinlan status?

"Not at all," says one doctor when I ask if the feeding tube means that Al is veering toward brain death. "New findings show that the brain consumes enormous numbers of calories while it tries to repair itself. The brain takes those calories from wherever it can find them, even destroying muscle tone in the process. So we've found that feeding comatose patients from the very beginning aids in recovery."

"Why is he the only one naked?" asks my mom when she first arrives at the intensive care unit in Kingston. Alan, newly tanned from six days at the lake, lies on the bed like a Goya Christ, with only a small white towel covering his crotch. The doctors and nurses want to keep him cold. The colder the brain injury patient, the less chance of brain swelling. (Nowadays traumautic brain injury victims are even packed in ice to lower their body temperature, with great results.) The ICU has a towel-warming machine, but the only one who gets to use it is me. Every few hours one of the nurses wraps a warm towel around me in a comforting gesture.

"You *would* look good in a coma, you know," I tell my inert husband. "If I were in that coma, I would look all pale and sickly and my hair would be plastered to the pillow. But on you, the coma looks good!"

"Your husband is a handsome man," says Kathy, his second night shift nurse. Later, I will kid Alan about this: "Hey, you were picking up the broads, even in a coma!" Yet now that I have gotten used to seeing him in this strange otherworld of the ICU, I have to agree with the nurse. Alan looks unnaturally good. His weight is down (that special crash "coma diet"), his hair looks long and full, and the pillow hides his bald spot. His tan has stayed. He looks taller in bed. There's just the little problem of him being made into a total machine. The ventilator breathes for him; he is catheterized, and the feeding tube pumps in nutrients. An IV filled with a heavy diuretic courses into his vein, removing excess fluid from his cranial cavity.

"I don't understand it," says his mother when she arrives two days later. "He's usually so lively!"

I leave the room. "Your son is in a coma!" I want to tell her. "He is not going to be lively now!"

But I can understand her perplexity. Comas do seem magical, somehow. The comatose person is exempt from real life. There, but not there. The events taking place during that time will never be recovered. The comatose person is living a narrative that he will have to take on faith from other people, once he wakes up. Rip Van Winkle. Sleeping Beauty. Snow White.

As a writer, I'm accustomed to dealing with steep learning curves. It's not uncommon for me to know absolutely nothing about something one week and then produce an article or script about the subject a week later. But the topic of closed head injury is the steepest curve I've ever been thrown. I spend the first day just getting up to speed and learning all the jargon.

First of all, they're not really called "closed head injuries" anymore. Alan has TBI—traumatic brain injury—and assuming he lives and doesn't succumb to the pneumonia or staph infection that plagues nearly everyone after such an accident, he will henceforth be known as a TBI survivor or, in more politically correct terms, a person with TBI. He's stayed alive in part because there has been no damage to his brain stem, the section in the back of the head on the top of the spinal cord that regulates breathing, heartbeat, and other involuntary functions necessary for life.

At this point Alan responds to pain stimuli. Every hour a nurse comes by to prod Alan's feet and hands with sharp little steel rods. I rejoice as he instinctively draws back his appendages and grimaces in his deep sleep.

Alan has extensive damage in the frontal lobes of his brain. The official diagnosis is DAI—diffuse axonal injury— with subdural hematomas all over his frontal lobes. What does this mean?

His brain is very messed up.

The axons are the connecting parts of the neurons that send the messages that let us think, talk, and walk. The neurons and the axons are the brain's "fiber-optic" system, through which information passes. Diffuse axonal injury means that axons all over Al's head have been jangled, perhaps sheared off. He has pools of blood and swollen tissue all over his brain, but particularly in his frontal lobes, the area of the brain that governs speech, memory, movement, and personality. The frontal lobes are the part of the brain, essentially, that makes us who we are. The dura mater is the hard, skinlike covering right beneath the skull; a subdural hematoma is a bruise beneath the covering that has nowhere to go as it bangs up against the skull. Brain cells drown in the blood and fall apart as the swelling continues, increasing the pressure inside the skull—the intracranial pressure, or ICP.

Sometimes a TBI patient develops particular problem spots where the intracranial pressure becomes so high that a surgeon must drill a hole in the skull to relieve it rather than risk total brain death or stroke. As Dr. Asshole has already pointed out, this is not the case for Alan. His injury is global; his head was walloped so hard that the brain just bounced back and forth against his skull. If you have ever heard of "shaken baby" syndrome, this is similar to what Alan has, I am told.

I learn a lot of this information from booklets around the hospital and from constantly asking about Alan's condition. Thanks to my whining, we already have a new neurosurgeon, Peter Ellis, who patiently answers all my questions.

Also, while I am waiting around endlessly in the ICU, I call many friends in Philadelphia and start a chain of information-gathering. Soon I get several messages all saying the same thing: "Call Dr. Andy."

Of course. How could I have forgotten Dr. Andy? A good friend during our student days, he and his girlfriend, Dr. Gwen, lived in a communal house in West Philadelphia, the site of many fun parties when we were graduate students at the University of Pennsylvania. Andy plays the bass; his jazz band performed at our wedding. He has never lost that mellow, stoned-out demeanor of the jazz musician. But he also happens to be a well-known neuropsychologist at Dartmouth now, specializing in brain injury. He and Dr. Gwen are still together; she runs a rehab hospital across the border in Vermont. It gives me great pleasure to think that a connection made in our dissipated grad school years will help me get the information I need.

Even though Dr. Andy has seen hundreds of TBI patients, he is surprised that Alan has become one. He tries hard to keep his voice steady over the phone line, but occasionally he pauses for a little too long. "Oh, man. Oh, geez. I am so sorry." Then he tries to be cheerful: "Well, hey, I just keep thinking of Mr. Al stoned, asleep on the couch in our place on Forty-ninth Street fifteen years ago! Is that what he looks like now?" Andy is the first person who tells me about the long process of awakening from a brain injury coma. The next day, an overnight package arrives at the ICU waiting room from Dr. Gwen—a guide from her hospital called *Understanding Brain Injury: Acute Hospitalization.*

Two other families of TBI patients in comas are waiting at the ICU, and we learn from each other, gradually, as we lose our inhibitions. One, a family of cattle farmers, discovered that their nineteen-year-old daughter had fallen off a ladder in their barn and had been unconscious for who knows how long before they found her. She's in a coma, too. The other TBI patient, an older man who was doing some work on his house, also fell off a ladder. He has awakened and will soon be moved to another area of the hospital.

The time seems to drag, and yet it seems to go quickly. Mostly, it seems that time does not exist anymore, nor does the world outside the filtered, eerily lit environment of the ICU. I continue studying the jargon. There is, for instance, the whole concept of "outcome." The doctors explain that no one can really predict the outcome of any brain injury. That is part of the stress for the families.

I leaf through Dr. Gwen's book and learn the physical symptoms of severe brain injury: intense headaches, seizures, a decrease in muscular strength and coordination, paralysis, and difficulties with vision, speech, hearing, smell, and taste. As for cognitive and behavior disorders, it seems that TBI "sequelae" (another jargon favorite) can include deficits in short- and long-term memory; slow thinking; short attention span; difficulties in reading, writing, and speaking; inability to comprehend or process information; problems with planning, organizing, and judgment; mood swings; depression; confusion; irritability; and restlessness.

Whew. I think I want Alan to stay asleep. Yet, of course, I can't wait for that moment when I will find out if he still exists. In a way, the situation reminds me of how I felt when Kelly was born. I would read ahead in the baby book and try to imagine our little blob of a baby doing all those things they said she would do—roll over, sit up, walk, talk—yet I couldn't imagine the reality of it, any more than I can now imagine the future behavior of a brain-injured Alan as I read ahead in the literature. The only Alan I can picture now, as I sit next to his inert form and rub his chest between the electrodes, is the Alan of a few days ago, who would wake up and say "Ouch! What the hell happened?" An Alan who might suffer from any of these other scary symptoms seems inconceivable.

What I want back is the "premorbid" Alan—my favorite jargon phrase, a scary-sounding word that really just means what the person was like before the brain injury. In the future I will spend hours describing Alan's premorbid behaviors and traits to doctors and therapists.

On the phone to concerned friends I affect a certain bravado: "Well, if he doesn't wake up, we'll just put him on the couch and pretend he's watching ESPN." One of the nurses, trying to be kind, tells me that Alan will probably never practice law again. This is a fork in the road of our lives, she says. These things happen. I turn it into a joke, almost a routine, during long-distance calls. I hear myself hiss the lines too forcefully into the receiver: "Hell, who cares if he can practice law? He hates the law anyway!"

Dr. Andy, who calls every day, tries to clue me in, and so do the nurses, but I have to find out firsthand that rebirth after brain injury is slow. Messy. Not like in the movies. The coma patient does not suddenly open his eyes and begin bantering with his family, as did the handsome love object Peter Gallagher in *While You Were Sleeping* or the reborn lawyer played by Harrison Ford in *Regarding Henry*.

It has been three days, and Al shows no signs of waking up.

"Coming out of a coma is like wading out of very deep water," says Maureen, a fiftyish ICU nurse with a sensible cropped hairdo and a faraway gaze in her eyes. "First we see the tip of your head, and then your other features, and then you come slowly, slowly out with great difficulty. The water is heavy. It is hard to get out."

Maureen is very wise, very spiritual. She tells me to pay attention to Kelly because I really can't do anything for Alan now. Rationally, I know she's right, but I feel obsessed with Alan's blank presence. I sit by him. I stroke him constantly and whisper into his ear.

I start going back to the hotel late each night to crash in the crowded room with Honey, Sarah, Benjamin, and Kelly. But I don't sleep. I slip out of bed and go downstairs to the lobby, where I call the nurses' station at four in the morning from a pay phone. It is stupid. There is nothing else the nurses can tell me about Al's condition.

But soon there are new problems. Although Al is still in a coma, he has begun to thrash around in fits that raise his blood pressure by tens of points. One afternoon I see the high number go over 300. He has developed mysterious scorching fevers the doctors don't seem able to control, even with antibiotics. The fevers reach their highest at certain parts of the day: the late afternoon and the very early morning. They report them dutifully to me, though since the temperatures are recorded in Celsius, they never seem as serious to me as they should. (A fever of 39 degrees?) In spite of the feeding tube, Alan is getting thinner every day.

Kathy, the intuitive nurse who worries so much, tells me that she wonders if Alan is concerned about the others in the boat and is, in some way, reliving the physical turmoil of it during his fits. In the midst of one of his agitations, she sits with him and says, "You are in a hospital. Everyone survived. Your daughter is all right. No one else got hurt." She claims it calms him down.

I'm not sure that Al's agitation isn't just a physical stage of coma. It seems to match pretty much the description of Rancho Los Amigos' Level 2: "Generalized response. The patient moves around, but movement does not seem to have a purpose or consistency." Alan is moving a lot now, so much that they don't need to put elastic stockings on him, say the nurses—there is no fear that he will develop blood clots. "Is he always like this, squirming all around?" asks Kathy, pushing him to the middle of the bed.

I'd like to believe that Alan is hearing everything in his comatose state, but I wonder. I dabble in the idea, neurotically worrying that if I don't stimulate him properly, he will not have the best recovery possible. I talk to him a lot, although sometimes I feel stupid. The nurses provide a radio/tape deck and I play music, hoping it will soothe whatever is hurting him. One night, as I am about to go back to the hotel, a nurse asks what kind of music Alan likes. Classical, rock, jazz, I tell her. The next morning when I arrive, the radio is tuned to a hokey country music station. I pass the time imagining that Al will wake up with a powerful craving to buy a pickup truck with a gun rack.

Late one night I sing "Chapel of Love" to Al as an oldies station plays in the background. We've always sung it together, and I find that I miss his harmony. "Last night I sang a song that Daddy and I sang together at our wedding," I tell Kelly the next morning.

"Daddy sat up and sang?" She claps her hands. I hate telling her she is wrong, explaining once again that we don't know when Daddy will wake up.

Kelly is starting to fall apart. Or rather, she is starting to come together in a strange, upsetting way. The day after the accident, she threw herself at me on the Holiday Inn queen-size bed and started crying. As I held her tight, we rolled back and forth as she asked why I had left her alone and gone with Daddy after the accident. Why, why, she sobbed, did her daddy have to get hit by a boat? Her clinginess and emotional turmoil seemed natural. The first time she visited the ICU, she went up to every nurse she saw and hysterically informed them that she had broken her arm in the accident and needed an X ray. This, too, seemed like normal kid behavior.

Now it is the fourth day of her father's coma, and I overhear her calmly talking on the phone about *CT scans* to one of my friends. She asks if she can get on the line with her uncle in California and then tells him, "They're changing Daddy's feeding tube."

"Your little girl is amazing," says Maureen. "I asked her, 'Do you want to talk about what has happened to your father?' and she said, 'Not really. I'm not ready to talk about that.'" Maureen sees it as a sign of composure. I see it as a warning flag. Kelly is not as mature as she seems, and an ICU is a terribly depressing place for a seven-year-old.

Benjamin, Honey's son, is a year younger than Kelly and has the same coloring, so many people around the hospital automatically assume that I have two children. The social worker counsels both kids in a session, talking about how we don't know why accidents happen. Benjamin goes in to see Alan a few times and always comes out nearly in tears. Just a few days ago, Al helped Benjamin bait his fishing rod. "He's my best friend!" Benjamin tells the other families in the ICU waiting room.

Honey and Sarah are great. They keep Kelly and Benjamin amused with shopping trips around Kingston and swimming sessions in the hotel pool while I loiter obsessively in the ICU, waiting to snag the doctors on their rounds. My mother and Alan's parents arrive, and one day they watch the kids while Honey and Sarah make the trip back to Bob's Lake to be interviewed by the police and pick up our car and possessions. They make their statements about the accident, and then the officers take them in a special police boat back to the cabin, where they scramble around and quickly throw whatever they think is ours into bags and suitcases. I can't imagine how going back to the lake and cabin affects them. Sarah marvels at how well I am functioning and tells me she feels upset, off kilter all the time. She and Honey are surprised, too, at how little curiosity I have about the details of the accident. I am focused completely on Alan.

"It must be the difference," Sarah says. "Honey and I are still processing the accident, being there, and you're one step ahead, having it just presented to you." By this time, Honey's bruises from where the boat collided with her body are ripe, purple and brown and yellowish, covering an area of about two feet extending along her back and buttocks. She shows them to me in the hotel room, and I gasp. The swollen marks make her look as if she had been tortured and beaten by a particularly brutal prison guard. Somehow they seem an external link to what I imagine is happening inside Alan's skull.

. . .

I don't realize how accustomed I've grown to hospital life. When my mother and Al's parents first see him, the expressions on their faces jolt me back to reality. His immobility and all the tubes and the ventilator and the monitors beeping frighten them. Alan's father is too upset even to approach Al's bed. He hovers in the doorway of the ICU cubicle for only a few minutes at a time and then goes out to the waiting room. Later he roams all over town on foot, unable to bear the sight of his son so incapacitated.

By now the ICU waiting room has become home to me, and I know everyone's stories. The family with the brain-injured teenage daughter are having a terrible time of it—their daughter has had two emergency surgeries to relieve the pressure in her brain. I see her being wheeled off to one of them, her head shaved and bandaged. One night I glimpse the father, a shy farmer not given to many words, comforting a sobbing teenager in the hallway. It is his daughter's best friend, he tells me later: "It's hard on the young kids, I think. We tried to prepare her. She knew Janie had the accident, but she didn't know she would look like that."

"How's it going then, Cathy, eh?" a pudgy thirtysomething man yells to me in the hospital cafeteria. "Did he wake up yet?" He is the brother-in-law of a gravely ill man in the ICU.

I tell him no, Al is still asleep.

"The goddamned kids! They drive those boats crazy on the lakes," he says. "And look at what happened to your hubby. They've got to stop this." I find out from him that the boating accident was mentioned on the radio and television. I make a mental note to look for it in old newspapers around the waiting room, but I never do. Al was the first person to be airlifted from the highway to Kingston General in this new type of helicopter ambulance service sponsored by the Canadian government. That's something for our scrapbook!

In the ICU waiting room, there is a big message board with paper and pens and thumbtacks. Everyone is so nice— they pretend not to mind that every other call is for me. It becomes a joke, though. The phone will just begin to "tingle," as they say in Ontario, and if I am there they will say, "Cathy, it's for you!" Everyone makes tea, real British-style tea that tastes delicious. I put sugar into mine for the first time in quite a while. I don't think I've ever drunk so much tea in my life. One night I start to doze on the couch and an elderly man puts an afghan over me. You couldn't ask for a kinder place than eastern Ontario to be in the midst of a crisis.

Each night the Holiday Inn clerk asks about Alan and gives me the many messages that have come in.

On the third day, Dave, the paramedic who worked on Alan at the scene of the accident, shows up. At first I don't recognize him out of his uniform. It is awkward between us; he knows about the seizures and that Alan hasn't awoken from his coma.

"Kind of a hairy time, eh?" he says, standing in the doorway of the waiting room. He explains that his wife is having some trouble with her pregnancy and he had to drive her to Kingston for an appointment with a specialist, so he thought he'd drop by. I realize with a start that I am still wearing the dirty dress I threw over my bathing suit the day we were taken away by ambulance. Sarah and Honey haven't yet gone back to the cabin to get my clothes, so I am sporting borrowed underwear, the dirty dress, and my reef shoes, still slightly soggy.

"Listen, do you need any money?" Dave asks. "Because I could lend you some if you need it." I stammer no, thanks, and he thinks I am embarrassed. In fact, I am deeply touched and afraid I will start crying. I have a real problem that way: once I start crying, I find it hard to stop. "Well, okay," says Dave. "We'll send you those sandals. We will. And his T-shirt."

I talk with Sarah, and we decide that Kelly should go home with her. She and Honey will drive with the kids to Honey's house in Oneonta, where they will spend the weekend. Then Sarah and Kelly will drive on to Philadelphia. Kelly is supposed to start Girl Scout day camp the next week, so she can live with Sarah and her sister, Joanne, and be picked up by a camp bus near their house. We are planning for the long term, because we have no idea how many weeks or months Al will be in a coma.

I feel relieved and fortunate. Sarah and Joanne Babaian have been caring for Kelly since she was nine months old. They adore children and are wonderful with them, probably because they are a little like kids themselves. Their house, in a leafy suburb of Philadelphia, is filled with dolls and games. Kelly has always called them her "sisters." Thanks to Sarah and Joanne, she knows all about shopping malls. She has taken two trips to Disney World with them. When younger women ask me how I can have a child and still work as much as I do, I always tell them: If you want to be a mom, make sure you have lots of single, childless friends to help out! I think about how nice it is that Kelly will be someplace safe and familiar. A few years before the accident, when Alan drafted our wills, we designated Sarah and Joanne as Kelly's guardians should we die together, thinking it would be an easy transition for Kelly to live with them. She even has little friends in the neighborhood; they go trick-or-treating together. Now it all seems comforting and yet somehow . . . spooky, as if our posthumous arrangements are being carried out even though neither of us has actually died. Sarah will be taking Kelly over the border back to the United

States, so I write and sign a statement that gives her the status of temporary guardian.

Kelly has been told that when her father comes out of his coma he may need to learn to read again, and since she has been learning to read this past year, she thinks she will be the perfect teacher. She imagines making up flash cards with words on them. On the morning she leaves, Kelly gives Al a little stuffed moose dressed in a Canadian Mountie's uniform and a lucky American penny that we tape to the metal railing of his hospital bed. We tuck the moose under his bare armpit, which makes him look quite ridiculous. Someone gives Kelly and Benjamin brightly colored helium balloons, but Honey and Sarah say they cannot possibly fit balloons into the overpacked car. Kelly starts getting tearful, and I get an idea: "Let's release the balloon into the air and wish really hard that Daddy wakes up," I tell her. This catches her fancy, and we go outside and stand on the hospital lawn. We close our eyes and concentrate, and then she lets go of the string. It's a clear, sunny, breezy day and we squint as we watch the balloon go up and up. Then it suddenly takes a sharp turn and heads out over Lake Ontario, where it disappears.

We go inside the hospital to fetch Honey and Sarah and tell them we have made a special balloon wish for Alan.

"Gosh, that's supposed to be bad for the fish if it lands in the lake and they swallow the balloon," says Honey.

"Fuck the fish," I say. I imagine the good-luck balloon soaring ever upward.

3

Level 3—Localized response. Patients begin to move their eyes and look at specific people and objects. They turn their heads in the direction of loud voices or noise. Patients at Level 3 may follow a simple command, such as "Squeeze my hand."

—Rancho Los Amigos Hospital Scale
of Cognitive Functioning

Dr. Peter Ellis, the neurosurgeon, meets with me and Alan's parents. The best news he can give us is that Alan will definitely wake up. He doesn't know when that will be, and he doesn't know how he will progress afterward.

"You'll know better than we do when your husband is about to wake up," says Dr. Wood, the attending internist. He stops by frequently to tell me to take care of myself and gather my strength for the next phase: "You will know, and, believe me, it will be amazing."

It *is* amazing. It happens late on the fifth morning after the accident, only a day after Sarah and Honey leave with the kids. I am sitting at Alan's bedside, yammering away as usual. His head is turned toward me on the pillow, so I don't feel quite as silly talking to him. In the last day or so I have been experimenting with asking direct questions.

I am telling him how much we all love him, about how I

already miss Kelly and how much she wants him to wake up. "Alan," I say, "can you hear me? Can you?"

His eyelids flutter, taking me by such surprise that I almost scream. The lids raise halfway and there, again, for about twenty seconds, are his beautiful hazel eyes. He looks right at me. I can't manage anything but a gasp.

"Mwah," he says through the ventilator.

His lids fall shut quickly, like the peepers on a plastic baby doll. The effort has been enormous, and I won't see his eyes again for another twenty-four hours. But he is in there, I think. He looked right at me, I tell everyone after rushing for the phone. I am crying. He knew me. He knew what I was saying!

At least I think he did.

Once Alan shows signs of awakening, the hospital staff begins to reduce his morphine, and they "wean him" from the ventilator. His face looks empty, beautiful without the vent. They still give him extra oxgen through a small tube in his nose.

About a day after I first see his eyes, he awakens briefly, to find all of us—his mother and father, his sister and brother-in-law, my mother—standing around him. He says each of our names, haltingly, slurringly, as if he has big wads of cotton in his mouth. The only one he has trouble with is "Marcia," his sister's name. He calls her what sounds like "Mary."

Marcia has brought along a symbolic gift, a figurine of Glinda the Good Witch from the movie *The Wizard of Oz*. Last year she gave birth prematurely to her third child, Jaclyn, who weighed only one pound, thirteen ounces. Not knowing what to do, we sent her Glinda, with a note that read:

Dear Jaclyn,
Welcome to the world! Click your heels together three times and you will get home!

Plastic Glinda, pink and perpetually smiling, sat next to Jaclyn's isolette for her entire stay in the neonatal nursery, until Jaclyn did come home, small but intact, at about the time she was supposed to have been born, three months later. Like most preemies, Jaclyn endured many near-fatal crises along the way, so naturally Marcia believes fervently that Glinda is a good-luck charm that will work for Alan's recovery, too. As we put plastic Glinda next to Al's bed, I think of that scene at the end of *The Wizard of Oz* where Dorothy wakes up in her dingy little bedroom with a white bandage on her head. She is amazed that all the people in her "dream" are sitting around her: the Wizard, the Scarecrow, the Cowardly Lion, and the Tin Man in their Kansas incarnations. In those first times when Alan is conscious for but a few moments, he seems to have the same reaction. He'll see my mother and grunt, "Bette! Huh!" and knit his brow. "Moooom," he slurs, squinting at his mother in disbelief. All the people who are close to him in his life are gathered around, and he can't quite figure out why.

"I love you," I say when Alan "comes to" every few hours. He gazes at me blankly. Then one afternoon he says, "I wub youuuu," his first full sentence. During two semiconscious days, he mostly grunts, and when he does speak, he has the limited vocabulary of a toddler: "Who dat?" "What?" and "Huh!" One day he says, over and over again, "Okaaay. Byebye," and the fingers on his left hand go up slightly, in a minimalist wave. We are lucky he can speak at all. Some people must learn all over again. I stop wondering why the paramedics and the emergency doctor all asked if he was right- or left-handed. Being left-handed, it turns out, was a lucky stroke in an unlucky situation. Al was clobbered on the left side of his head, the side of the brain that in a right-handed person contains the speech centers. But since Alan writes and bats and eats with his left hand, his speech centers are scattered around his brain, rather than concentrated on one side. We must watch and wait to see how much of his vocabulary comes back on its own.

The agitation is worsening. Alan flails and grunts as his blood pressure soars, making the monitors behind him beep. Other times they beep because he has managed to pull out all of his IVs. Once he even pulls his feeding tube out through his nose, driving the nurse crazy.

"Mr. Forman, you should not pull out those tubes. You need them. You are in a hospital. You are very sick. You need the tubes."

"Uhh. Okay." The nurse leaves, and Alan immediately starts tearing at his intravenous lines. He thrashes and screams. I try to hold him down, to calm him, but he rolls his head back and forth frantically.

One night, as Alan thrashes, I sing him my "Kelly repertoire" of lullabies. He immediately quiets down, and when I get to "Kumbayah," a song he's always detested, he sings along on the verse, slurring it. "Kwumbaaaaayaaaah," he croaks, his throat still sore from the removal of his oxygen tube.

Alan becomes a well-trained semicomatose patient. Sometimes I think I am torturing him, making him perform for me and the nurses and the family.

I never lose interest in seeing how much he can respond. "Squeeze my hand," I say. "Blink your eyes." "Raise your foot."

But he can't do everything. When the doctors ask him to raise his right foot, he picks up his left. When they command him to lift his right arm, he puts up his left. The right side of his body no longer matters to him. It has been erased.

"The motor strip for the right side has been damaged," explains Dr. Ellis. (Unlike Dr. Asshole, he is a wonderful, sensitive man who rubs Alan's legs or puts his hand on his shoulder as he is talking to him.)

On the CT scan of Alan's brain, says Dr. Ellis, he can see a large hematoma, or bruise, splayed over the area that controls motion for the right side of his body. A nurse says they had a young woman with a similar injury pass through the ICU only a little more than a year ago. She has learned to walk again but still drags her right foot. Of course, she was only nineteen when she got hit on the head. They don't know if Alan, at forty-four, will ever walk again.

"Where is the Mango Princess?"

Alan has been out of coma for two and a half days, and his speech is gradually sounding less fuzzy. But I don't understand what he is trying to ask, and no one else is around.

"Where is the Mango Princess?" he repeats. I give it a try. "Your nurse?"

"No. The Mango Princess."

He makes me nervous, staring with liquidy eyes that roll back into his head slightly.

"Do you mean Kelly, our daughter? Alan, she's back in Philadelphia." I think, for a desperate second, that he is asking for "My little princess," but I am just grasping at straws. Besides, Al would never use a pukey phrase like "my little princess" to describe our kid, who in less politically correct times would qualify as a tomboy.

"*No.* Mango Princess. Where is the Mango Princess? Where is the Mango Princess?"

Disappointed, he keeps repeating the question, more imploringly each time, as the warning sounds of the blood pressure beepers screech behind him.

When I address him now, I tend to speak too loudly: *"Who is she, Al? Who is the Mango Princess?"*

His eyelids flutter. "I spoke with her earlier today," he says softly, drifting back to sleep.

Where does he go when he passes from frenzy into stupor so suddenly? Where was he during the coma? Is this his longest dream or a nightmare? Perhaps the Mango Princess is there, in that other place.

4

Level 4—Confused and agitated. The patient is very confused and agitated about where he is and what is happening in the surroundings. At the slightest provocation, the patient may become very restless, aggressive, or verbally abusive. The patient may enter into incoherent conversation.

—Rancho Los Amigos Hospital Scale
of Cognitive Functioning

I peel the tape off the lucky penny on Alan's metal bed rail and put Glinda and the stuffed toy moose into a box with the Ella Fitzgerald and Louis Armstrong tapes. They're moving Alan to the eighth floor, to the neurological intensive care unit, a definite step up. Dr. Ellis says he will probably not need a ventilator again, but his other vital signs must still be monitored. The feeding tube has been pulled out. Soon they will bring him some pureed food and we'll see if he can regain his swallowing reflex.

This next step begins to worry me after a nurse mentions that many brain-injured people can never swallow food again, and most at least not for weeks or months. I don't know why this side effect seems so startling. We had a cat, Edie, who got hit by a car and was in intensive care at the University of Pennsylvania's veterinary hospital for weeks, all trussed up with IVs and racking up astronomical bills. After a while the people from the vet school called and said that they could either put her to sleep or release her to me, since she wouldn't eat and they couldn't keep her alive artificially forever. Now, Edie was a stupid, annoying cat even before her head bounced off a fender, but I couldn't let her die without giving it a try. So I brought her home, still hooked up to saline solution, and sat with her several times a day, pushing her nose into the smelliest tuna-flavored cat food I could find. Edie was too weak to get away but would look crookedly at me each time I sat down, as if to say, "Please! Not the squooshy stuff up my nostrils again!" By the third day I was beginning to think it was hopeless. I could see her pelvis and ribs starting to show through her fur. Then, just as I was about to take her to our vet for her trip to Kitty Heaven, Edie got up, wobbled over to the bowl, and took a small bite of food.

It is easier with Al, although the moment he first takes semi-solid food is one of great awkwardness for me.

I am not Florence Nightingale. In fact, once when I was on deadline for a project and Al was home with a bad flu, he started calling me Florence Kevorkian, a name that has stuck in our household. I worry that I will not be as good at dealing with Al's disabilities as I was with a stupid cat's.

At this point Alan's left arm is not paralyzed but very weak. He's already been raising it, though with some difficulty. His right arm, immobile, is curled in a spastic way, his fingers pointing to his armpit. Very Joe Cocker. The first time the orderly sets down the tray with the little plastic cups of brightly colored purees, I realize with a start that I'm going to have to feed Al. He can perform erratic actions, such as grabbing at his IV tubes, but nothing as purposeful as holding a spoon. I can't just say "Okay, mister, chow down!" What makes it worse is that his mother and my mother are both there. I feel as if this is a test of my feminine skills.

"Open up," I say, placing a spoonful of baby pink stuff that looks like gelatinized Kaopectate right at his lips. He obeys but makes no move to suck the glop from the spoon. I have to thrust it toward the back of his mouth, way beyond his tongue, sort of the way I give the cats their pills. He looks stunned for a moment but feels something tickling the back of his throat. He swallows. He is so thin I can see his Adam's apple bob as I hear the exaggerated gulping noise.

My mother and mother-in-law beam. As I scoop out another small spoonful of glop, the Bigger Picture hits me: I am spoon-feeding my husband.

For once I am glad to see a doctor swooping down like a god. Dr. Ellis arrives, a deus ex machina with a sense of humor: "How are we doing today, Alan? Looks like a meal from *The Jetsons,* doesn't it?" Al, wide-eyed, grunts a little, pink goop oozing from the corners of his mouth.

Alan's first nurse in the neuro ICU stops me in the hallway as I am going out to the bathroom.

"Your husband is so cute!" she says. "Last night, every time the monitor bell rang, he said, 'Hello, this is Alan Forman. How may I help you?'"

I smile, but my heart sinks. Yesterday, when asked if he knew where he was, Al said, "The swim club."

"Who's in charge?" Alan says over and over again, like a demented version of Abbott and Costello.

"I'm in charge," I say.

"So when are we going to have the meeting?"

"What meeting?"

He sighs impatiently. "If someone else is going to be in charge, then we have to have a meeting so I can tell them what to do. When's the meeting?"

"Al, there is no meeting. It was a coup. I'm in charge."

"That's what I was afraid of."

Then there are the demands.

"I've got to send this fucking fax."

"Al, you're in the hospital. You don't have to be sending faxes. They are taking care of it at the office."

"The first four pages went through, but not the fifth. Damn fax machine. I've got to send the fifth. They called."

"Al, you are still on vacation. You don't have to worry about the fax."

"I have to get the fifth page to them before I leave."

"Al, you're in the hospital. Don't worry about the fax."

"I've got to send the fax. It's important. They have to get the last page by five o'clock."

I turn away for a few seconds, then turn back.

"Al?"

"Yeah?"

"I sent the fax for you. The fifth page. They just called to say they got it."

"Oh, okay."

And the questions.

"How many grandchildren are we going to have?" asks Al.

"Excuse me?"

"How many grandchildren are we going to have? I need to know."

Al is not very fond of children, except for Kelly, who hasn't even hit puberty yet.

"Well, Al, I can't say how many grandchildren. I think that is going to be up to our daughter. To Kelly. That's not anything we can control."

"Yeah. Right. So how many grandchildren will we have?"

"Did we win the game?"

"What game? Alan, do you think you were in a baseball game? Do you think you got hurt playing baseball?"

"Yeah."

"Why are you here, Alan?"

"Ummm. Because I fucked up?"

I expect the agitation and confusion, but somehow I also expect Alan to be interested in what has happened to him. But at this stage that's impossible. He doesn't even know we are in Kingston, Ontario. He still sleeps about twenty hours a day, and when he is awake, he has no memory of recent events. He might be in Philadelphia, or he might be in Montreal. He tells everyone that he is from Brooklyn, where he hasn't lived in more than twenty years. He is twelve years old, he says. The blankness of the coma was somehow easier to take than his complete lack of self-awareness now. I have an intense desire to relive every detail of the accident, so I do it with my mother and Naomi, my mother-in-law, who are still here in Kingston, staying at the Holiday Inn. I can barely face the desk clerk anymore as The Wife of the Man Who Got Hit on the Head by a Boat. Every day she asks me how Alan is doing, and I can't explain, so I say, "Better." Every night I stay awake far too late, drinking wine and crying into the phone with friends around the country.

The neuro ICU is less flexible about visiting hours, and I feel as though I've been thrust out of the nest. The waiting room in the regular ICU was warm, womblike. Here on the eighth floor we hang out in a communal waiting space, which has a beautiful view of Lake Ontario. Large ships steam by, and small boats with striped and neon sails billow past, dreamlike. But there is no tea, no message board, and no companions who are in a similarly intense predicament. People come and go, and I form no bonds. We have more time now, and every night after feeding Al his plastic gruel we stay at the hospital for some of the evening, then go out to eat in this cute tourist town.

One night as we're walking out of the hotel, down past the harbor, we come upon a Scottish dancing troupe and bag-pipers performing in a cobblestone square. "Al would love seeing those pipers," I mumble, the words catching in my throat. Alan loves Scotland and everything Scottish, from haggis and neeps to caber tossing. When we met, he was thrilled to find out that I had played the bagpipes as a kid. When we were grad students, we took a summer trip to Scot-land, traveling from Edinburgh to Glasgow and then into the Highlands. We visited tiny regimental museums displaying stuffed dogs and Bonnie Prince Charlie's socks and traveled by ferry to the moonlike landscape of the Isle of Skye, where the MacCrimmon clan, my ancestors, were the court bag-pipers for the MacLeods, the ruling clan. At Inverness we took a boat out onto Loch Ness, where Al asked me to snap a picture of him as the legendary "monster." He wanted to tell all our friends we had seen it. Back home, Al moaned in agony when he saw the photo of him grinning stupidly, with his two hands cupped and stretched out past the boat. "No, no, no!" he said, marveling at my hopelessness as a photogra-pher. "You weren't supposed to take a picture of my whole body! You were supposed to take a picture of *just my hands* over the water, so it looked like the Loch Ness monster's head coming up!"

"I am beginning to understand the phrase 'lack of companionship,'" I say to my mother and mother-in-law as we sit eating dinner in a nice outdoor café on Kingston's main thoroughfare. "He's not here," I say tearfully. "He might never be here again." They don't know how to answer. After a while, we begin joking that maybe we can make a tape recording for Al and play it every few minutes at his bedside:

You were in an accident. You got hit on the head. They flew you here by helicopter. We are in Canada. You have to stay in the hospital until you get better, and then we will go back to Philadelphia, to another hospital. Your brain is hurt. You have bruises all over your brain.

These are words we have said to Alan hundreds of times in the last few days.

On Al's last day in the neuro ICU, Rabbi Steve shows up. Dark, bearded, wearing Birkenstocks, he was visiting an elderly member of his small congregation (the only one in Kingston) when he discovered another Jewish patient listed at the desk. He walks into the waiting room and begins asking us about Alan.

"Doesn't he look like Alan?" says Naomi. "Like Alan, only ten years younger."

Rabbi Steve seems uncomfortable. "I tell you, if there's one place that's *bad* to be," he says, "it's the neuro ward. Oy."

"You look so much like my son," Naomi says. Naomi thinks Al would wear Birkenstock sandals to a hospital, too. He's known for his fashion gaffes.

The rabbi, it turns out, is moving in the next few days to Bala-Cynwyd, right outside Philadelphia. We marvel at the coincidence. He has been ousted from the congregation in a bad political situation, and Naomi tells him the story of her Brooklyn rabbi's problems.

"Can I see Alan?" he asks.

Naomi and my mom stay behind, and I lead Rabbi Steve into the hallway toward Alan's cubicle and put my hand on his shoulder. "Listen, please don't tell him you're a rabbi, okay? He hasn't been in a synagogue since his bar mitzvah, and I'm afraid he'll think he's dying." I'm still projecting Al's old personality onto this new semicomatose stranger who is thrashing a bit in the bed as the rabbi and I go in.

"Hello, Alan," says Rabbi Steve. "I'm a friend, and I just wanted to see you."

"Huh?" Al says. He looks sedated and confused. The rabbi asks him about the accident, and Al doesn't know what he is saying. After a few one-sided attempts at conversation, the rabbi gives up. "Well, take care," he says, and pauses at the foot of the bed for a semiprayer: "May God be with you and give you the strength to help you overcome this terrible accident and regain your health," he says, leaving. Al doesn't even ask who he was.

A few minutes later I find Rabbi Steve buttonholed by Naomi in the waiting lounge. We need someone to drive our car back to Philadelphia, and she wonders if he can do it, since he's going that way. She is, as they say in Yiddish, a *noodge*. The poor guy. He's moving in two days, and his wife is taking their one car and he is driving the moving truck, towing their other car behind him for seven hundred miles. He has two children under the age of four. Rabbi Steve looks as if he is registering pretty high on the stress-o-meter.

The next day he calls me at the hotel, anguished. He's still trying to figure out a way to help us, he says. He's putting himself through hell, and I begin to regret checking off the religion box on Al's hospital admission form. I try to let this nice man off the hook easily, but what I say comes out too harshly: "Look, you're not responsible just because some Jewish guy got hit on the head by a boat!"

·   ·   ·

As the days progress, Al's empty trances grow more alarming. A stupor seems to descend upon him shortly after he gets his Dilantin, the antiseizure medication. I ask Dr. Ellis about it. Does Al really need this heavy-duty medicine? Isn't it keeping him a little hazed?

"He had a major seizure," says the doctor, "and in a case like that, we recommend that a patient take Dilantin for a year after a severe brain injury, to prevent recurrence. Subsequent seizures could kill even more brain cells."

"Will being on a drug like that affect his recovery?"

"Let's put it this way: taking Dilantin will definitely put Alan in the *slow class* in rehabilitation."

A year on Dilantin. God. It's beginning to sink in that Alan's recovery will be a long process. Dr. Ellis tells me that it takes six months to a year to recover from the physical and some of the cognitive symptoms of brain injury, although there is a catch: during recovery, a patient may get "stuck" in any phase, and few recover fully, especially in the cognitive realm. So the way Alan is now could be the way he will remain forever.

"The time for recovery keeps getting pushed back, though," explains Ellis, who says some experts now think there is still potential for improvement for even a decade postinjury. "I think one year is unrealistic. It takes, really, at least two years. During the first year, you might see ninety percent recovery. That last ten percent, if you are going to get it back, comes after another year."

Perspective, I need perspective. I get some from the parents of the nineteen-year-old girl who fell off the ladder. She is still in the ICU. Her father says he has heard that Al is speaking again. As I start to ask about their daughter, the mother begins to cry. No speech, not even an attempt, says the father, putting his hand on his wife's arm. Their daughter

Janie can look at them, and she can track movement with her eyes. She seems to recognize her parents. That's all.

By contrast, Alan is progressing quickly—it's just that my expectations are still way out of sync with the timescale of neurological recovery. I hear "six months to a year" but still secretly believe this whole recovery thing is something Al can breeze through faster than anyone else. Trained to be an overachiever, I just can't accept that there is little we can do but wait for Alan's brain to heal.

My self-centeredness shows up in other ways, too. Speaking to Janie's parents, I tell them how upsetting it is for me to feed my husband. "It must be easier, somehow, to feed someone who is your child, who was once your baby," I say. The mother says nothing, and I want to go out into the hallway and kick myself. How could *anything* be easier in this situation? I brood about my crass comment for hours.

They're moving Al to a "real" hospital room, and I've been busy making arrangements for our eventual return to the States. It hasn't been easy. Sometimes I think they'll need two stretchers—one for each of us—after I have a heart attack screaming at HMO representatives.

Foolish me, I never thought to contact Alan's "primary care physician" (read: gatekeeper) when he was first brought in by helicopter. I was too busy worrying that he was going to die. By the time I try to call the HMO a day later, I find that the toll-free number on our insurance cards doesn't work in Canada. So, standing in a phone booth in the hospital hallway, I ask my mom in New Jersey to dial the number and then call me back after she has reported Alan's accident. I give her all the pertinent data and member numbers.

"It was the weirdest thing," she says a few minutes later. "I called and explained the whole thing, and then the man on the other end just said, 'Uh, I don't think you're covered for any accidents up there at all,' and hung up."

Eventually I patch my calls through to my friend Joellen at her office, who then dials the HMO office's toll-free number and listens as I try to explain what's going on. There are starts and stops and many screaming sessions. Every phone call is grueling, since I must explain the accident and Alan's condition over and over. Dr. Andy has recommended a number of neurosurgeons he knows in Philadelphia, because I can't get Alan flown back home until he is officially accepted as a patient by a neurosurgeon at an acute care facility. We will then move him to a rehabilitation hospital. But both places have to be approved by our HMO, as does any doctor. If we could stay in Canada, he would immediately go into the rehabilitation hospital attached to Kingston General. One Philadelphia neurosurgeon, a friend of Dr. Andy at Thomas Jefferson Hospital, speaks with me on the phone for a half hour. He says he will accept Alan, and I become very emotional before I hang up, saying we will see him soon. Then I find out he's not a part of our health care provider network, so I have to start looking all over again. My writing partner, Tom Maeder, calls doctors he knows at the Hospital of the University of Pennsylvania, which everyone in Philly calls by its odd acronym, HUP. "Cathy is not only looking for a good neurosurgeon," he tells them, "she is looking for someone who can communicate with her. She gets pissed off real easily at pretentious doctors." Dr. Eric Zagar's name emerges as a possibility: "You'll like him," Tom's doctor friend says. "Eric is not only good, he's a mensch." That's just what I want to hear.

I'd never met David Nicklin, Alan's primary care physician. Al had switched to him only a few months before because he had been impressed by David's caring attitude toward an elderly client. I enter David's life screaming. He is a very patient man. He gets involved, talking to me on the phone and trying to sort out just what Alan needs and how we're going to get it for him. He speaks with Dr. Ellis and sets things up with HUP. Now there is the matter of getting Alan down there by plane ambulance.

"HUP HUP," says Ellis on his next rounds, amused at the acronym. By this time he's become accustomed to being harassed by all sorts of doctors from the States on Alan's behalf. Al's brother, Gary, who works as an administrator at the University of California, San Francisco, has already gotten neurosurgeons he knows to call about Alan's case, and Dr. Andy has spoken with Peter Ellis, too.

"We're not so sure that your husband's condition warrants an air ambulance," says Timothy Somebody, Al's so-called case manager from our HMO. (I often wonder why these people don't proudly print the title Benefits Denial Specialist on their business cards.)

"I don't think you understand that my husband has suffered a *severe* brain injury. No way is he going by land ambulance. That's over eight hours!"

"Well, I am doing my best. I will let you know."

That is just the first conversation about Al's transfer to the United States. Eventually Tim Somebody angers me so much that I start swearing as soon as we begin talking. I imagine him, his top shirt button undone, tie askew, sitting in a cubicle in a corporate park in North Carolina. He goes to work each day, puts on a headset, and listens to some crazy lady in Canada scream.

"Well, Christ, why don't I just tie my husband to the top of the goddamned car like a dead deer and drive him down to HUP? Or maybe you could hire four teenagers on Rollerblades and they could wheel his gurney across the border and down Route 81?"

There's always a dead silence after one of my tirades. Poor Tim Somebody. His job is to count the beans and try to give as few away as possible. I think I'm giving him an ulcer, or maybe, I hope, some more exotic condition that isn't covered by his health care benefits.

Alan has only one brain, so I decide to borrow the money from my mother to get him a good air ambulance. Then I'll worry about reimbursement. We had planned that when we left the island on Bob's Lake we would visit Alan's trusts and estates client James DaCosta and his wife, who live on a small farm outside Toronto. Jim and Susan had come down to Philly rather recently. We'd had a wonderful dinner together, and then they had urged us to visit Canada. They had been quite excited when they found out we were coming up their way.

Now Jim feels personally responsible that something this awful has happened to us in Canada. He calls me every morning at the hotel to find out how Alan's doing. He's on the board of a hospital in Toronto, so he knows how to help me get a good air ambulance, a Learjet from an outfit called Angels of Mercy. It's expensive, and I have a hard time making the commitment. Then another outfit calls me at the hospital, determined to woo me away with a lower bid. It is surreal—I am actually looking at catalogs and glossy full-color brochures for air ambulances, the way I would shop for a vacation cruise. The Angels of Mercy boast a Learjet with a pilot and copilot, a pressurized cabin, and an attending registered nurse. The other company has the same services, except that it is a twin-engined prop plane instead of a small jet. The difference is about seven hundred bucks American and a little bit of airtime, and, after worrying about it far too long, I decide to go with Jim's recommendation, HMO be damned.

Now that he is in a "real" hospital room, Alan seems even more out of it, if that is possible. He can't focus on anything.

I try to point out the boats on the lake—there is a beautiful view from his bed when the back is cranked to a right angle—but he doesn't seem to notice. I turn on the television, but he couldn't care less.

The physical agitation worsens. He thrashes from side to side and flings himself over the side of his bed so that he dangles by his waist on the metal railing, his head nearly touching the floor. One afternoon the nice Malaysian nurse decides he should try to sit up. She and another nurse prop him up in an orange vinyl chair next to the bed and go away.

"Gotta get up!" Al says, grunting. I am all alone with him, except for his roommate, a nice fiftyish schoolteacher who is in the hospital awaiting tests to determine the cause of his severe headaches. He wears sharply creased pajamas and reads long novels and probably thanks his lucky stars that he is only in for tests. I can see him watching us anxiously from his bed.

I lean over the chair with each of my hands resting on the vinyl arms. "Al, you can't get up. You are paralyzed on your right side. You can't stand. Just sit."

"No!" Al screams through clenched teeth. Then, with every ounce of his strength, he lowers his head and hurls himself forward, knocking me down. He tries to stand, but his right side collapses beneath him as if he's an inflatable doll with a quick leak. He lands in a heap right in front of me, and the nurse arrives only seconds later—the nice man in the creased pajamas has run into the hallway to summon her.

Alan will not sit up again until we reach the United States.

Day ten after the injury—Al enters his "Rain Man" phase. He still dozes a lot, but when awake says only, "Uhhhhh. Okaaaaaay. What are we gonna do?" This is said slowly, oddly, like Gomer Pyle or the cartoon character Deputy Dawg.

"Uhhhh. Okay. What are we gonna do?"

"Well, Al, we're going to go back to the United States, and you are going to another hospital for a while, until you get better."

"Uhhhh. Okay. What are we gonna do?"

After a half day of this, the schoolteacher with the headaches begins to lose it. He's been a really good sport up until now; he even tried to make conversation with Alan about the All-Stars baseball game, which was broadcast from Philadelphia last night. Al seems to have no awareness that he lives in Philly at all.

"Uhhhh. Okay. What are we gonna do?" Al says, for maybe the thirty-fifth time.

"Listen!" says Al's roommate. "You know how your wife married you for better or worse? Well, buddy, this is the worse! So just shut up!"

We're going home.

Everyone at Kingston General asks if I am excited. Actually, I'm scared. Canada is a comforting cocoon, a retro-type place where people are friendly and caring. It seems twenty years behind the callous, moneygrubbing, consumer-oriented American culture. Kingston is clean, perky, and perfect, like the artificial town in the movie *The Truman Show*, only *real*. And I am now a convert to socialized medicine—the national health care system up here means that no one has hassled me about Alan's care; he gets what any brain injury patient in Canada is entitled to.

In short, I know we are in for a rude awakening once we hit native soil. Philadelphia is our home town, but HUP is a huge urban hospital. As soon as we land, the HMO vultures will be circling, looking for any way possible to turn down our benefits. The night before we are scheduled to fly, I lie awake wondering why I am in such a rush to get Alan home. He's safe here, and I don't have to explain anything. I get a mad impulse to let everyone know in the morning that I want Al to go into rehab in Canada. The hell with it, we'll stay. I'll rent an apartment here for me and Kelly. Maybe I can get a job teaching English at the university. What can they do to us? No one has ever said we *must* return to the States; I have just been acting on the advice of everyone who assumes that Al will get better care back home. I like Canada. I like this hospital. We will become Canadian citizens. Everyone has been warning me that Alan's injury will create a huge change in our lives. So why not just do it up big? We'll stay up here, eh? Talk about life changes.

But when I wake up the morning of our departure, I know I can't change our plans. My mother and Naomi are going to drive to Syracuse, where they will drop off the rental car and get a flight back to New York. I am going in the air ambulance with Al. My mother thinks I should relax. "The worst is over," she says.

Ha!

A social worker shows up to interview Alan and evaluate his level of independence, using the Functional Independence Measure (FIM). She explains that even though we are U.S. citizens, the Canadian government tracks all head injuries. They will even follow up on his injury six months later. Realizing immediately that Alan cannot answer any questions, she asks if I will accompany her to the lounge, where she begins: Can your husband walk? Can he use the bathroom? Can he dress himself? Can he feed himself? Can he groom himself? "No" on all counts. Al scores a perfect zero on the FIM scale of independent living. He is now officially totally disabled and dependent.

We're finishing up the interview, and Al's roommate slides into view, skidding up the hallway in bedroom slippers, his reading glasses slipping off his nose. "He's wiggled himself out of the bed!" I go bounding to the room, where Al's entire torso and arms are draped over the metal railing of the bed, nearly touching the floor. He's huffing and moving his good leg, flailing it back and forth, so that soon, even with the dead weight of his paralyzed side, he would have totally hurtled himself over the rail. Does he have a death wish, I wonder?

The roommate, looking even nattier today in a navy blue flannel bathrobe, tries to help me hoist Al back into the bed. The best we can do is kind of hold him in place, poised between the bed and the floor. Finally the nurses show up, and as we stand back to let them do their job, the roommate looks at me with what I fear is pity. "Good luck, dear," he says softly.

In a very formal show of farewell, the three neurosurgeons parade into Alan's room. Peter Ellis leads, saying good-bye and good luck, warmly taking Al's good hand into his own two as Al stares at him vacantly. Then a nice doctor from Italy who occasionally attended Alan steps up and shakes hands, too. Last in line is Dr. Asshole, who never even looks at me. I assume he is required to do this upon discharge, as part of the neurosurgical team. He goes up to Al and nods, mumbles something, and then makes a hasty retreat to the end of the bed. The three surgeons leave the room together. It is a very quaint, almost European ceremony.

The ambulance people were supposed to arrive at ten o'clock, and now it is nearly noon and there is no sign of them anywhere. So much for Jim DaCosta's recommendations, I think. I ask at the nurses' station, and they have no answer. We were supposed to take off at around eleven and land at HUP at two o'clock.

I've insisted that they dress Al in a pair of roomy boxer shorts and a T-shirt I retrieved from his suitcase in our car. I want him to look somewhat dignified for the trip. They took out his saline IV yesterday. For the last few days, since they removed his Foley catheter, he's been wearing a "condom" cath, attached to the end of his penis, but now they put on a diaper for the journey. The stitches in his ear have healed and dissolved, and even the abrasion on the left side of his face is almost gone. Ever since they took off the cervical collar, he has looked nearly normal, at least when his eyes are closed and you can't see that wild and stoned expression.

They deliver to the room a lunch Al can't eat, and I am wolfing down some gray sludge over bread that is supposed to be an open-faced meat sandwich when another social worker comes in. Al is asleep. This woman has been very nice to me throughout our time here, in spite of how hard it has been for her to understand the private American health care system. She's the one who finally set up the pickup time with the Angels of Mercy air ambulance, after Jim DaCosta made the arrangements.

"Oh, I am so sorry," she says. "They canceled it."

"What?"

"Yes. Your insurance company. They called up early this morning, and when I told them you were taking the air ambulance today, they canceled it. Said they are sending their own."

Now I am mad *and* embarrassed. All those arrangements Jim DaCosta went to the trouble to make, canceled without my knowledge. And who is coming? And why aren't they here?

The social worker feels for us, she says, adding, "I don't really understand why this has to be so difficult. But they said if they were going to pay, it had to be an air ambulance they authorized." This is news. Up until the last minute the HMO had been trying to transport Al by garbage truck or yak, I thought.

An hour later we are still waiting when a middle-aged man wearing a dark blue windbreaker enters the room. He immediately approaches Al's bed and looks at him closely.

"Oh, God, you're finally here!" I say, and start jabbering about how the hospital in Philadelphia is expecting us *now*.

He gives me an odd look and hands me a business card. He is not an ambulance driver, he is the claims adjuster for the girl's insurance company—the girl who ran over Alan. "Please leave," I say unsteadily.

Finally, at around the time we are supposed to be landing in Philadelphia, the land ambulance crew arrives to take us to the airport. I assume they're just going to wheel Alan down to the ambulance in his hospital bed, but of course that's not possible, and they begin sliding a rigid wooden body board under him. They strap him down to it like a mummy as he smiles goofily. The image opens the floodgates of a too-recent memory, and I begin sobbing, seeing him tied down to a stretcher again. I try to say good-bye and thank you to the nurses at the station as they wheel Alan by on the gurney, but I can barely speak. Nasal honking noises are coming out of me. Water streams down my wide face and soaks into the top of my blouse.

"Don't be sad, you're going home," says one nurse. I put on my sunglasses and try to make the best of it.

I have only a tiny bag and Al's CT scans to carry with me. It's as if we are leaving without a trace of Kingston General. There are no cards or flowers—one time, during one of his more lucid moments, when I tried to tell Al he was in the hospital, he said, "I am not. How come no flowers, no cards?" We're in Canada, I explained—everyone would send cards and flowers when we got home to Philadelphia. I looked over, and he had fallen asleep.

The tiny airport is only about twenty minutes away from the hospital. Bill, one of the paramedics on board the ambulance, was on duty at Bob's Lake the day of our accident and treated Honey, Sarah, Kelly, and Benjamin. "Oh, that was a bad accident," he says now. "People are still talking about it.

I wondered how you made out." He leans over to Al. "How ya doin? You're sure a lucky man, aren't ya?"

The motion of the ambulance lulls Al to sleep. We arrive at Kingston Airport and—surprise!—there is no air ambulance. We wait on the tarmac for a half hour. It's nearly ninety degrees, and when they turn off the ambulance it heats up. So they put the air back on periodically to cool things down. Al awakes and becomes agitated. Then Bill contacts the airport tower by radio. Not only is there no air ambulance here, there is no sign of any such airplane within a hundred miles of Kingston in any direction.

I swear under my breath. "I gotta get out and call somebody," I say to Bill, who opens the back of the ambulance and helps me down. The small airport building is locked, but I can see a place big enough to crawl into where the baggage comes out on the conveyor belt. It's less than four feet high, with those heavy rectangular black vinyl flaps hanging down over it. I hunch down—I'm almost six feet tall—and, getting down onto my knees with my ass in the air, squeeze into the space. Once in the terminal, I have to walk along the outside loop of the dead conveyor belt, jump to the center, and then climb across another section of conveyor to get to the "people" side. Only there aren't any people.

It's like a bad dream. The deserted terminal seems spooky, like a ghost airport or the terminal for transport to Heaven or Hell. It's small but ultramodern, with gleaming marble floors and state-of-the-art ticket counters, all shut down. No lights, but banks of pay telephones that work.

First I call Timmy Somebody: "Damn it! My husband would be in Philadelphia now if it weren't for you! There *is* no fucking airplane coming from your company." I tell him that Al has been strapped down for more than an hour, that he is without seizure medication, that he is probably already sitting in his own excrement.

"I just want to warn you, Ms. Crimmins, that this call is being recorded. I do not appreciate your using such language."

"Oh, what are you going to do? Play it back for my mommy? Oooh. She is saying bad words! *I don't appreciate you canceling our air ambulance without telling me and then making my severely brain-injured husband suffer unnecessarily!*"

Timmy says he just can't imagine what is holding them up.

I call Alan's primary care physician, David Nicklin, and leave a fairly hysterical message. Then, after using one of the fourteen stalls in the spooky women's bathroom, I climb back out the conveyor belt orifice and return to the ambulance.

Bill says the tower still insists that there are no planes in the vicinity.

"They are such assholes at that HMO," I say. I turn to Al, who is awake and dazed. "Good thing you didn't get hit on the head back home. You know what our HMO's brain surgery plan is? They give your wife a Black and Decker drill and an instruction booklet."

Bill laughs. "Is she always this way?" he asks Al.

"Yeah," says Al. "Yeah." Bill seems to think they are having a conversation.

We wait another forty-five minutes or so, and I crawl back into the terminal.

This time I reach Dr. Nicklin on the phone. He is hopping mad. "Take him back to the hospital. Just take him back in the ambulance. Admit him to Emergency at Kingston General. We can't have Alan in this situation."

We start driving back and are about five minutes away from the hospital when a crackling message comes over the ambulance radio: there *is* a plane, and it's on its way from Cleveland.

Cleveland? Once we return, we still have to wait on the runway another twenty minutes, and then the airplane lands. Bill and I are shocked: it's a flying bucket, a single-engine Cessna. I figured the Learjet was probably a no-go, but *this thing?* My dad was a private pilot, and it looks like the flying jalopies he used to rent at the local airport to take the family up for weekend joyrides.

This is the flying bucket's seventh airlift of the day, I discover. There is an exhausted, bewildered crew of two, neither of whom is a registered nurse. I had insisted, back when I still harbored some hope that the HMO would fly us home, that Peter Ellis talk to the people there and tell them Al would need nursing on the flight. They listened really well, evidently. In fact, they listened so well that they sent a plane for an *ambulatory* patient. The pilot is very distressed that Al cannot walk onto the plane by himself. I begin laughing when he asks if he couldn't just try doing that. Bill watches the overweight pilot and his even fatter assistant sweat and pant as they try to load Al, strapped to the rigid body board, into a tiny door at the side of the plane. "I wouldn't let my dog go on that plane," he says. I ask him if he would write that down and detail all that we've gone through, and he does, giving me his account on small notebook paper.

Meanwhile, we watch them tip Al almost onto his head as they tackle the geometric problem of getting a long, totally stiff object into such a small opening. It's like watching movers try to get a hutch up a narrow, twisty staircase. The situation has gone beyond surreal, and I can't summon up the strength to yell "Stop!" Unbelievably, they eventually get him in. I realize with a start that of course this is not a pressurized cabin. I have second thoughts. Should I demand that he be taken out again? But I just want all of this to be over. I can't take any more battles. So I surrender. The heartless HMO has worn me down, which is what managed care is all about.

Al is now dehydrated. It's been nearly five hours since he had his semisolid food or any water. I ask the assistant, whom I assume is a paramedic, if they have liquids and a straw aboard. No. I have my own little bottle of water with me. How about just the straw?

Not even a straw. How can an "ambulance" not contain a straw? Al hasn't sipped from a cup yet, and I wonder if I can get any liquid into him. I drizzle water onto his lips from the bottle; most of it falls on the floor.

As soon as the plane climbs into the air, my ears begin to pop and pop. It hurts. We are flying pretty high for an unpressurized plane, about as high as we can go. I think of Alan's brain popping, too, of the swelling inside his skull increasing once again. His head is full of swollen brain tissue already. I start weeping, and the fat sweaty guy crammed into the back with me thinks I am scared of flying. Blessedly, Al falls asleep. I wonder if he will be even worse off when he wakes up.

After an eternity—the flight takes nearly two hours instead of the one hour it would have taken in the jet—we land on the private-plane airstrip at the Philadelphia International Airport. The only land vehicle in sight is a hearse. "Oh, look!" I say to Al, "It's the Aetna Managed Health Care ambulance!" Why pay for brain rehab, I think, when you can kill them with the ambulance ride?

The indignities continue. A customs official comes out to detain the plane because it does not have the right sticker for international flights. The engine is off and the interior of the cabin is nearly a hundred degrees. I see that the land ambulance has finally arrived, and I throw myself on the mercy of the customs guy.

"Please," I say, sounding pitiful, "my husband is severely brain-injured. We were supposed to be at the hospital at two o'clock, and it is after seven now. He had a terrible seizure after his accident, and he hasn't had his medication in hours."

"Okay, yeah. Unload him," says the customs official to the land ambulance crew. "But you," he says to the pilot and assistant, "you stay *right there*."

The guys in the ambulance have heard the words "brain injury" and "seizure," and they want to get Al out of the plane as quickly as possible, but they run into the same problem as when he was loaded back in Kingston.

"What was he doing on this airplane?" asks one guy, tall and lanky, with a ponytail. "He shouldn't have been on this plane in the first place."

He and his partner work for about ten minutes, rocking Al's body board slowly up and then sliding him almost vertically out of the small opening. They put the siren on as we make the fifteen-minute drive to HUP. The squealing sound comforts me as we breeze down the Schuylkill Expressway. Finally—someone is paying attention!

Al is not asleep, just out of it. His eyes are rolling back into his head again, as they did the first few days out of coma. "We're almost there," I say to him as we turn onto the exit ramp. He seems not to notice the screech of the siren. Does he even know he is in an ambulance? How many more of the axons in his brain fell apart or fried in that unpressurized cabin?

I will never forgive myself for letting them take Alan in the Cessna. Never. I'll always wonder if that nightmare flight increased the damage to his brain.

When we get to HUP, it is nearly eight at night. Al is dehydrated and totally disoriented. For the first time since he awoke from his coma, he cannot respond to simple commands. And when the doctors at HUP ask him who I am, he says in a slurred voice, "I don't know."

5

Mr. Forman is physically and medically stable. Cognitively, he is amnesic for events prior to and after the accident. Mr. Forman also demonstrates lack of awareness of being head-injured and is impulsive in his behaviors. Functionally, Mr. Forman has right-sided weakness which prevents him from being able to stand or walk without assistance. . . . My prognosis is guarded/fair for Mr. Forman returning to his previous occupation as a probate attorney.

—letter from Dr. Everett C. Hill, a rehabilitation doctor at the Hospital of the University of Pennsylvania, to our disability insurance case manager three weeks after the accident

The Hospital of the University of Pennsylvania is only a block away from where Alan and I first met back in the fall of 1976. The first thing Al remembers about me, he likes to say, is that I once dressed as a worm at a costume party: "It should have been a warning, Crimmins, but I married you anyway."

I was twenty-one, a first-year graduate student in English, a gung-ho medievalist, attending my first big student party at Penn. Alan, a veteran second-year student, was on the party committee, in charge of buying cheap beer and sherry and setting up the Penniman Lounge in Bennett Hall, which had been the library for the College of Women. The once grand two-level room was a wreck of its former self, just a dusty, depressing place with a few ripped books and mostly empty shelves. But it had a nice wooden library counter that made a great bar, and in those days, broke as we were, a Penniman Lounge party was a big event.

My Halloween costume wasn't a *worm*, as I always remind Alan, it was a *bookworm*. Anyone could tell that, because I was coming out of a huge cardboard *Oxford English Dictionary* I'd made out of poster board. I was wearing a green-striped floor-length T-shirt, and I had painted my face green to match. I also sported green pipe cleaner antennae and some false sharp teeth. Al, one of those bearded, serious types, was too busy minding the party to dress up, so I didn't talk to him too much that night. "I thought you were so weird, Crimmins. You freaked me out," he told me after we started living together.

Why did I fall in love with Alan? At the time we met, Alan was twenty-four, a complex, bright young man. Yet he was also charmingly honest and a bit naive. Many of the other grad students never realized how smart he was because he had little ego and didn't wear his intelligence on his sleeve like the rest of us. An urge to impress people was never a part of Alan's personality. He'd led a sheltered life in Brooklyn, where he had been the black sheep of his family, dating non-Jewish women and reading avant-garde plays. He'd dropped out of premed to become first a philosophy major and later a student of modernist English literature. Alan had a wonderfully eclectic sense of humor, and I loved that he didn't take himself too seriously. He liked playing and singing along to corny Harry Belafonte calypso records. On my first visit to his apartment, he showed me his copy of the *MAD* magazine cartoon book *Don Martin Steps Out,* which he kept right beside his tomes of literary criticism.

Alan's strong practical streak appealed to me: once I began living with him, I never again had to get my car inspected, pay a utility bill, or do my taxes. He liked pushing paper, he used to say, and he loved getting the best price on any consumer good. I didn't know quite what to make of his obsessive frugality, but since I was living on $2,600 a year, I often took his advice. "I can tell you where to get the cheapest sodas," he told me one day on his way out of Bennett Hall. "There's a machine that's twenty-five cents over on Locust Walk."

One night, the spring after my debut as a bookworm, I joined a group of graduate students walking home, and Alan was among them.

"Geez, look at that baby," he said, pointing to a totally wrecked yellow Ford Maverick at the end of my block. The back looked like an accordion, and it was crunched up against the car in front of it. "What a crash."

"That's my car!" I said, and everyone started laughing.

"No, it's *really* my car," I said, and the giggles abruptly ceased. Someone had rear-ended my cute little yellow car and fled. I was pretty sure it was totaled.

That night, Alan helped me find the correct police station a good fifteen blocks away in a terrible neighborhood, and he and a few others even went in with me to fill out the accident report. My parents had given me the '71 Maverick, my mother's old car, when I graduated from college, and I had been pretty attached to it. Alan understood. He treated me as a fragile case, a new member of the wheel-less bereaved.

Yet it took a few weeks of dating for me to discover that Alan's practicality was a veneer that disguised, beneath it, an adventurous nature I'd seen in few men. He was open to new and exciting experiences and willing to share them with a partner. He liked the theater, music, and exotic foods. He was an excellent companion for a creative, restless woman— he could offer stability without being dull. When I met him, Alan had many female friends, and he still does. He is the least sexist man I've ever met, and I sensed almost immediately that he would always be fair in our relationship. Some of my friends have even said he was "feminized" rather than feminist, and that is probably true. He didn't mind that I did better than he did in graduate school or that I was more ambitious about my career. He didn't even care that I was six inches taller. Amazingly, he was also good in bed and enjoyed doing dishes and laundry.

I fell in love with Al completely when we went with four other people to rent a communal house from a slum landlord in West Philadelphia who had a reputation of being so lazy, he would literally roll out of bed for his lease signings. We knew that the guy would appear in pajamas for our meeting, looking like a cheapskate Hugh Hefner. I suggested to all our housemates that we also appear in nightclothes when we went to sign for our rental property. Alan was the only one besides me who arrived in his pj's, and when I looked over at him through the curlers in my hair, shifting in my chair and adjusting my giant fuzzy slippers, I knew Alan was the man for me.

As graduate students we knew HUP as the place where Student Health sent you after a nervous breakdown. Going totally bonkers seemed to be a rather common side effect of the pressured, competitive grad school existence. We had a phrase for it, "going Tenth Floor Gates," alluding to the psych floor at HUP, where you would end up after you cracked. You knew a fellow student was really stressed if he or she said, "Oh, man, I'm almost Tenth Floor Gates." Alan and I visited two of our friends there, and sometimes when I thought I just couldn't cope with learning all the dead languages, prepping for the freshman comp courses I was teaching, studying for orals, working on my dissertation topic, and mourning for my recently dead father, I envied the people who had just thrown in the towel and surrendered to the comforting hospital beds of Tenth Floor Gates.

We weren't still supposed to be in Philadelphia twenty years later. That had never been the plan. We were supposed to finish our Ph.D. dissertations and get the hell out of there. California, Massachusetts, Texas, New York—anywhere but Philly. We were like cultural soldiers awaiting our postings.

But the bottom fell out of the academic job market and I became a copywriter and later a freelance writer, and Al worked as an administrator for a program for disadvantaged students and then went back to Penn's law school, where he did really well and we got our first taste of serious financial debt. Many of our friends stayed in Philadelphia, too.

So we fell in love, lived together, got married, and bought our first dilapidated house, then another one in slightly better shape. Kelly was born seven years into our marriage, and before we knew it we were longtime residents of urban Philly. HUP is less than half a mile from our house in Center City, a hop, skip, and a jump across the Schuylkill River.

And now here we are again, Alan and I, at HUP in 1996, and he is brain-injured, and the neuro ward seems an even scarier prospect than Tenth Floor Gates.

The first night, they've put Alan in a double room. He's seriously regressed since the ordeal of the flight. Even his speech is less clear. He is fascinated by the other guy's television set. "Wha dat?" he keeps saying, trying to move his head to catch the images. I turn on his TV and that only confuses him more—his eyes go back and forth from one set to the other, like the ball in a Ping-Pong match. Then he fumbles with the remote control for his set. He turns off the picture and looks upset. "Huh!" he grunts. So I turn it on again. "Uh. Okay," he says, then takes the remote and turns it off again. On. Off. On. Off. He stops, then two minutes later looks down at the remote in his hand. "What dis?"

The neurosurgeon doesn't come around that first night (we've gotten to HUP too late for rounds), but some residents do, and we have our first skirmish. Exhausted, I can't believe I have to start pissing all over my turf again.

The neurological resident orders a neck brace for Al, and I tell him I don't want it.

"But we don't know for certain that his neck isn't involved," he says.

"We do," I say. "His neck is fine. The chart will tell you. Check the chart. He's been cleared. Please don't put a collar on—it will make him even more nuts."

"The neurosurgeon recommends it."

"Well, I refuse it. I don't want it."

"I'll have to note that you are refusing our recommendation."

"Fine."

The resident writes "WIFE UNCOOPERATIVE" on the chart.

A team of rehabilitation doctors comes by, and Al does terribly. He has ceased playing with the TV remote and is now a zombie. He won't even respond to commands—no lifting his arms and legs, no squeezing hands. I try to tell them that he is "oriented in one sphere"—in other words, he knows who he is but not where he is or what day it is. But now he doesn't even know his name. He no longer seems to recognize me. I feel like the guy in that old Warner Bros. cartoon who finds a singing frog: every time he tries to show off his performing amphibian to the world, the thing just sits there silently. Now I can tell that the doctors think I am exaggerating Alan's progress in the last two weeks.

"He was an *attorney?*" says one young rehab medicine resident who should know better.

"He *is* an attorney!" I snap back.

I wake up in our own bedroom the next morning feeling as disoriented as Alan. I want to think that none of this ever happened. I dread going in to see Al at HUP. I dread the next step of rehab, too, which I know I must start planning immediately. Kelly is still staying out in Cheltenham with Sarah and Joanne. Our house has never felt so empty.

I walk down to the Schuylkill River, two blocks west, to our little plot at the community garden. As usual when we've been away, I'm shocked by how much everything has grown. It's like the time-lapse photography in those PBS nature specials Alan likes so much. The plot is blazing with color and weeds, full of flowers Al planted last April and May, as well as our beloved perennials. There are zinnias, cosmos, snapdragons, foxglove, bee balm, black-eyed Susans, dianthus, gladiolus, Queen Anne's lace, asters. I cut a bunch and arrange them in our French gardening bucket with the romantic notion that when Al sees the flowers from our plot, he will surely know we are home.

"Look, Al," I say, thrusting the bucket in front of me as I enter his room. "They're all from our plot. At the river. Aren't they beautiful?"

"Uh," he says. I bring the bouquet right up to his face, but he barely seems to notice it.

Eric Zagar, the neurosurgeon, comes to see Al that first morning, and afterward we go to his office to talk. He's wearing his scrubs and bright yellow rubber clogs. He apologizes for the neck brace. I like him a lot. He's interested in what our lives were like before this accident and who Alan really is. He has ordered some MRIs and other tests. The diagnosis is not a surprise: severe traumatic brain injury (TBI), with no real certainty of a good outcome. He says it will be a long time before Alan gets better and that he won't be exactly as he was before. I tell him the whole story of the accident, and we discover that Eric worked with Dr. Andy, too, and really admires him. Whether it is because Al is obviously going to drive any roommate crazy or because Eric

Zagar likes us, I find out that Al is being moved to a private room.

The room, tucked away in a corner behind the nurses' station, has only one drawback: it's next to the rooftop helicopter pad. HUP is a well-known, respected hospital. People and organs are flown in and out nearly hourly, but Alan never seems to notice the deafening whirring noise of the choppers outside his room's tiny window. It's like being in a *M*A*S*H* episode. The copters are so loud during a landing or takeoff, you can't hear a person speak even a foot away, but Al never even asks about the noise.

Yet other, smaller noises or stimuli now plague him. I will be trying to talk to him, and he'll hear a phone ring at the nurse's station fifteen feet away. "What dat?" he will say immediately. Or a nurse will be taking his temperature and he'll suddenly become disturbed about an open paper bag sitting on a radiator across the room. He won't be happy until I go over and close the bag or move it somewhere else. Like a child, he can be distracted by the tiniest things.

Distractability. So far Al's biggest symptoms have been agitation and confusion, but I am learning that he will manifest more side effects, adding them like lasagna layers to the casserole of bizarre behavior that constitutes TBI. The injured brain loses its ability, either briefly or forever, to filter out distractions and concentrate on the task or conversation at hand. Sometimes such behavior is called "inattention." In physical or occupational therapy for the brain-injured, the therapist must get the patient to pay close attention to the task at hand, whether it be learning to walk or creating a list of chores. HUP's physical therapy area is terrible for Alan— it's big, with lots of swirling action all about. When they take him down there daily, they just drape him over some parallel bars, and he does nothing. He never makes any progress. Later, on the brain injury ward at the rehab hospital, he will be sequestered in a small, sheltered gym, one designed to cope with the distractability of TBI clients.

About three days into our stay at HUP, I am helping Al drink from a cup with a straw. He can't concentrate on swallowing soda, though, because I'm wearing a big white blouse with pockets that billow out. He stares into the pockets wordlessly, marveling at their depths. I think of our friend whose son was diagnosed with autism. She told me her first hint that something was wrong was that Joe would spend minutes staring into the hole of a Cheerio floating in his bowl.

Our second day back in Philadelphia, Alan's brother, Gary, arrives from California. I am relieved, and so is he. Anxious to be with Al, he's left his wife and three small children to take a thousand-dollar plane ride. He wanted to come to Kingston, but I knew we would eventually come home, and he agreed to wait. I tell him he can help me more now. It is strange, though, because his voice sounds so much like Alan's. When he answers the phone at our house, he has to say immediately, "Hello, this is Gary," because several people have called and started telling "Al" how glad they are that he is better already.

Gary knows how serious brain injury is. He is a dentist and an administrator with a lot of medical friends, and he has been talking to them. I can tell it is painful for him to see Alan.

"Well, he looks stoned," Gary says. "I can't believe how stoned he looks."

Al has a kind of loony, wild-eyed look about him, and his mouth drops open slightly when he stares at things. His right arm is still curled up toward his armpit, and there is no tone in the hand—it just extends limply. The nurses straighten him frequently and crank up the back of the bed, but gradually, over the course of an hour or so, he starts to lean over toward the right, until he is at about a forty-five-degree angle to the bed. He often looks like a human Leaning Tower of Pisa.

"Al, do you want me to help you sit up straight?"
  "Huh?"
  "I can help you sit up straight."
  "I thought I was up straight."

In addition to controlling body movement and our senses, speech, and thought, the brain also governs our spatial sense, the idea of where we are in space at any given time, which enables us to balance our bodies and exist in many different planes rather quickly. Sitting down, standing up, lunging forward or backward, all require instantaneous adjustments of our sense of balance and the gestalt of where we are in space. My writing partner, Tom, has gotten me textbooks, monographs, and collections of articles about brain injury from Penn's medical library, and before I go to sleep each night I read them. I panic at the case history of a brain-injured man who never regained his spatial sense: although there was nothing wrong with his motor functions, he remained in a wheelchair for the rest of his life.

Right now, Alan is not even ready for a wheelchair. He's like a toddler who would do well, perhaps, in a big round walker with bumpers on it, the kind where he could just flail his legs around and move back and forth erratically.

He's like a toddler, too, in that he could play peek-a-boo endlessly. He's lost his sense of object permanence. As soon as someone leaves the room, he forgets entirely that the person has been there. I can be with him for hours by his bedside and then go to the ladies' room out in the hallway. When I return three minutes later, he's genuinely surprised to see me. "Wow," he says. "Hi!"

One night Gary and I go out for a quick dinner after spending the whole day with Al. Jimmy Schank, a friend, shows up shortly after we leave.

"No one has been here all day," Al tells Jimmy, who calls Joellen later that night, upset that Al is abandoned, alone.

Toward the end of Al's stay at HUP there are signs that he is regaining his sense of continuity. One day the nurses ask me and Gary to step outside for a moment while they change his diaper. (They call it a "pad," though, in deference to our feelings.) I go out into the hallway, but Gary just stands behind the curtain at the doorway. From the bed Al yells out, "Gary, is that you? Are you still there?" Gary has tears in his eyes as he tells me about it later: "It made me feel for the first time like he knew, a little bit, what was going on, that he had begun to remember."

Two amazing things happen on the day our friends Larry and Sally come to visit at HUP:

    1. We discover that Alan can still read.

    2. Alan begins to masturbate incessantly.

Sally is one of our oldest friends—she lived with us for a year in our huge, drafty house out in the Mount Airy section of Philly back in the eighties. We even survived the winter without a furnace, huddled together in one room in front of kerosene space heaters. She met Larry while she was living with us, and they got married a few years after we did and had two sons.

"You remember Sally and Larry, right, Al?"

"Of course I fucking remember them," he says, surly.

He's tied down to the bed on one side because he tries to get up all the time. After he pitched himself over the side and cut his nose badly, the nurses resorted to bondage.

Sally walks over to kiss him, and I see with horror that Al's left hand is stroking his penis. He's got it totally pulled out of his diaper. I move in, grab his hand, and pull his gown back down over his groin. Al half sits up, gazing toward Larry's chest. Larry is a runner and a fine athlete. "The blah blah marathon," says Al, reading Larry's T-shirt. I'm stunned, because for days I've been showing him Get Well cards he's been unable to read. But while I'm focusing on Larry's shirt, Al whips out his penis again and begins going at it. I try to move his hand away, and he resists. For the rest of Sally and Larry's visit, I play tug-of-war with Al's onanism, finally deciding that it's better to just give up and pull a sheet over him so he can masturbate out of sight.

"Sorry about that," I say, walking Sally and Larry to the elevator. They laugh nervously, assuring me that they understand. Then we all begin to cry.

From that moment on, for weeks, masturbation becomes Al's hands-on public hobby. Yet it never seems to get him anywhere. His disinhibition just makes him stroke his limp penis, openly and constantly, without results.

"Al, what are you afraid of? That it's going to fall off?" asks his brother.

"Yeah. Ha. Fuck. Yeah. Afraid of that."

"Al, give it a rest," says Gary. "It still works."

"No, it doesn't still work," says Al sadly.

Once we get Al into a rehab facility, the incontinence and masturbation are taken in stride by the staff. But at HUP, both become a big issue. One nurse tells me that Al is upsetting everyone and it's up to me to keep him from masturbating. At first I explain it to him the way I've explained it to our daughter: touching himself is a fine and fun thing to do, but only in private. That strategy gets me nowhere. Pushing his hands away also gets me nowhere.

"Al, stop that, please. Please stop it."

"Why?"

"You're upsetting the nurses."

"But I like touching my penis."

"I like it, too, but this is not the place."

Finally, I come up with a desperate strategy.

"Al, you have to stop that."

"Why?"

"You have to stop that because the Dick Police are coming."

"The Dick Police?"

"Yes."

"Oh. Okay."

A few moments later, Alan sighs and asks, "Are the Dick Police real?"

Did I say yes or no? I don't remember. Probably I said nothing because I wanted him to remain scared of antipenis storm troopers. When I get home that night I blush, reliving the episode. Shame on you, I think, making up lies and telling them to a brain-injured guy just so you can get some peace and quiet.

The frontal lobes control our sense of propriety, and when they are damaged, disinhibition becomes a major symptom. Like a small child or a sloshy drunk, the severely brain-injured person just says or does whatever pops into his head, especially in the early stages of recovery.

The masturbation is just the first sign that Alan has entered an extreme disinhibited phase. He now has two speeds: zombie and loony. In the loony, disinhibited phase, he calls the nurses "bitches" and "assholes." "You're a fucking idiot!" he screams at his brother, who is trying to get the right channel on the television. A few minutes later he begins to cry and says, "I love you, man. You're the best brother in the world."

He throws things, too. One day his parents are visiting. Someone hands Alan a nectarine and he looks at it closely, as if he doesn't have the slightest idea what it is. Then, without warning, he hurls the fruit directly at his father's head a few feet away. Later he will do the same with oranges, plastic forks, and hard candies.

We have many friends who work on the Penn campus, right across the street from HUP, and they pop over to see Alan a lot. I read in all the booklets that it's bad to overstimulate a brain injury patient, but somehow it's hard to control the visitor flow. Besides, I am determined not to fall into the trap of being ashamed of Alan's brain injury. It is a physical injury, caused by an accident, I tell myself. He would have visitors if he were in a body cast, so why not when he is lamebrained?

Alan couldn't care less about the visitors, with the exception of our friend Kay Dowgun, who seems to calm him down. Later I will find out that he doesn't remember a single moment of his HUP stay. A constant stress is what he will say to people in this new disinhibited state. I try to explain before they go in to see him, but he looks rather "normal"—not a mark on him now that his facial wound has healed—and they are taken aback when he has one of his loony episodes.

"What does Jimmy do?" asks someone, pointing to our friend, who is a development officer at Penn.

"Jimmy's a homosexual," says Al very authoritatively.

"Oh, Al, you know that's only my avocation!" protests Jimmy good-humoredly.

On a day when I must leave Al alone in the hospital to go to a meeting, I arrange to have his friend and former coworker Kathy bring in lunch and visit. At around noon I call the hospital room and get Al. Kathy is there, helping him eat. How nice, I say, that she has brought him lunch.

"Yeah, it is nice," he says. And then, suddenly: *"She's a fucking asshole!"*

One time, overwhelmed by his nastiness, I go into the tiny bathroom next to his bed. I sit on the toilet and cry.

"What are ya doin in there, huh, Crimmins? Playing with yourself?"

"Alan, you sound like Don Rickles," I say when I emerge ten minutes later, eyes swollen. "Do you think Don Rickles has frontal lobe damage?"

"Don Rickles has no fucking frontal lobes!" he screams back. ·

Aside from its general entertainment value, disinhibition after brain injury has its bright side as a brain injury sequela. Dr. Andy is glad to hear about Al's shenanigans. He tells me over the phone that it's much better to exhibit disinhibition than its opposite symptom, a general withdrawal from life. He says a brain injury patient like Alan can eventually learn to control his disinhibition.

Nurse Megan, a tall, sturdy blond woman, is particularly good at jollying Al into doing things. Megan doesn't cringe when he yells obscenities at her or throws his food.

One day Megan is there with Alan when I arrive, and rolls her eyes as I enter the room.

"We were a little wild today already," she says. "He's a wild thing."

"Wild Thing," I say. "That's Al's favorite song. He sang it at our wedding. Right, Al? The song 'Wild Thing,' remember? Wild Thing, I think I love you—but I gotta know for sure!"

Al stares at me with the poker face of brain injury. "There *is* no song called 'Wild Thing,'" he says.

Of all his addled comments, this one hurts the most. We have a painting done by a friend that shows Al singing "Wild Thing" to me. He's also sung it at four other weddings. Oh, God, to lose "Wild Thing"! It is tantamount to saying that our past together doesn't exist, and right now that's all we have.

Today they've put Al into something that looks suspiciously like a straitjacket. Megan takes me aside and explains that earlier this morning Al had shat the bed and then proceeded to smear his feces all over himself. "Oh, he's a devil, that one!" she says, a merry twinkle in her eye, as if she were discussing some unruly toddler.

A day after the feces incident I'm sitting in the lounge, crying, when Megan comes in and sits down beside me.

"This happened to my brother," she says. "And he did all of these things. We're just beginning to tell him some of the crazy things he did after his brain injury."

It took eight months, she says, but her brother, who sustained his injury in a car accident, eventually went back to work. An engineer, he now needs to carry a book with him at all times to remind him of people and dates and specific tasks. But he has gone back to work. "It passes, this stuff," she says as I sob.

While he is untied for a little while, Al tries to get off the bed and begins to fall over the side.

"Now what are you trying to do?" demands Megan.

"I gotta go to the fucking bathroom."

"Well, let us wheel you there."

"I can walk."

"No, you can't."

"She's a fucking asshole. She is such a goddamned bitch," he says to me and his brother as we stand by helplessly.

Megan gets Al into the wheelchair and takes him into the bathroom. She pulls off the diaper and hoists him onto the toilet. She's being a very good sport about this, since we all know that Al is basically incontinent. He's just hassling her, like a child.

"Give me a book," says Al. We hand him one of the paper-back mysteries some unknowing soul has brought as a gift.

Megan stares at him as he sits on the toilet.

"Leave me alone," he says.

"You know I can't do that—you'll fall off," she says, standing in front of the sink. "Read your book and just go."

The door is wide open—an unpleasant standoff, since Gary and I are also staring at Al sitting on the toilet. Al looks down at the book and screws up his eyes in an exaggerated expression of concentration. I realize, suddenly, that he's holding the book upside down. He raises his head and glares at me.

"You know I can't fucking read anymore," he says.

Often after head trauma a person becomes totally disconnected from the feeling of having to defecate or urinate. It's a classic symptom of severe brain injury, which makes sense, since it is only when toddlers' brains develop to a certain point that they can even recognize and concentrate on the need to go to the bathroom. Our daughter, Kelly, began to use the toilet at about two and a half, the very day she first made a drawing of a human face. I went around telling people, back then, that I was convinced continence was a brain thing.

Now I have a new occasion to find out just how right I was. For the first few weeks after his injury, Al is like a little kid in the toileting area. He has no idea he has to go. Then he gets to the point where he has about a ten-second warning, like a toddler in the supermarket who pees on the floor. There are many wacky piss episodes, with me attempting to get the urinal bottle onto his penis before he soaks the bed and both of us.

He seems to pick the most inopportune times to let loose. A HUP nurse has just changed his diaper, and he's lying naked from the waist down on the bed as she goes to fetch another. Gary and I, just returning to the room, notice that he is choosing that very moment to take a dump on the bed, raising his rear up with great effort. Hips in the air, Al hovers precariously over his own dirt. If he lowers himself even slightly, he'll begin smooshing shit all over his backside. I look at Gary. I know I can't deal with this.

"I'll get it," he says, reaching over deftly with a paper towel to snatch up the excrement the instant before Al lowers himself onto it. "What's the big deal?" says Gary. "I still have a kid in diapers. It's just a little poop." Then he magnanimously takes a washcloth and wipes his brother's ass. Gary's gesture makes me feel like a failure. How real is my devotion to Alan if I can't even leap in to keep his hindquarters clean?

Al still doesn't know where he is exactly, but he thinks he is being tested.

"Would you like a pillow under your head, Mr. Forman?" asks an orderly.

"I don't know. Should I want one? What's the right answer?" Alan asks, looking over at me.

"Yes, please," I say.

When the orderly has left room, I ask Al if he thinks it was a test.

"Yeah. It was a test."

I tell him he's not being tested, that the orderly just wanted him to be comfortable, but he seems doubtful.

The neurosurgeon, Dr. Zagar, comes by again. He asks Alan the usual questions: his name, his age, where he is from. Alan only ever gets the first question right, but now he knows who I am again, too. ·

"Do you know where you are, Alan?"

"No."

"Really?"

Al looks at him blankly.

"Well," says Eric Zagar, "I'm wearing a white coat and I'm a doctor. You're in a gown, in a bed, and I'm examining you. Take a guess."

"Ummm. A hospital?"

"Good, Alan, but do you know why?"

"No."

Al is also being attended by another doctor at HUP, Everett Hill, a rehabilitation specialist. Soon he will make the transition to a rehab hospital, and Everett is evaluating his strengths and weaknesses.

The first time Dr. Hill arrives, Al is in one of his agitated states. He seems to have particular hours, like a colicky baby, when he is impossible, especially at the end of the afternoon. I feel protective and wish that the doctors would stop by when he is "sharp," although I've lowered my definition of that term considerably.

This time, Al is an inarticulate mess. He is moaning and groaning. He squirms as if in excruciating pain. "Do you have a headache, Mr. Forman?"

"Nah."

"How about your legs or your back?"

"Nuh."

"Mr. Forman, can you tell me where it hurts? Where does it hurt?"

"It hurts in my soul," Alan says.

It has been two weeks since Kelly has seen her father. I've been talking on the phone to her daily, trying to explain that Daddy is awake but not himself. Now it's a Saturday, and

Sarah and her sister, Joanne, bring her to HUP for a visit. By all accounts, it is a disaster. Somehow Alan seemed more appealing to Kelly while in the coma. She focuses her comments on his hair and beard, which are longer than she has ever seen them. His wild-eyed look scares her, but she can't describe it.

"Daddy looks funny," she says. No matter what Sarah and I try, we cannot get her to approach her father in the bed. It's a shame, because Alan actually seems more "with it" when she is here. He puts his arms out to her, a gesture he still hasn't made with me.

"C'mere," he says, but she won't go to him. I watch vigilantly. If he starts masturbating, I plan to get Kelly out of the room as quickly as I can.

Sarah and Joanne have helped Kelly make a big poster that says "We Love You, Al," and everyone signs it. Joanne has brought lovely yellow roses. My mother and her friend John have come bearing hors d'oeuvres, asparagus rolled up in ham. Al can now grab things in his hand and eat them, and he devours the finger food. It's our approximation of a party, but Kelly isn't buying it. She looks as scared as the day she came to fetch me in the boat. She wants to leave with Sarah and Joanne after only a few minutes. But Sarah hasn't seen Al since he was still in the coma, and Joanne hasn't been with us since before the accident. Sarah, who is short and dark like Al, jokes around, saying stuff like "Don't you remember me, Al? I'm your long-lost sister," and we all do funny amnesia-type riffs from the soap operas. I am sorry when they go, but it is clear that the visit has upset Kelly more than it has reassured her.

One day, around lunchtime, I return from an errand to see Al propped up in bed, regaling visitors with his mastery of baseball statistics. Our friend Kay is there, and she's brought along an old acquaintance from grad school, John Shea, whom we haven't seen in years. Jimmy Schank is there, too, and so is Tom Maeder. I've never seen Al quite this comfortable being the center of attention—this is the good side of disinhibition. He appears totally confident in his power to entertain. He looks great, he sounds totally lucid. These people are probably wondering why I've been making such a fuss about his brain injury.

But all of a sudden Al stops talking and turns to me. "I want to call Cathy."

I laugh lightly. "Al, I'm here. You don't have to call me. Here I am."

"No, I want to call Cathy. The Other Cathy. The one at home."

The relaxed tone of the room collapses as Al continues to insist on calling "the Other Cathy." Eventually I hand him the phone. The visitors shift uneasily in their seats.

Alan remembers our phone number and dials it, getting the answering machine. It is a very odd feeling, hearing him leave a message for me while I am sitting right there beside him. I try to keep smiling. He doesn't say much, just that he is calling me to say hello and that everyone is there with him and they wonder how I am doing. "This is your husband," he says. When I get home, I play it back, and I realize how appropriate it is that he wants to talk to the Other Cathy; after all, he is now Another Alan.

Looking through the literature from the medical library, I find many examples that are similar to Al's way of denying his paralysis—denial of physical disability is standard post-brain-injury behavior. One case I find particularly fascinating involves a woman who disowns her paralyzed hand, even though doctors point out that it is wearing her wedding ring. It is not her hand, she insists, and posits that someone stole her wedding ring and is wearing it on "their" hand.

But I have a harder time finding descriptions of behavior in which a brain-injured person creates duplicates of people or things. The closest parallel I find to the Other Cathy incident is in a medical case study of a man in Britain in the 1970s who was hospitalized with a brain injury for a year. The entire time, when his wife and children came to visit him, he would insist that they were not really his family but another family that looked very much like them. His real family was at home, he said. Then, when he was discharged and went home, he found what he described as another family, quite like his own but not really his old family. Under questioning, he did agree with the doctors that it was amazing how all the children in this family were exactly one year older than his own children had been at the time of his accident. But he chalked it up to coincidence. At the time the case study concluded, the man had still never accepted this other family as his own.

Reading case histories, I realize, gives me the same feeling I have about the odd things Alan is doing. On the one hand, I am fascinated. It's like being inside an Oliver Sacks story. On the other hand, Alan is my husband. This British man's story is a terrifically entertaining story, but I can only imagine how the man's wife copes with being regarded as a lookalike imposter.

There is a term for this phenomenon of making doubles of things: "reduplicative paramnesia." When I tell Dr. Andy that Alan is doing it, he is impressed. "Whoa! That is rare," he says. "He's really a cool TBI person." Andy says that based on this information he is almost positive that Alan was also hit on the back of the head, even though it did not show up on the MRI or CT scans. I wonder if it happened when Al fell down into the boat after the impact.

Al not only perceives duplicates, he believes he can create them. One night he performs a piece I will forever think of as The Man Who Mistook His Daughter for a Plant.

"What are we going to do about the Kelly device?" he asks me and Gary and Joellen. "Should we keep it or get rid of it?"

"What do you think, Miss Brown?" Alan asks in a professorial tone, addressing Joellen. "Because we could create another Kelly device, one that would fit better into everything."

The three of us are silent for a moment.

"What is the Kelly device, Alan?" I ask.

"Or maybe we shouldn't *have* the Kelly device," Alan says.

"What is the Kelly device, Al?" He's upsetting me.

"Umm. A plant?" says Al.

"No. She is a child. Kelly is our child. We can't get rid of her."

"But maybe we should create a second Kelly. The character Kelly," says Al. "One that could fit better into our lives."

I try to kid him: "Gee, I don't think we could handle a second Kelly. We've talked about how one is enough."

"So what are we going to do?" he asks, childlike.

No one says anything.

He puffs out his cheeks and blows air through his lips in an angry rasp. Why, oh why can't we understand? Then he gives up. "Okay, let's just keep the Kelly device. Okay." A big sigh, this time more resigned than hostile. "Gee, this creation stuff is really exhausting."

Another day, late afternoon. Al begins sighing heavily. Then he moans.

"What's the matter, Al?"

"I was just thinking. Thinking about the does. I mean, why do we have so many does, why do we keep them in the backyard? And they just keep having babies and then there are more does."

"Deer? You mean deer?"

"Yeah. So many does."

"Alan, do you think we keep deer as pets?"

"Yeah."

"Cats. We have cats. You're right, there are too many. Remember our five cats?"

"I wish we could do something about those does."

"The defective Alan Forman versus the second Alan Forman that we could create, what do you think?" Alan asks his visitors one night toward the end of his stay at HUP.

It's Joellen and Gary and me again, and we don't answer fast enough. We don't know what we think. Al, impatient, makes a sweeping gesture with his good hand, as if he is lecturing to a huge group in a Socratic-method class. He begins speaking more loudly to get his students' attention.

"*Okay*. I'm talking about a second Alan Forman, who could just hang out in the universe. What do you think? And what do you think about the defective Alan Forman? Should he really have a right to exist in the universe?"

"How do you think Alan Forman is defective?" I ask.

"Ummm. I don't know. What do you think, Miss Brown?" he says, pointing to Joellen. Joellen is a natural diplomat and one of the most articulate people I've ever met. She explains gently that Alan probably *feels* defective, since he can't move or think the way he could before the accident.

"That's right!" says Alan, smiling at her as if she's his star pupil. "But he could decide if the defective Alan Forman still had a right to live in the universe."

"Who's 'he,' Al?" I ask.

"Mr. Finkelman."

"Who? Who's Mr. Finkelman?"

"He creates the Al Forman and Kelly characters."

"Who *is* Mr. Finkelman, Al? Is he a writer?"

"Yes. A writer."

"So you mean he writes your character? What is he, sort of a playwright?"

"Yes."

"Does he write my character, too?" I ask anxiously.

Alan looks grave. Professorial. He sighs and then explains the situation patiently: "Oh, no. Mr. Finkelman could *never* write the Cathy Crimmins character. He could not write that character at all. That's not to say that the character doesn't have a right to exist, just that Mr. Finkelman could never create her."

I am devastated. Later, Joellen, Gary, and I go out to dinner at a cheap Thai joint in west Philly, and I keep asking them why Kelly and Alan are part of the play and I'm not. If Mr. Finkelman isn't writing my character, who is?

Dr. Everett Hill returns with his resident to evaluate Alan's cognitive skills. They ask me to leave the room—standard procedure, since evaluators don't want a brain injury patient to try to get clues or answers from a well-meaning relative.

Al flashes me a "thumbs-up" sign upon my return. "I fucking aced it. Aced the test, man," he says, smiling goofily. The two doctors glance up, avoiding eye contact with me.

Outside later, in the corridor, the soft-spoken Everett shows Gary and me what he calls "very disappointing results." When asked to draw a clock face, Al could not do it. The doctors show us the paper. Al's clock starts with the number one at the top and ends with eleven. He also cannot copy a simple pattern. On the test they showed him an alternating border of squares and triangles, but he could not duplicate it. Instead, he has written down, with great effort, A B A B. He knows the two shapes are different, but he cannot copy them. His script looks like a second-grader's. In the hospital chart the doctors write that nearly a month after his injury Alan "is still oriented in only one sphere": he knows who he is but not where he is, why he is here, or what day or time it is.

"I think we are looking at months of rehabilitation in a good facility," says Dr. Hill.

Gary and I hug, both of us shaking. The test results have made it official—we are not just imagining how bad it is. This afternoon, I'm catching a train to New York, where Tom and I are supposed to go on the radio to promote our most recent book. Gary has promised to hold down the fort. I try to tell Alan that I am going, but it doesn't register. On the way back tomorrow I'll check out Bryn Mawr Rehabilitation Hospital.

When I get to New York to meet Tom, it turns out that we're doing a *television* interview about our book, not radio at all. It's one of those gang-bang satellite interviews where we'll sit in a studio and be broadcast to many stations around the country. I'm wearing ratty clothes, and my hair is long overdue for a cut. I've been existing on three hours of sleep a night for weeks. I'm white and blotchy and bloated. How will I remember anything about our humorous novel? It seems as if I wrote it in another life. At least on the radio I could fake it by looking at notes.

"I can't do this!" I tell Tom as the makeup artist commences her salvage operation.

He tries to console me: "Hey, wouldn't it be funny if Al were watching television in his hospital bed and he sees you and he tells everyone his wife's on TV, and they think he is just hallucinating?"

The next day I'm on the cell phone we bought for our big, exciting Canadian vacation, zooming down the New Jersey

Turnpike in Tom's car. Our Toyota is still stuck up in Canada, so Tom has agreed to take me to Bryn Mawr Rehab Hospital on our way back from the New York interviews.

I know that Al must start rehab as quickly as possible. Evidence shows that the sooner a TBI survivor starts a rigorous program, the better his chances of improvement. There's nothing nurses or doctors can do for Alan in an acute hospital setting, as they call it, except tie him to the bed and wheel him down to an overcrowded physical therapy gym once a day. If we'd stayed in Canada, he'd have started a rehab program by now.

Bryn Mawr is on the list approved by our HMO, but I'm also looking into Magee Rehabilitation, which is in downtown Philadelphia, only minutes from our house. Magee is not approved, but I have made vague noises about suing the HMO because of our air ambulance trip and what it might have done to Alan's brain. It feels strange to be shopping for rehabilitation centers, the way we looked at day care centers or schools for Kelly.

Bryn Mawr is an impressive place. The director of the brain injury program talks to me on the cell phone as we drive there, asking all about Alan's case. The hospital is set on a beautiful campus outside Paoli, Pennsylvania—the outer limits of the Main Line, an exurban paradise of upscale housing and horse pastures. There's a pond, a greenhouse, and a state-of-the-art indoor therapy pool. I'm appalled and somewhat amused to find out that the brain injury patients do equestrian therapy. "You *do* know that my husband got hit on the head?" I say. Al can't even sit up straight, so I imagine him falling off a horse. When we would ride horses or mules at places like the Grand Canyon or out in Yosemite, Al was always the guy whose pony would buck or run out of control. After one close call, when a loose windbreaker frightened his steed and Alan nearly took a seventy-five-foot tumble off a narrow ridge, he told me he was thinking of hanging up his spurs. Boys from Brooklyn weren't made to ride horses, he said.

Yes, there's definitely a Main Line Suburban/Devon Horse Show preppy connection. Of course they would do equestrian therapy at Bryn Mawr Rehabilitation Hospital! Does Dr. Muffy Biddle-Pepper supervise? I imagine Al in jodhpurs and a little *National Velvet* riding hat. The thought actually makes me laugh aloud. I cough into the cell phone to cover myself.

Of course, there are good reasons to put a brain-injured man on a horse. Horses are used to help a patient regain his own natural gait: by sitting astride a horse, the patient gets the idea of walking again. The animal's natural motion reeducates the brain and helps a person understand where he is located in the spatial frame.

The woman in charge of intake gives us a tour of the facility, with special emphasis on the brain injury ward. It is locked to prevent "elopement," the romantic term assigned to escape attempts by the mentally impaired. The beds are low, padded, playpenlike things on the floor that prevent brain injury patients from falling out of bed. The gates of the beds are locked from the outside so that the patients are securely contained.

I feel a mixture of embarrassment and fear as I ask the woman about basic issues: how the staff deals with incontinence, how often they provide cognitive and physical therapy. Having Tom there is hard; I'm self-conscious, and I can tell he is overwhelmed by the grim reality of the facility, however appealing its campus. My thoroughness in asking questions is just another sign that I have crossed over to the realm of caregiver.

I've been clutching the large films of Alan's CT scans from Canada, which I show to the director of the brain injury unit. There's not much he can tell me about them, except to note that Alan is severely brain-injured. He's kind, though, and talks to us for quite a while.

Our last stop on the tour is the scariest one. There is an apartment within the facility, complete with kitchen, living room, television, and bedroom. Once a loved one is nearly ready to come home, the spouse spends a night or two there with him, pretending to have a normal life again. The guide stresses the privacy of the place, which makes me think she is alluding to resuming sexual relations. Just the way she keeps emphasizing it makes me think sex will be a problem. The apartment is equipped with several panic buttons throughout the rooms that will summon staff should the brain-injured person begin to become "agitated or confused." I can tell that this apartment is a good idea, but I find it overwhelmingly sad that I will have to come to a motel-like setting to see if Alan and I can live together again. Our tour guide talks about how in the program patients learn to cook and clean—washing dishes, vacuuming, dusting.

"Hey, can I send my husband there?" asks my friend Robin, when I tell her that night about how Al will learn to cook and vacuum. We joke about opening a Husband Rehab center. Forget brain injury, we'll just send *all* married men to rehab. I'll tell Al he was a gourmet cook before his accident: "Honey, don't you remember that fabulous coq au vin you used to make for dinner parties?"

My night is sleepless as I weigh what to do with Alan. The brain injury evaluators from Magee tested him while I was in New York, and I am going to see their facility in the morning. Bryn Mawr seems wonderful, a top-of-the-line Mercedes-Benz type of place. I especially like the greenhouse, since I know how much the old Alan liked to garden. But the hospital is well over an hour from our house, and I wonder how I'll manage Kelly and my work and still get out there every day. Should I get a small apartment and enroll Kelly in school out there? Maybe that would be the right thing to do, since Al might be in there for months. Yet every psychologist I've spoken to has said that Kelly needs continuity at this point. I get tired just thinking about relocating for Alan's rehab time, although not tired enough to sleep.

Magee, which I tour the next day, is not as pretty as Bryn Mawr. It's an urban, gritty place. There's a greenhouse on the roof but no horses or pool. Still, I am convinced this is the right place for Alan. It's close to home, and as city people we'll feel more relaxed there. And it pleases me to think that I can force the HMO to pay for it, even though it is not in our "network." (I have been making a colossal stink about our harrowing air ambulance ride.) Maybe I just can't face a decision to move to a temporary apartment an hour away in the suburbs. Or perhaps I feel more confident with the people at Magee. I meet Lisa Gordon, the case manager who would oversee Alan's rehabilitation, and her empathy and honesty impress me. She tells me that she will be there for me and Kelly as well as for Alan and that she understands the tremendous stress we're under.

The day before Al is moved to Magee, I try to talk to him about rehabilitation and how important it will be for his future. "This is the biggest challenge you're ever going to have," I say. "But you'll do fine."

He looks at me with dull eyes. Above his salt-and-pepper beard, which is getting longer by the minute, his mouth turns up in a tiny smirk. "Yeah. I think I would do okay in rehab. *If* I had another wife."

"Oh great. Thanks. So who would you want, Al?"

"Umm. Kay. I think Kay," he says.

Gee. I want our friend Kay for a wife, too. She's even-tempered and thoughtful. She's visited Al every day while he's been at HUP. I love her. And I'm sick of doing this stuff. Let someone else make the decisions!

It's funny, I think, that the damaged Al alludes to my inadequacies as a nurturer quite a bit. He's right. I am lousy at taking care of people. Wife of Brain Injury Victim is a really bad role for me. And in his disinhibited phase, Alan can only tell the truth. I wish Alan had another wife, too.

6

*Patient was somewhat lethargic, naked. . . . He was alert and
oriented to person; however, not to place or year, for which it was
1963. He was able to get the year 1996 on repeat with
rehearsal. . . . He was able to spell "world" forwards; however,
not able to spell it backwards.*

—notes from Alan's admissions exam record,
Magee Rehabilitation Hospital

The Magee Rehabilitation Hospital on Race and Sixteenth
Streets is a scary place to many Philadelphians. It's where
you end up if you've been in a car accident and are paralyzed or you've had a major stroke and can't speak or move.
On hearing that Alan's at Magee, one of his coworkers says
to my mother, "Oh, he must be really bad, then."

That first weekend at Magee is awful.

Al arrives by ambulance from HUP late on Friday afternoon. His childhood friend Gerry Sussman and his wife,
Judy Wein, come down to visit from Queens and end up
helping me move all the flowers and cards from HUP to
Magee. They're shocked by how out of it Al is—the stress of
the move seems to make him slip back into a semiconscious
state, and when awake he is very agitated.

Initially, I feel as if I've been sold a bill of goods: rehab was supposed to be different from an acute hospital like HUP, but I don't see any sign of it yet. On the weekend, without scheduled therapies, Magee seems pretty much like a regular institution. Al's case manager, Lisa Gordon, and I have discussed "timed voiding," the technique of asking a brain-injured patient every two hours if he has to go to the bathroom. She assured me that they would begin this immediately with Alan, but the whole first weekend he is still in a diaper, and it is changed less frequently than at HUP.

The first morning after we arrive, on Saturday, while Gary is still there, I try to overcome my natural awkwardness and learn how to push a wheelchair. Maneuvering Alan through doorways and around corners takes time, and I'm very bad at figuring out how to back him into elevators. I'm surprised by how heavy the wheelchair is and by how Al's feet keep falling off the little metal platforms at the bottom. I can't even get the thing to roll straight—it veers to one side or the other, and I have to ask Gary for help as we wheel around the hallways, trying to become oriented to Alan's floor.

"I'm tired," Alan says repeatedly in a flat voice. He shows no interest in being out of his room and no curiosity about where he is.

Kelly has stayed overnight with her best friend, Jennifer, whose parents bring Kelly over to Magee in the early afternoon. Kelly is delighted to see Al out of bed and sees his wheelchair as a new toy. She begs to push her father, but the chair is too much for a seven-year-old to handle, and whenever I let her take over, even briefly, poor Al goes careening into gurneys at the sides of hallways or catches his legs on garbage cans and water coolers we don't seem able to avoid. "Fuck!" he yells, a standard comment these days.

With Gary by our side, we take our first hike around the hospital, up to the roof, which has tables and big planters all around. Alan criticizes the decor and especially the lack of attention to the plants.

"Goddamned law firm!" he says. "The goddamned law firm never knows how to take care of things. Look at this! It's pretty fucking pathetic!" Whenever visitors come that first week, he will complain incessantly about his law firm's inattention to detail.

The last big law firm Al worked for, Montgomery, McCracken, Walker & Rhoads, is but a stone's throw from the rehab hospital. Does he sense that? I point out to Al how we can see part of the firm's building from the rooftop garden at Magee, but it doesn't register. He thinks he's *in* the law firm, so why would he be interested in seeing where it is?

At times, before Kelly was born, I'd pick up Alan at Montgomery, McCracken early in the evening and end up parking near Magee, an imposing brick fortress on the edge of Chinatown. Walking by the hospital, I'd notice the mostly young men in wheelchairs or on stretchers out on the balcony, smoking and laughing. I pitied them. I looked away.

Now we, too, seem to have descended into the innermost circle of Hell, where normalcy is aberrant. Fresh horrors appear during every hallway stroll or elevator ride on that first weekend, and I spend most of my energy pretending not to look at the other patients. Spinal cord cases on their stomachs on rolling stretchers, catheter bags beside them. Boys in neck braces, strapped into wheelchairs with high backs. Former jocks with metal rods sticking into their heads or open holes in their shaved skulls. Joellen, who suffers from degenerative rheumatoid arthritis, will end up at Magee a few months after Alan for rehabilitation after getting both a knee and a hip replacement. She remembers crying every time she was wheeled into the cafeteria, which "looked like the intergalactic bar scene in the first *Star Wars* movie."

Kelly seems to adjust better to the strangeness than I do. To her, Magee is less boring than the hospital, full of nooks and crannies to explore, and the wheelchairs, gurneys, walkers, crutches, and canes are "cool." By the end of our first tour, she is even comfortable sitting on her father's lap as I wheel them around.

As we're waiting for the elevator to leave the rooftop that first day, a young man in a wheelchair, a counselor at Magee, attempts to strike up a conversation. "What is your disability?" he says to Alan. Clueless, Alan turns his head toward me. Kelly, sitting on his lap, looks up at me, too.

I must seem as blank as Al, because the man repeats the question:

"What is your husband's disability?"

I open my mouth, but the words won't come. I've been perfectly comfortable discussing Al's brain injury with doctors, nurses, and therapists up until now because it was, I thought, a temporary condition. But here's a young man, disabled himself, who's asking a simple yet unacceptable question, one that implies immutability. I feel panicky, embarrassed, and pissed off at the same time. *My husband is not disabled,* I want to say, *he just hit his head.*

"Brain injury," I mumble.

"Well, we'd love to have him play in our basketball league. We practice a couple of times a week."

"Can he, can he, huh, huh, huh, Mom?" asks Kelly, jumping up and down on her paralyzed dad.

I look at Al. "That would be cool," he says goofily. His eyes still have that glazed-over look; his right arm is still curling up strangely.

I take a breath. "Well, let's see how your dad does, okay? I mean, he was just in an accident." I can't even imagine Al playing wheelchair hoops. He's strapped into his chair and still can't move his hand well enough to wheel himself. He continues to slump over toward his right side, as he did in his hospital bed. I know I'm disappointing Kelly, who still wants to see her dad as a jock. The only question she asks the rehab doctor that first day is when her father will be able to go in-line skating again.

Al's room resembles a dormitory room, with built-in dressers made of blond wood and a large bulletin board. A big calendar announces the year, month, and day of the week. The staff has suggested that we bring in photographs from home to keep Alan oriented, so on that first Saturday I set up pictures on his nightstand of Kelly and of us at our wedding and at a formal dance. I tape photographs of his nieces and nephews on the wall. I feel as though I'm dropping my husband off at summer camp, since I'm told that every few days I'll have to take home his laundry and bring him a fresh supply of T-shirts and shorts. On his night table is a big bowl of candy and Cheez Doodles and potato chips that people have sent or brought, and we've taped all his get-well-soon cards to the walls. From his room you can see the clock tower of the *Philadelphia Inquirer* newspaper offices.

After our Saturday wheelchair tour, a male nurse transfers Alan to his Vail bed, a mesh contraption that's like a cross between a pup tent and a mosquito net. Zipped up from the outside, the Vail is designed to keep a brain-injured person from getting out of bed unassisted and also to minimize the damage he can do to himself when agitated and thrashing around. The staff at Magee tell me that families are often upset when they first see their loved ones confined inside the Vail bed, but to me the zippered compartment seems more humane than bonds or a straitjacket. Alan still refuses to believe that he can't walk and will try to stand up whenever given the chance.

That first weekend, Al appears to enjoy the soothing, womblike atmosphere of the bed. He seems like a happy toddler content in his playpen or crib, and he sleeps a lot, exhausted by the move from HUP. When I kiss him good-bye to drive Gary to the airport, I zip up his bed and he drifts off immediately. Joellen has arrived for a visit, and she says she will sit with Al and watch Kelly while I take Gary to the airport, which is only fifteen minutes away on a weekend day without traffic.

It's hard to see Gary go, because he's been such a help. Every night he's been there with me, in our house, so that I haven't felt so alone. He has even started helping me sort out the bills and Alan's insurance policies. Gary was glad to be there when Alan left HUP, since he'd been eager for his brother to get into rehab. "I wish I could stay to see him get better," he says, hugging me before he jumps out of the car to catch his plane.

As I leave the airport I feel empty. I decide to stop quickly at the small supermarket around the corner from our house before I go back to Magee. I realize that I haven't done anything "normal" in nearly a month. I buy a few staples and a few kiddie items—Popsicles, bubble gum, macaroni and cheese in a box, soda—things I know Kelly will like, since this is the first night she will be home. Joanne and Sarah are going away for the weekend, so Kelly has no choice but to stay with her mom. So far she has refused to come home to sleep, and her reluctance to spend time with me hurts.

For the last week and a half, ever since Alan and I arrived at HUP, Kelly has insisted that our house is dangerous and something might happen and she doesn't want to be there. "It's too scary," she says every time I beg her to come home to stay with me. We've developed a routine: she sleeps overnight at Sarah and Joanne's, where she boards the bus for Girl Scout camp each morning. Then she takes another bus home to our neighborhood at about three-thirty, where either I or her babysitter, Ali, picks her up. A lot of times it has been Ali, since in the afternoon I am always busy with things relating to Alan's care. Sometimes they go to our house or to Ali's to play and watch television. Sometimes they take a cab to meet me at the hospital. Then I see Kelly for dinner and drive her back to Sarah and Joanne's. If I say she *must* stay home, she starts crying, so I always give in. I'm too tired. Some nights I'm even too tired to drive her out to Cheltenham, and I call Joellen or someone else to do it. I try telling Kelly that she can't go because I can't drive her, but then she gets on the phone herself and begs Sarah and Joanne to pick her up.

Her terror seems real, but why would she be afraid of our house? The accident happened so far away and in a rural place. Later, psychologists explain that Kelly, at age seven, is just at the end of the "magical" stage. Seeing her father knocked unconscious was terrible but also somehow random and supernatural. When she is with me, say the shrinks, she fears that I might disappear or be injured in the same unexplainable, sudden way. So it's easier for her not to see me—that way I am safe. And the experts also say it's natural for her to have transferred her feelings of evil and foreboding to her home.

But explanations offer little comfort. I keep thinking about what would have happened if Alan had died. Would it be months before I could even get to see Kelly, to hug her and hang around watching television or reading? I feel like a widow, but it's not like in the movies, where the widow and her only daughter bond and have adventures together.

As I enter the grocery store, I think about how important it is to have a perfect and fun time with Kelly that night.

The aisles might as well be the surface of the moon. I am disconnected, spacey. I go through the checkout, and then, on the way out, I hold the door for a young mother with a stroller. But as I clutch the door I let my cart go, and it drifts down the sidewalk, over the curb, and into the middle of busy South Street. Disaster. The cart overturns, my bags spill out, and several cars whiz by, running over the groceries.

The guy in the delivery van who pulls over to help me is clearly puzzled that I'm not making a move. I've gone from astonishment to resignation in about thirty seconds flat. I just stand there, laughing and laughing.

"Gee, lady, how could this happen?" he says, salvaging my gallon of milk from the middle of the street but abandoning the partially crushed carton of eggs.

In the end the delivery man saves quite a bit of the stuff, while I just look on, giggling hopelessly. I open my trunk and he throws pasta, produce, and Popsicles into it, bagless. I can't stop laughing.

"I still don't understand how that could have happened," he says again, getting back into his van.

"Oh, I wouldn't be surprised at anything that happens," I say, forcing the words out between guffaws.

I decide to stop at home briefly to unload my ragtag pile of groceries before meeting Joellen and Kelly back at Magee. I'm just coming into the house when the phone rings.

"Cathy, it's Al," says Joellen. "He's very agitated. He's upsetting Kelly, and he's, well, moaning and thrashing, and, well, you know."

Oh God, poor Joellen. Why has everything turned to shit? Why didn't she just take Kelly home immediately? "Get her out of there," I say. "I'll come right over."

Al turned on a dime, Joellen tells me when I get to Magee. He seemed so nice and peaceful, sleepy, really, and then suddenly he was awake and exposing himself to Kelly and shouting swearwords.

When I arrive, Joellen and Kelly are sitting in the lounge on Al's floor, looking red-eyed and grim. The stage is set for one of the worst nights of my life.

As soon as I get Kelly back to the house, I order Chinese food, her favorite, and then we settle down to watch TV in the living room for a few hours. I ply her with what's left of the mangled supermarket treats. At around eleven Kelly finally seems tired, so I suggest we go upstairs to bed.

"No, no, I can't. It's bad up there!" she says.

No amount of reasoning helps. Worn down, I find myself yelling at her, "Daddy's accident was in *Canada*. *Canada!* Not here. This is the city. We're safe!"

She cries piteously. She doesn't even want to be hugged. I drink another glass of wine. Then I drink one more. Before I know it, the bottle is finished and I'm feeling very sorry for myself. My husband is a mentally deficient pervert cripple, and my daughter hates me.

There's no way I am going to get Kelly upstairs. She's too heavy to carry, and I've never felt so tired or alone in my life. Eventually I drag a futon mattress from my office into the living room, where she sleeps fitfully, waking up every hour or so, screaming. I can't sleep at all, so at about two in the morning I begin watching a movie by Paul Auster and Wayne Wang, *Blue in the Face*. What a mistake. The movie features Harvey Keitel as the owner of a cigar shop in Brooklyn, and the characters are constantly talking about being from Brooklyn and how unique Brooklyn is. All I can think of is Alan, zipped into his bed. He's from Brooklyn, he tells people constantly. In his mind he still lives there, stuck in 1963. Watching the movie, I dissolve into drunken blubbery sobs until I finally fall asleep. The next morning, Kelly accuses me of drifting off before she did. She says I was asleep while she was awake. She's inconsolable.

"You lied to me," she yells. "You said you would stay up when I went to sleep!" She must have popped up again after I had finally conked out.

I ask her if she wants to go to the hospital again to see her father. "No," she says, "I want to be with someone else. Daddy scared me." We have the first of many discussions about how Daddy doesn't know he is acting strangely. He doesn't mean what he is doing, I tell her. I explain, too, that most people are away on this nice summer weekend, so she'll have to come to the hospital. But she doesn't have to see Alan if she doesn't want to. I offer to take her to the pool before we go to Magee. "I don't want to go there," she says, and starts to cry. Desperate, I call Sally, and about an hour later she arrives to take Kelly to her house to play with her sons.

"Oh, God, you look awful," says Sally. "What happened?"

Although Kelly relents within a few days and begins visiting Alan, it is weeks before she agrees to stay overnight with me again.

Fortunately, a rehabilitation hospital has its own microcosmic order. After a few days at Magee, it seems perfectly natural to see people whizzing by who are half human, half machine. A middle-aged man perched on his stomach on a gurney playing poker with his friends in the roof garden is unremarkable, as are the giant buzzers announcing the floors to the blind and the wide automatic doors and raised window boxes. It takes me three days to figure out that the faucets in all the bathrooms operate on automatic sensors, but once I do, it makes perfect sense, and when I return home at night I almost resent having to twist something to get water.

Rehabilitation is an equalizing process. No one much cares what you did before; they're focused on what you can do now and how you can learn to live independently once again. Going from an acute hospital to a rehabilitation environment represents what current sociological jargon calls a "paradigm shift": at an acute hospital, you are sick and being taken care of. But once you arrive at a good rehab hospital like Magee, you go from being a passive patient to becoming an active participant in your own recovery.

. . .

Only a few days into his rehab stay, Al is chosen to be transported along with other paraplegics to Veterans Stadium for a Phillies baseball game. Magee believes in integrating the disabled into every facet of life as quickly as possible. They call this approach "community outgoing."

"I'm going to a baseball game!" Al tells me over the phone when I call him that afternoon. It's strange, since before we left on vacation he'd actually bought tickets for a game this very week. I immediately decide that he's confused. Yet how on earth did he remember having baseball tickets when he doesn't remember anything else? Still, he mixes everything up. "No, you're not going to the Phillies," I say gently. "You were supposed to go, but now you're in the hospital."

"Yeah, I'm going," he says flatly.

The next day, I discover he's right. After dinner in the hospital's rooftop garden, we go downstairs, where a special little bus with a hydraulic lift waits to take Al and four other guys in wheelchairs to the game. While we're waiting for Al's turn to board the bus, a blond young man approaches us. He drags his foot as he walks, and his body, particularly his neck, is twisted to the left side. He slurs his words as he talks.

"Ya got TBI?" he asks.

"Yes, he's brain-injured," I say, patting Al's shoulder in the wheelchair. Al is staring ahead, distracted by the spectacle of the bus and the lift.

"Me, too," says the young man. "Motahcycle accident. Six yeahhs ago. Drunk. Ma-a-a-an. Dey had to teach me everyting all ovah again. Howta walk, howta talk, howta read, ya know." The man leans down, putting his face near Al's.

"Dey teach you real good. Dey fix you up real good here. But, let me tell ya, *dey are fuckers, fuckers dey are.* Dose speech terapists. Dey make ya work, dey fuck with ya. *Fuckers!*" He laughs, sounding maniacal. Alan hardly reacts at all to the exchange.

Oh, hell, I think, this guy is a walking poster child for

frontal lobe damage. Is he the ghost of brain injury future, some sort of warning about what will happen to Al? That's a terrible way to respond, I know, and a rotten attitude to have toward a survivor, and I feel guilty. Think of how far this man has come, I tell myself, how hard his life must have been these past six years. But the plain truth is, he scares me. I want to hang on to the back of Al's wheelchair until my knuckles are white. I want Al to get up from the wheelchair, look me in the eye, and admit that he's been faking. I've been reading more about the tendency toward disinhibition after severe brain injury and about the frequent use of profanity. I've seen these traits in Al already. And here is someone, years out of injury, still manifesting these problems. A wave of pity hits me, but it is not pity for the young man, it is pity for myself. Is this what my husband will be like forever? The young man is talking to me, and I seem to be listening. I arrange my face in a happy, inquisitive mask as I ask him more about his condition. He still comes back to Magee for activities, he says. "How nice," I say. And then finally it's Al's turn to board the minibus. Loaded backward on the lift, he smiles and waves as it hoists him aboard. I wave back and then turn away quickly so that he won't see me start to cry.

During the first week at Magee, it takes me a while to switch my communication strategies. In acute hospitals, you only have a few seconds to talk to the Mighty Doctors as they stroll by. At Kingston General and HUP, I planned my quest for information like guerrilla attacks, pouncing rabidly to make the most of those few moments. Rehab is much more relaxed, and the doctors have a more human touch. A few days into Al's stay, Kelly and I pull into the parking lot at the same time as a young resident, John, who's driving a hip utility vehicle that impresses my daughter enough to make her want to speak with him.

"How is my dad doing?" Kelly asks John. It's the first day she's agreed to come back to visit Al.

He looks right at her, and for a moment I'm worried about his response. "How is he doing? How is he *doing*? Man, he's doing *awesome*, babe." I want to kiss him when I see how Kelly starts beaming. "He said my dad is doing *awesome*," she tells Sarah later.

I'm still devouring everything there is to read about brain injury, and when I first meet Dan Weinstein, Al's physiatrist (rehabilitation doctor), I come on strong, flinging around medical terms like some insecure cub reporter.

"I've been reading a study about indications for prophylactic Dilantin in TBI cases where there was only one seizure incident," I say to Dan. "And I really think that I don't want Alan on Dilantin much longer. I believe it's slowing down his cognitive recovery. This study said that it could be discontinued after two weeks in cases like his with no ill effects."

He looks at me for a moment. "Yeah, I read the same study. Sure, let's take Al off Dilantin."

"What about heterotopic ossification?" I ask Dan another time. Al is experiencing excruciating shoulder pain. I've dredged up the most arcane possibility: in rare cases after brain injury, signals get sent to the shoulders or hip to form more bone, so the muscles in the joints become ossified. No one knows why, exactly. I'm convinced, with our luck, that HO is causing Alan's severe shoulder pain.

"Okay, we'll do an X ray of the shoulder," says Dan, practically sighing. "But I can guarantee that it won't be heterotopic ossification. It is really rare, Cathy."

Dan is right. Al turns out to have just a garden-variety torn rotator cuff that goes undiagnosed until I take him to an orthopedic surgeon weeks later.

. . .

"My wife is a genius! She memorized the code!" From his wheelchair, about a week into rehab, Al is watching me punch in the numbers that let us enter or exit the locked brain injury ward. Alan says that if he could just remember his bank machine code, he'd be able to open the door. He tells all his visitors that the touchpad at the door is his ATM machine, and he tries, almost halfheartedly, to look over people's shoulders to figure out what his personal identification number used to be. He's upset that he can't remember his ATM number. Yet, oddly, he never asks me what it is. Does he think the other people are using their own special codes? Even if someone were to give him the numbers, he wouldn't be able to keep them in his mind very long, perhaps not even long enough to punch them in.

Short-term memory disturbance is one of the many deficits noted in Alan's admission diagnoses at Magee. He's also described as having "acute confusional state," "right hemiparesis" (paralysis of his right side), "aphasia" (failure to locate words), "dysarthria" (slurred speech), "memory disturbance," "mobility deficit" (inability to walk), "self-care deficits," and "deficits in activities of daily living."

At Magee, Al is pissed off a lot. Most of all, he hates his logbook.

The big black book, a staple of rehab life, goes everywhere with him. It's next to his bed at night and in the bag on the back of his wheelchair during the day. Because brain injury patients tire easily and can't concentrate for very long, Al's therapies last only a half hour each. His physical, cognitive, occupational, and speech therapists record what he has done in the logbook, and Alan is supposed to write down comments, too, although in the beginning he is incapable of scribbling more than a word or two.

The logbook is designed to help Al remember what he has done—he still can't recall anything that happened more than a few minutes ago. But he thinks he doesn't need mnemonics. He feels as if Big Brother is watching him, he says. Lacking self-awareness, a common symptom of brain injury, he tells all visitors that he can remember what the hell he has done all day, thank you very much. Yet whenever I ask him what happened that afternoon, he has no idea. He reminds me of Kelly in kindergarten.

At the beginning of the logbook is a section of "autobiographical information" I filled out on his first day here. It lists his age, occupation, family members, and hobbies, which include gardening, softball, baseball, roller hockey, reading, the theater, music, and travel. Someone must have gone over the information with Alan, because there's an addendum at the bottom, in someone else's handwriting, that says, "Why I'm here—I hit my head in a boating accident and have trouble remembering things."

I filled out the form during my first interview with Lisa Gordon, Alan's case manager. She's sensitive to my emotions about the rehab process and in particular to my snobbish determination to let people know how smart and well-educated Alan is. Sensing this, Lisa makes a point of telling nurses and other staff members that Alan is "a very intelligent, very-high-IQ patient." She listens to me patiently when I get bristly about gender roles. I want her to know, I say, that Alan was equally responsible for taking care of Kelly. I am not just a typical female, I tell her. I have a career that I can't give up. Alan and I are equals. I sound like an asshole, defensive and elitist. But Lisa is wonderful at handling stressed spouses. (Is there any other kind after a severe traumatic brain injury?) She tells me that she's there for me and Kelly as much as she is for Alan.

About a week after getting to Magee, when Alan seems to have figured out that he is not in a law firm but in a rehab

hospital, he begins complaining vociferously about "the god-
damn social workers, the ex-hippies," who work there.
They're always late and not very smart, he says. He sounds
like a cantankerous old man.

Alan has a full day of therapies and group meetings. The
attitude at Magee is that the patients are here to work, and
they are kept busy in sessions from nine until three-thirty. In
the morning Alan has orientation group, physical therapy,
occupational therapy, and speech therapy. After lunch he
attends recreation therapy, physical therapy, occupational
therapy, a third session of physical therapy, and a psychology
session with a neuropsychologist.

The nurses have time to shower Al only every few days, and
they ask me if I want to help so I can do it myself on the
"off" days. They show me the drill. First they strip him and
transfer him to a shower chair, a padded, waterproof wheelchair with slotted cushions that allow the attendant to reach
up from underneath to wash the patient's backside and
genitals.

I see how wet the nurse gets, standing there shampooing
Alan's hair and soaping up and rinsing off his body, so I
make a mental note to wear a bathing suit when I try it. The
next night I change into my sensible black tank suit and manage the whole process rather successfully. It feels strange to
wash Al in intimate places as I would a baby. But I feel like
I've come a long way from the first days at Kingston General, when I could barely spoon food into his mouth.

Lisa Gordon is excited about Al's progress. "Alan is clearing," she tells me over the phone at the end of that first week.
"He is really clearing quickly." Al's rehab team, consisting of
the doctors and Lisa, has just come from seeing him. I've

heard from Lisa frequently this first week, which I appreciate. Not being able to see Alan during the day, when he undergoes his therapies, has made me feel cut off.

But what does she mean by "clearing"? Pressed for a definition, Lisa explains that Al seems to be better oriented. He shows some awareness that he is in a rehab hospital. He is not as agitated.

"And your husband is much less self-centered than he could be, which is amazing for someone as severely brain-injured as he is," she says. He has been asking about his wife and child, she says, and asking how we are doing. Lisa sees this as a very good sign.

I guess it is, but every time I see Alan he refers to his "wife and child" or his "wife and daughter." Kelly and I can be right there, but he still refers to us by generic titles instead of our names. Is this because one side effect of brain injury is a propensity toward concrete thinking? He is Alan. He is a husband. He has a wife. He has a child. This much he knows, and he clings to those basic roles and definitions. Before his injury, he never would have called me his wife over and over like this. Another odd quirk has emerged, too: he's added a year to Kelly's age. No matter how often I tell him she is seven years old, he insists that she is eight. It seems a small problem, perhaps, but, as a friend points out, not being able to get single-digit numbers right could certainly preclude returning to work as a bank trust officer, his current position.

He's developed a strange, childlike reverence toward authority. Whenever I talk about Lisa Gordon, he says, "She's the boss. The head of everything." I explain that Lisa is a social worker, and a wonderful one at that, but he just says, "No, she's the head of the whole unit. She rules everything. She's my boss, too." He tells elaborate stories about his doctors talking to him, and in the narrative, he is always addressed as "son," even though I know that Alan is several years older than his physiatrist, Dan Weinstein, and certainly much older than the residents who accompany Dan.

After the first week at Magee, Al starts railing against any restraints. The Vail bed is no longer comforting. He thrashes around and pushes at the mesh. He asks me to unzip it before I leave, which, of course, I can't do. He also hates the seat belt they've put on his wheelchair to keep him from standing up and falling over. He begs our friend Sandy when she visits to untie him and later appeals to Kay, too, saying he really *needs* to be free.

"What's the first thing you remember about the accident?" I ask Alan two years later.

"Waking up in that damn zippered bed! I hated that bed!"

Al's continence is beginning to return, too, although sporadically. He goes through a condensed toddler-type period, when he begins to develop awareness of the urge to go. He'll often announce that he has to urinate only seconds before it happens. Once during the first week at Magee we are on the roof when he says he has to go. I wheel him into the men's room, but I've never thought about how a guy strapped into a wheelchair can pee into a toilet. Then I see that there's a bottlelike portable urinal available, but before I can help him get it over his penis, the whole cubicle has been sprayed. Another time, while he is resting in his room in his Vail bed, he suddenly gets the urge to go. We try to use the "no spill" urinal the nurses have provided, but somehow I get it wrong and all his urine flows back out onto his legs. "You stupid moron bitch!" he says.

Once he does partially regain continence, Alan becomes obsessed by the bathroom and resents having to call the nurses to help him get there. Sometimes the staff still dresses him in a diaper when they are busy or they know he will have visitors and might have an accident.

More than anything, Alan wants to walk. He's begun to admit, under direct questioning, that he is paralyzed. And he seems to understand that walking is something he can do again, possibly, even if he can't do it now. He's working toward that goal in the three physical therapy sessions he has each day, and by all accounts he is making wonderful progress. In one of our first interviews at Magee, a counselor questioned me about our house layout. How many stairs? Would it be possible for Alan to live on the first floor? We live on the first two floors of an old brownstone town house, with steps up to both the front and back entrances. Our bedrooms are on the second floor. I'd begun to browse the yellow pages to find a contractor to build a ramp, and to think about how I would turn my office, on the first floor, into a bedroom.

But once he starts intensive physical therapy, Al surprises all of us.

For the first few days, he practices "transfers"—how to get himself from the wheelchair to the bed when he is not tied down. He is strong enough to do it, despite his weakened right side. Then a few days later an entry appears in his log-book, from his physical therapist: "Walked with a rolling walker." A week after he arrives at Magee, I see Al's brain-injured scrawl appear in the logbook: "I walked 150 feet PT w/Colleen." On the same page is an entry from his occupa-tional therapist: "You got up and dressed yourself with very little help. Stood very well by the bed to pull up your pants— Great Job!" I ask him about both entries, but he doesn't remember anything. I never see him walking, because I'm not allowed to participate in his therapies until the official "fam-ily training session," and he is not permitted to walk in the halls by himself or even in his room. By the time I get to the hospital, at around four, he's always back in his wheelchair.

That's why it is so startling the next week when my mother and I are visiting with Al one evening and he just gets up and walks across the room. He's been in physical therapy only about nine days.

"I gotta pee," he says suddenly, then stands up and stiffly walks across the room toward the bathroom. He's not quite upright, and kind of bow-legged, like Popeye, moving each leg stiffly from the hip. But miraculously, he's walking without assistance.

"Alan!" my mother and I yell together in the shock of seeing him upright. He's pretty fast. Running after him, I say his name again and come up behind as he slams the bathroom door in my face.

"I can't believe it," my mom says when I return to her side. Her eyes are filled with tears.

Seeing Alan stand up and walk is a revelation, an affirmation, a redemptive moment. I think back to the day he first opened his eyes in the ICU in Canada. I remember the dramatic moment when we saw Kelly walk her first few steps right before her first birthday. Alan's rebirthing is proceeding apace.

Al comes out of the bathroom, looking sullen as he perambulates awkwardly toward us.

"Al, you're walking!" I say, still astonished.

"Yeah, yeah, I'm walking," he says, sounding disinterested. "I can walk."

At this point, Kelly visits Alan at the rehab hospital every other day or so, one of our friends bringing her around. I get to see her every day, if only for fleeting moments. I feel very inadequate as a mother, with a child who doesn't even want to stay with me. I start thinking of myself as the opposite of a vampire—Kelly will tolerate me during the day but never through the night.

I also have mixed feelings about Kelly's visits to Magee. She should see her dad, sure, but I worry about having her encounter more disinhibited or agitated episodes. And the other people on the brain ward are no picnic, either. Al's roommate is a middle-aged man recovering from a brain tumor operation. Half of his head is shaved where the surgeon dipped into his skull. He stares down at his feet or watches television with the volume turned way up. I say hello to him every day when I arrive, but he never responds. In the hallway outside Al's room there's a little old black lady who sits, speechless, in a wheelchair, hour after hour, with a stuffed toy dog in her lap.

But the worst ones are the screamers. From the moment you enter the ward, you hear them. There's one who yells "Help me, help me, help me, Mary!!!!! Mary!!!!," another who shouts obscenities, and one guy who issues a deep, protracted wail.

"These people can't help it," I say to Kelly as we ride the elevator to Al's room. "It's not their fault—"

"—*because* their brains are hurt. Yeah, I know, Mom," says Kelly, rolling her eyes. At odd times she seems sophisticated, bored with the idea of having a father on a brain injury ward. Especially when she isn't cowering in our house, begging me to check the closets for intruders.

The best times for Kelly, I think, are when I bring along another child to keep her company, and they ride up and down on the hydraulic beds or race around in Al's wheelchair. They can go up to the big rooftop space to play and run around. There's a car up there, airlifted in by helicopter, so that patients in wheelchairs or crutches can learn to get into and out of it. Kelly and her best friend, Jennifer, climb in and pretend to drive. One afternoon Kelly and Natalia, our neighbor and her Girl Scout campmate, sneak into the rooftop greenhouse and play with bags of potting soil, flinging it all over the floor.

Sometimes I wonder if I should be exposing Kelly's young playmates to the world of rehab, and I know I should describe the ward to their parents before taking them along. ("Oh, by the way, you don't mind if your child sees people screaming, zipped into beds, do you? Or guys with bolts through their heads?") I know this, yet I don't do it. I just invite the kids and it makes my life easier, and I need them.

When you see a brain injury firsthand, it plunges you into thinking about the mind/body problem. Like a lot of people, I'd never thought seriously about the brain as a *physical* organ that regulates the body, like the heart, lungs, or kidneys. For most of my adult life, I'd never really considered the role it plays in walking, sitting, running, and jumping.

But as a child I thought much more about the brain's physical role. In the first grade my teacher showed a movie about the brain that featured tiny workers operating levers inside a person's head. A crowd of little guys scurried to and fro in "mission control," working frantically just to help their person walk down the street. Others manned buttons and levers to enable the human machine to see, hear, think, and smell. I got the message, at six, that much of the brain's power is expended on just lugging our carcasses around and keeping us from falling down. We're motorized meat and as such can't separate—ever—the mind from the business of bodily function. And when the brain is damaged, the results show up quickly in other parts of the body. In a few seconds Alan lost most of what he prized about his body: his easy sense of movement.

For up to a year after the accident, Alan's paralysis would return whenever he felt mentally overstimulated or threatened. He'd walk past a noisy group of people in a restaurant or on the street, and suddenly his right arm would curl up. His right leg would buckle a bit. In brain injury jargon, this sudden return of paralysis is called "inattention." The brain, overloaded with visual or aural stimuli, lets go of something else it is doing, in this case keeping Alan's damaged side functioning. The balance between the mental and the physical is delicate, almost magical, as any excellent athlete or ardent lover knows, and that balance is exactly what is threatened after TBI.

I'm in awe of Lisa Gordon's level of commitment. She's always at the hospital late. She sees each patient on the brain floor as much as, if not more than, the doctors, and is intimately familiar with each of their tiny gains. She goes through HMO hell for every case she manages: the weekly review, in which the bean counters try to discontinue therapy, and Lisa argues them out of it.

I call Lisa almost daily, and she always asks how I feel. One day I tell her how tired I am: "I feel exactly like I did right after my father died. I know that sounds silly, because Alan didn't die."

"Of course you feel that way. You're experiencing grief. You're in mourning."

I am so thankful for her words. Up until now I have felt secretly guilty that I am not more ecstatic about Alan's progress. I should be overjoyed that he is alive and doing so well, but I just want him to be uninjured. I want to turn back the clock, make our little boat leave the dock a few minutes later or earlier and miss the reckless teenager's speedboat altogether.

"You've experienced a crushing loss," Lisa continues. "The man you married is no longer here. Think about the summer you were going to have, the life you were going to have, and how it has turned out."

What a relief, to have someone else say I have a right to feel crappy. Ever since we got back to Philadelphia, friends and neighbors have been coming out of the woodwork to tell me how lucky we are. Alan didn't die. He's already learning to walk again. They seem to enjoy enumerating our blessings. "Don't you feel lucky?" they ask after they feast upon all the gory details of the accident.

No, I don't feel lucky. I feel scared. I have no idea what's going to happen next. And Lisa is right: Alan is still not here, however much he is "clearing." I thought he would be coming back a little more each day, but each day just seems to emphasize that I am alone, that Al is never coming back—or at least not the old Al.

Late one afternoon, when Al is still in his wheelchair after his therapies, I come into his room as he is talking to a coworker from the bank. The woman is leaning over, listening carefully.

"So, you see, I saw her, outside on the street, and she came up to me, the poor kid," says Alan. "She told me that she was sorry that she ran me over. But she said it isn't the first boat accident she's had. She doesn't want me to tell her parents."

"Oh, my," says the coworker, a nice older woman.

"Al, what are you talking about?" I ask.

"The girl. The girl who hit me. I saw her on the street, and she told me she was sorry. She's real sorry. Gee. She's so young, and here she's been in two accidents! I told her it was okay."

I'm about to correct him, to say it isn't possible that he met the girl, but there's something about the concerned look on his coworker's face that stops me. If I try to confront Alan with the blatant untruth of the story he's just told, this nice woman will go back to the office and tell everyone that Mr. Forman has lost his marbles. A group of coworkers was here a few days ago, and as Alan was giving advice about certain changes in the law governing bond investments—very confidently, I might add—he was also playing with his diaper through his shorts.

So I don't say anything. The woman leaves soon afterward, and I ask Alan to tell me the story again. He tells it in exactly the same way, not varying a single phrase, except that when I ask what the girl looks like and what her name is, he has no idea.

"Al, I don't think you saw her. Maybe you dreamed about it."

"No. She came to see me. She said she was sorry."

"Al, you don't even remember the accident. You couldn't recognize the girl. Even I don't remember what the girl looked like. Besides, she's in Canada."

"No, I saw her. Did you know she was in another accident before mine?"

I perch on the edge of the bed and reach out toward his wheelchair, putting my hands on his shoulders. I look right into his eyes. "Alan, let's think about this. Have you been outside at all yet?"

He is silent.

"Al, you can't walk that well yet. You can't have met the girl on the street. You haven't been outside. You weren't walking down the street. It's impossible."

"But I did. I did meet her."

.   .   .

Confabulation is one of the more interesting side effects of brain injury. It usually occurs at the stage when the person is still suffering from posttraumatic amnesia—that is, when the brain, scrambling to repair itself, is still incapable of dealing with short-term memory. When we were little, our parents called it lying, but the term "confabulation" is actually more accurate for children, too, since it refers to a "lie" in which the person is incapable of knowing the truth. Confabulation after brain injury or at the age of three stems from the same developmental problem—as kids, we didn't always understand what was true and what was not, and neither does the brain injury patient.

All of Alan's confabulations during this phase of his recovery contain a grain of truth, however microscopic. His brain takes little bits and pieces of whatever it can gather and cobbles them together into a narrative. He'd probably overheard some of us talk about the girl who had run him over with a speedboat, and so his brain annexed those comments as real memories. When my mother visits at Magee, he tells her stories about going swimming every day. Sounds plausible, but in fact the hospital has no pool. Maybe he saw a scene of someone swimming on a television commercial, or maybe his brain is hearkening back to all the other times in his life when he did go swimming during the summer. When Kelly was two, my mother took us to Sanibel Island in Florida, where we saw a few alligators in the swamps of the Ding Darling Nature Area. For weeks after we returned to Philadelphia, Kelly would insist that she saw alligators swimming in the Schuylkill River.

The wife of a caregiver I met on the Internet wins the prize as the most creative confabulator: after her severe brain injury, she told everyone at the rehab hospital that Adolf Hitler was staying on the same floor. She couldn't go out of her room, she said, because she was a little Jewish girl and

Hitler would find that out and kill her. There was no way my friend could convince his wife otherwise, despite his attempts to point out that it was 1998 and Hitler couldn't possibly be alive and that she was a grown woman in her forties. He has no explanation for the confabulation other than her lifelong interest in the Holocaust.

In addition to posttraumatic amnesia, Alan is suffering from retrograde amnesia, which in his case means that he not only recalls nothing about the accident itself but has also lost the memory of the three months before the accident. He remembers nothing, for example, about the big wedding we attended two weeks before our trip, or our anniversary weekend in New York about a month and a half before the accident, when we saw four plays in three days and went to the Met. I kid him about this: "Okay, so you don't remember the plays. What about the sex?"

Explanations of how the brain works seem to beg for metaphor: in the case of the memory problem, even experts will resort to comparing the human brain to its man-made counterpart, the computer. When we have experiences, they go first into short-term memory. Think of those memories as "computer files" we are working on at the moment or saving on floppy disk. Our long-term memory is stored in something more like a hard drive, which explains why, when the brain is damaged, long-term memory is often left intact. When Al's brain got walloped and began to swell against his skull, it discarded its current files, the ones that hadn't been "saved" to longer-term memory storage. That's why, his neuropsychologist Barbara Watson tells me, he cannot access memories that occurred a few months before the accident. They've been discarded, or at the very least, temporarily lost as the brain repairs itself.

Alan's short-term memory is already improving, though. He remembers, sometimes, what has happened that day. If you leave the room, when you return he knows you have already been there. One Sunday afternoon, after running around getting things together to take to Alan at the hospital and making phone calls and trying to sort out our bills, I decide to take a brief nap on the couch in my office. I haven't been sleeping well, so it's surprising how fast I fall asleep. It's also surprising when I wake up and it is nearly nine o'clock at night, when hospital visiting hours are over. My phone has been ringing, I later find out, but I never heard it. I feel as if I've been in a kind of minicoma myself. I call Al and apologize over and over. I can't believe I didn't go to see him. It is the first time I haven't seen him during visitors' hours since that day at HUP a while ago, when I had to go to New York. Alan doesn't sound particularly upset. He sounds sleepy and rather flat-toned. He had other visitors, he says.

Later that night his mother calls me. "Alan is still confused, I guess," says Naomi. "I asked him if you were there, and he said, 'My wife has not been here today.'"

"Well, no, actually he's right!" I feel terrible about not seeing him but mildly encouraged that he was able to remember enough to tell his mother of my absence.

Alan is developing new problems as his therapies proceed. Chief among them are sudden fluctuations in body temperature, or at least the perception that his temperature is changing. "It's as if I am swimming," he says, "and you know how when you're in a lake or the ocean, you hit a real cold spot? Well, that's how it feels when I am going through the air."

I'm stunned by his eloquence. He is so much more creative than he was before. In our marriage, I've always been the fanciful one, the writer. Alan is smart as a whip but prone to paper pushing. As he puts it, "I've got accountants' blood running through my veins." It was a joke when we were in graduate school—Al was so literal, he couldn't really analyze poetry. Our friends used to wonder why he had become an

English major. Law, with its minute, painstaking interpretation, seemed to suit him perfectly.

But now that he's been conked on the head, Alan is wild-eyed, imaginative, while I'm stuck paying the bills and filling out insurance forms. I haven't paid so much as an electric bill for fifteen years, and now everything financial is up to me. It's not a pretty sight. We have bills I never even knew about. Al always compared doing our finances to keeping an insolvent Third World country afloat. Now I see what he means. Dunning notices begin appearing right away. "Why wasn't *I* hit on the head?" I ask friends. The old Alan, with his practical streak, could have managed this whole situation much more competently.

I'm with Alan several times at the hospital when the temperature thing happens. He gets a funny look on his face and begins to shiver. One time his teeth actually chatter. Even though it's August and over 95 degrees outside, he is forever turning off the air-conditioning unit next to his bed. His room is often as hot and muggy as a sidewalk café in Miami.

"Have you asked the doctor about why you get so cold all of a sudden?" I ask when I see the sudden chill descend upon him a third time.

"Umm. No."

"Why not?"

"I forget."

I leave a Post-it in the logbook, prompting Al to ask his doctor or social worker about what he's feeling the next day on rounds. Dr. Weinstein runs blood tests, but everything turns out normal, and he doesn't have much to say about Alan's cold spells. One time Al has a spell when I am watching him do his walking exercises in the small brain injury gym. As Al shivers, Colleen, his physical therapist, mentions that she sees such problems quite often in brain-injured patients. Wild fluctuations in temperature, she explains, occur because the small center that regulates the body's temperature, the hypothalamus, has been damaged. It's not that Al merely perceives a chill, he really feels it. Later, I find out that the hypothalamus is very estrogen-sensitive and that the declining estrogen levels of menopause affect its function. So the hot flashes some menopausal women experience are related to the "cold flashes" Alan is feeling postinjury. The hypothalamus also regulates appetite and the sense of satiety. A damaged or hormonally altered hypothalamus can trick a person into thinking he or she has eaten when in fact it's not true. That could be why Alan continues to lose weight at Magee, to the point where the doctor prescribes a liquid food supplement. Months later, the damaged hypothalamus will begin to trick him in the opposite way, making him eat thousands and thousands of calories and never feel full.

Al detests occupational therapy, where he's asked to cook eggs and bacon and bake a cake. Later, when he's more mobile, he goes to a nearby convenience store with the therapist to purchase simple items. She gives him twenty dollars to buy snacks for the floor, and he spends much more than that. Later he tells me that she gave him only two dollars—that's why he went over his budget, he says. All this is stupid, he thinks. He rants and raves about how he doesn't *need* to be able to bake a cake. He just wants to go to work again.

He doesn't realize that all the tasks he's being assigned require sequencing or organizing skills. Kitchens are chosen as environments for occupational therapy because the goal is independent living for the patient. Before a brain-injured person can work again, he must be able to dress, wash, and feed himself. Many of these tasks, which seem simple, are actually quite complex. Take, for example, the job of loading a dishwasher. The person loading must recognize different shapes and sizes of dishes and cutlery and make sequential decisions about how to sort them and how to place them in the dishwasher. Getting a meal onto the table, even a simple one, also taxes the decision and judgment areas of the brain located in the frontal lobes. Should I wash the lettuce first? When should I turn on the oven? How much time must I allow for my dish to cook? The kitchen is such a good environment for relearning organization skills that one computer software company has actually created a "virtual kitchen" for use by brain injury patients.

The OT kitchen at Magee is far from virtual; for Al it is a real live torture chamber. Plagued by fatigue and lacking initiative, he finds it hard to start anything or to finish it. In the middle of trying to scramble some eggs, he sits down and cries.

His occupational therapist, Grace, is tough on him. She puts aside the eggs and bacon he has been cooking and makes him finish them in his next session. When I visit around lunchtime one day, Grace explains that she is working on Alan's lack of "initiation" (another TBI jargon term). She sees his inability to start an activity on his own as one of his major deficits, not surprising in someone with so much frontal lobe damage. Grace has one major goal: she wants Al to come into the therapy room and begin a task for himself. For example, he is supposed to work on the ergometer, a machine that builds upper body strength, for three minutes. Each time he leaves the OT room, she tells him that the next time he arrives, she wants him just to go to the ergometer and start doing his three minutes. One day when I arrive early and go to his OT session with him, he enters the room and then leans on his cane, looking around, bewildered.

"Alan, remember what you are supposed to do?" says Grace.

"No."

"Over there—remember?"

"No."

"Okay, let me get you started."

"I hate that thing," Al says gloomily, sitting down with a grunt and reluctantly grabbing the ergometer's handles.

As Alan works with Grace in this session, I want to scream out, "That's not my husband! He can do that! You don't understand! He's just tired!" But it's more than fatigue holding Alan back. His brain's ability to tackle a task is as scrambled as the eggs he's been trying to cook.

After the session, Grace asks us to make a list of all the chores Al does around the house. For lunch we go up to the hospital's rooftop garden, where I discover that we're lacking pen and paper to make the list. So we bum a pen from another patient and use the back of one of the paper plates I've brought for our lunch. The list is longer than we thought it would be, which explains why everything is in such smelly disarray at our house right now—Al normally does the dishes, changes the cat litter, takes out the garbage, and so on. The front of the paper plate has a gaudy watermelon design on it, which makes Grace laugh when we return for the afternoon session. I'm relieved, since she has seemed a bit stern.

"This is going into your file!" she says merrily. She isn't as merry when she looks at the list of Alan's household chores. The last, and most important, one is "find things."

"Finding things is asking a lot of the brain-injured person," she says. I glance over at Al, who's wearing his glazed zombie expression. Everything feels hopeless.

"I don't think you understand," I say. "Unless Al can find things again, we are doomed."

You couldn't ask for a worse lifestyle than ours for brain injury rehabilitation, it turns out. A brain-injured person needs a steady routine, a minimal amount of stimulation, and a lifestyle that is not taxing in any way. One rehabilitation counselor later put it into perspective for me: "I see one client with TBI, an attorney who has never gone back to work. Our weekly session consists of me going to his house and making out a schedule for him that covers every fifteen minutes of every day of his week. Simple things, like "Get up. Brush teeth. Read Bible.""

Our household, with five cats and a seven-year-old, my erratic work schedule subject to extreme deadlines, and a swirling social life that includes a cast of neurotic friends calling at all hours of the day and night, is a kind of antilaboratory for the successful rehabilitation process. I might be looking for a plate in our china cabinet and find the hammer I misplaced six months ago. Don't ask me how it got in there. Kelly has never had a bedtime. We've never kept a schedule or a family calendar. We've never written instructional notes to one another. Up until now, we have been very much a seat-of-your-pants kind of operation.

Who would have imagined that some day we would be called on our lifestyle? Time's up! You've been crazed, disorganized fuck-ups for years, and now it's time to pay the piper.

7

Level 5—Confused, inappropriate but not agitated. The patient is confused and does not make sense in conversations but may be able to follow simple directions. Stressful situations may provoke some upset, but agitation is no longer a major problem. Patients may experience some frustration as elements of memory return.

—Rancho Los Amigos Hospital Scale
of Cognitive Functioning

By the end of the second week at Magee, Al is walking with a cane fairly proficiently, so naturally our HMO tries to deny him further benefits and throw him out of the hospital. They already tried last week, but they didn't have a great excuse then, like Al's returned mobility.

Lisa Gordon is very frustrated. She tells me she spends most of her day fighting with HMOs. One woman who has done better than Al cognitively still cannot swallow food. The HMO will not pay for her liquid food and feeding tube.

I'm shocked. What is her family supposed to do, chew up cheeseburgers and spit them down her throat as though she's a baby bird?

Lisa says that Al might have been better off, in terms of benefits, if he hadn't learned to walk again so quickly. Cognitive deficits are not really considered medical problems. "The HMO case managers are ignorant," she says. "I spend most of my time educating them about the effects of brain injury, although they don't care, since they don't want to pay for the treatments anyway."

Lisa tells me tons of horror stories, including the amazing fact that one of the area's most prominent (and expensive) managed health care program pays *no* money for cognitive therapies at all.

Aetna Managed Care doesn't care that Al is unable to find his way from his room to the cafeteria without written instructions in his pocket. To say nothing of the Goat Cheese Incident.

"I actually used the Goat Cheese Incident to illustrate how Alan needs more cognitive help," Lisa tells me, and we both laugh.

When Alan had been at Magee about a week and a half, I brought dinner one night: gazpacho, bread, goat cheese, and a nice gourmet chicken salad. Goat cheese is one of Alan's favorite things on earth, and that day I had gone to a gourmet shop to buy a very expensive, freshly made domestic type that comes in large square slabs. I placed the chunk of goat cheese on a plate and gave Alan his own plate and some bread. He looked at the cheese curiously. Then, childlike, with his hand made into a fist over his plastic fork, he pierced and lifted the entire one pound piece onto his plate. He then cut it into four pieces, stabbed a piece with the fork again, and quickly shoved it into his mouth.

"Al, there's bread to go with that."

"Huh?"

He turned back to his plate and continued shoveling the pound of cheese into his mouth. This was during a period when he would pick anything off his tray and eat it in any sequence. What was this big white thing? All he knew was that it was flat and on a plate and could be picked up with a fork, so that's what he did. He had no sense that eating a pound of goat cheese at a sitting was inappropriate. He had no idea that it was cheese at all.

"Gee, that's an awfully effete story," I tell Lisa. "I'm not sure the HMO will be impressed by such a gentrified tragedy—he's so brain-injured, he can't recognize chèvre!"

"Well, we're laughing, but this is *exactly* why Alan cannot be released from rehab. He has serious cognitive problems." Lisa is an intense, articulate woman in her midthirties, and I imagine she runs verbal circles around the HMO clowns. "And the way we judge the extent of Alan's problems is by how much he differs from his premorbid behavior. If you're telling me that goat cheese was a favorite food of his and now he can't recognize it or eat it in a socially acceptable manner, that indicates a pretty severe cognitive deficit."

As valiantly as Lisa is fighting for Alan's benefits, we pretty much see that it is a lost cause. In practical terms, the HMO's aggressive stance means that we all have to start planning the transition to home and a day hospital environment much sooner than we thought. Alan was supposed to be in rehabilitation for three months, not three weeks. Before he can go home, I must attend a full day of his therapy sessions and learn how to help him walk around and perform his daily grooming functions. Alan can walk with his cane, but he has not been allowed to walk by himself along the hospital hallways—either a therapist or a nurse must be with him, or he must stay in his wheelchair. We decide that I'll attend the therapies on the second Friday, so that Alan will have more freedom in the evenings when I visit and I will be ready to help him when he comes home for good, probably only a week later. I try to remain calm when talking about the immediate future, but in truth I stay awake most nights, wondering how I can cope with this rushed end to his formal rehabilitation.

The day I spend with Al at Magee going through his therapy sessions is exhausting. Not physically for me, but mentally, as I try to wrap my brain around just how far he's come and what I should be concerned about.

First, there is speech therapy. But why is Alan seeing a speech therapist when his speech is fairly good? Many people, after a brain injury as severe as Al's, have terrible trouble speaking. They suffer from aphasia (an inability to locate words), dysarthria (slurred speech), and sometimes speechlessness altogether. While Al is at Magee, I hear about a man with a similar injury who can speak only in jargonlike phrases.

The way that speech is learned, stored, and then articulated is, of course, still being studied. The most exciting tool is the functional MRI, which enables researchers to quiz patients and actually see the part of the brain being used for speech "light up" on the scan as the patient is talking. In one fascinating study at the University of Iowa, researchers were able to determine that people who had trouble saying action verbs all had damage in the same speech area, near the motor centers. Shown a picture of a person working with a broom, the subjects could describe the broom, say that the person in the picture wanted the floor clean, and mention that there was dirt but could not locate and say the word "sweep." Similarly, the researchers found that people with damage to the temporal lobe, a section of the brain along the lower-left side of the brain, over the ear, often have trouble naming objects. One person might lose the ability to name animals, for example. Another might lose the ability to name utensils. This suggests that our brain contains learned speech clusters, arranged thematically, and that even a tiny bleed or lesion can wipe out whole categories of our vocabulary.

It boggles the imagination to think of all those "files" and how the brain organizes them into tiny centers when it receives new input. "Hmmmm . . . tapir . . . put it in the animal file . . . arugula . . . vegetable area . . ."

About five months after Alan leaves his outpatient therapies, we get dramatic, firsthand proof of these speech clusters at the Philadelphia Flower Show.

The timing of this opulent floral display, one of the world's finest, is impeccable. Held the first week in March, the Philadelphia Flower Show caters to a crowd of gardening enthusiasts from all over the country. Outside, the skies are gray and there's a taunting promise of spring. Inside, you enter a world of re-created Tuscan walled gardens, wildflower meadows, demonstration vegetable gardens, and rows and rows of orchids, flowering bulbs, and shrubs raised in expensive greenhouses by people such as Mrs. R. Higgledepiggledy DuPont Vanderbilt IV of the $$$$Mews Garden Club.

We've never missed the Flower Show. We started going as graduate students, and when Kelly was only three weeks old, we took her to it during a blinding snowstorm when hardly anyone else was there. It was like paradise, wandering around in the huge uncrowded hall, taking in the buds as Kelly slept in her stroller.

Eight years later, at Al's first postinjury Flower Show, we discover a strange pocket of speech deficits that went undiagnosed at Magee.

"What's this?" Al says. At first I think he's kidding; he's pointing to a totally ordinary red geranium.

"Huh. A geranium. Really?" He acts as if he's never heard of the word, or the flower, before. And so it goes with gerbera daisies, jack-in-the-pulpits, ageratum, foxglove, delphinium, even, amazingly, the most common of flowers, such as marigolds, tulips, and daffodils. The flower speech center in his brain (how big could it be? perhaps microscopic!) has been destroyed. A few months later, when Alan goes bird-watching for the first time since the accident, we discover that not one of the bird names he's learned over the years is accessible to him, either. Now, what do Al's particular speech deficits mean? Are flowers and birds always together in a person's brain? Or were those centers more vulnerable in Alan's brain than they would be in others because he had developed an interest in gardening and bird-watching in his twenties and thirties? ("The idiosyncratic aftereffects of brain injury are what make it so fascinating," says one social worker I know who counsels TBI patients. "No two brains are the same premorbidly, and then no two brains are hit in the same way; finally, every injured brain bleeds differently.")

While Al is still an inpatient at Magee, he shows very few speech deficits. Yet his therapist, Sue, explains that it is through speech therapy that TBI patients' cognitive therapy needs are met. Speech is thought expressed; by quizzing Alan and doing oral exercises, she can gauge the extent of his cognitive deficits. She has him do her billing on the computer, which takes him a while. They go to the hospital library together and take out books on brain injury. They talk about reading—he is still having trouble with concentration and comprehension. Sue says reading is one of the mind's most complex tasks, involving letter and word recognition, long-term memory, short-term memory, and attention. It is Sue who first brings up the concept of cognitive fatigue: surprisingly, Alan's brain can still perform fairly complex mental tasks, but it takes longer, and the damaged organ is working probably five times harder than it did when Alan was well.

Al has tried to read some mystery short stories in *Ellery Queen's Mystery Magazine*. "I don't really understand what I am reading," he says. "I can do it, but I get tired."

I've seen Al's attention span improve gradually while he's been in rehab. At first he can't even watch television for more than a few minutes. By the second week we're able to view an Olympic track event together that lasts more than fifteen minutes.

It seems that Alan has lost the "topographical" center in his brain; that is, he has trouble sensing where he is at any given time or how he could possibly get somewhere else. Later I will see this problem when he comes home. All his therapists notice the topographical problem and worry, since getting confused and lost can pose major dangers to brain-injured people in the outside world.

Alan is defensive about it: "No one can get around here. It's so fucking confusing."

When I visit for the full day of family training, Grace, the occupational therapist, is working on Al's lack of geographical orientation. She wants him to be able to get down to the second-floor cafeteria and back again on his own. Alan is frightened, like a child, when she suggests he can do it. She gives him oral instructions and asks him to repeat them, but he can't. So she writes down directions for him to carry in his pocket. I'm allowed to go along but not to help him in any way, and he ends up consulting the piece of paper three times on the way down there and two times coming back.

That day, Sue, the speech therapist, also has him show her around the fourth floor, trying to strengthen his sense of location. Grace and Sue both hope that Al will learn to use the security code and move around the hospital freely before he is discharged. Thanks to the HMO, he never attains that goal.

During my training, Colleen, the physical therapist, decides that she wants us to be prepared for all real-life situations. We go up and down stairs together. We stop by the larger therapy gym so that Al can practice getting into and out of a bathtub. Then Al, Colleen, and I walk down Race Street for a few blocks. Al is on his cane, doing pretty well, and Colleen shows me how to "spot" him so he won't fall. I stand right at his side, my arm crooked up slightly, ready to grab his elbow if I see him falter. Colleen also points out any imperfections in the sidewalk and shows Al how to put his cane down first when he is stepping off a curb.

Colleen drums it into Alan's head that he must stop for all red lights and even then should look both ways.

"You wouldn't believe how many people with brain injuries get run over by cars," she says. "They get distracted or stop paying attention, and they walk into traffic." Driving is also out of the question. Colleen casually informs me that Magee has already written to the Pennsylvania Department of Motor Vehicles, asking that Alan's driver's license be suspended until he can once again pass a written test and one behind the wheel. It's hospital policy in dealing with any severe brain injury case. I know this makes sense, but still it's a blow, another reminder that Al is no longer independent.

But he is beginning to understand the future. I've told him that his parents are coming down to see him today, and while we walk back to the hospital he says he wishes they could see him walking outside. "Then they would know that I am really okay," he says.

He keeps obsessing about this idea long after we are back in his room. In brain injury jargon, he "perseverates" about the topic. Over and over and over again, he says how much he would like his parents to see him upright, just taking a stroll down the street. "I mean, what if they were just driving along and they saw me walking down the street? Then they wouldn't have to know anything is wrong with me at all," he says. Perseveration—the aimless repetition of a task or an idea—is a very common sign of brain injury. Some people cannot stop washing their hair or clapping their hands. Others, once they think they have to find something or do something, cannot stop talking or thinking about it. With Alan, mostly, it is ideas. He just won't let go of them.

I'm more than a little bit peeved with Alan's parents at this point, since they refuse to acknowledge the seriousness of his injury. "Everything is going to be okay!" says his mother in phone calls from Brooklyn, which is odd since she and my father-in-law are normally the most pessimistic people I know, but I guess denial is an amazing thing. They never want to hear any stories about what is truly happening, especially anything about the cognitive problems. God forbid that their brilliant son might now be an idiot. It is unthinkable, so they choose not to think about it. But someone has to. I resent that I've been making all the decisions about Alan's treatments and worrying about the outcome of his injury while they've been convincing themselves that it was just a knock on the head and he'll get over it. Sociologists have done studies about how stressful it is for the primary caregiver in brain injury families when other relatives refuse to come to grips with what has happened, and that's the situation that is brewing here. It strikes me as absurd that Al, who's been in a coma, sick with staph pneumonia, paralyzed, incontinent, and cognitively damaged, would be the one to worry excessively about someone else. Of course, another problem TBI survivors have is a lack of self-awareness. As far as Al is concerned, he's just had a rough time getting his legs to work. He hasn't acknowledged that he has a brain injury, and despite his strange fantasy about talking to the girl from the boat, he still sometimes acts surprised when I tell him about the accident. After he has said the thing about wanting to have his parents see him walking about twelve times, I blow up.

"Al! This is not about your parents! This is about you! You are injured! They are adults! They should be able to handle it!" He looks at me blankly, and when his parents arrive for the visit he is thrilled to tell them that he is okay, that he was walking outside, that they shouldn't worry.

Of course, when they first arrive we are both asleep in the Vail bed. I've found a whole day with Al to be more exhausting than I thought. I can only imagine what it's going to be like when the HMO kicks him out of here and he is home full-time.

Yet despite his many deficits, there is someone inside Al, a person struggling to return to what he perceives is normalcy. Two days after his parents' visit, I see a logbook entry in his handwriting, now about half the size of his preinjury script. (No one knows why, but after a brain injury one's handwriting becomes either much larger or much smaller.) His entry reads: "Did walking up stairs—various exercises. Getting ready to be a real person again."

The next day, a Saturday, Alan and I are walking in the hallway at Magee when a group of people pass by and the stimulation overwhelms him. Even though he's on the cane, his right leg buckles under him. I know instinctively that he needs more than an elbow hold, so I reach out and put my arms around his waist to keep him from falling.

"Oh, I fall all the time," he says. "I fall and I can't get up. They just leave me there."

The image of that old late-night television commercial where the elderly lady is screaming, "Help me! I've fallen and I can't get up!" goes racing through my mind.

When I see Colleen on Monday, I ask if Al's ever fallen and had no assistance.

"Not that I know. It would be impossible. There's always someone to spot him as he moves to the different therapies."

Al tells me a few more times that they just let him fall and lie around in the hallway. Another confabulation. But he is very convincing, and this time the story is within the realm of possibility, I guess. But where is the story coming from? Why does he feel that anyone here would leave him keeled over on the linoleum? It's a dramatic attention-getting story, like the ones Kelly tells when she pretends to be crippled and walks around on crutches.

Magee does not have a "test apartment" to simulate real living situations. Instead, the therapists encourage daytime passes to the patient's house, so that families can see how their loved one will do in the home environment. Al's home visit comes sooner than I think, during his third week there, only a few days before he is discharged.

I show up at around ten in the morning to pick him up.

"Al, you ready to go home for a few hours?"

"Well, are you sure it's okay? What did the doctors say? I don't want anyone to catch this from me."

Alan has been obsessing about being contagious for a few days. "Don't let her drink out of that!" he screams when Kelly reaches for his can of Coke.

"Why not, Al?"

"Because she might catch what I've got."

I explain to him that he has a brain injury caused by a blow to his head. There is no way a brain injury can be contagious.

"Yeah, well, you never know," he says.

Al is expressionless as we make our way to the elevator and then down to the desk, where we show our six-hour pass before heading for the parking lot. I expect him to be excited about going home, but he seems like one of those lifers in prison movies who can't adjust to the idea of being released to the outside world. He's been practicing getting into and out of the automobile on Magee's roof, so he has no trouble at all bending down, leaning on his cane, and plopping into the front passenger seat of our tiny green car.

His silence is eerie. No reply, no matter what I say. In his logbook he has written that he has difficulty with conversation. I think he has trouble whenever the conversation is not about something that is securely locked in his long-term memory—that's why he does so well talking about banking issues or sports trivia and very badly when the topic is what he thinks or feels or what he's done with his day. And it's no wonder he's not talking now—this drive along busy streets is distracting for him, too. He looks frightened, overstimulated, as cars pull out toward us or a light changes and streams of cars pass in front of ours. This is the first time in six weeks he's ridden in a motor vehicle without being strapped onto a stretcher or locked into a wheelchair.

I have plans. Kelly is away for the day at Girl Scout camp. I don't see why we should go right home. I think maybe a visit to our garden and even a quick dip over at our pool club would be nice. It's a beautiful day out, warm and, blessedly for Philadelphia, hardly humid at all.

"No, I don't want to go anywhere," Al says.

"Not even the garden?"

"I don't think I could walk down there. Too far." (The garden is a block and a half away from our house.)

"What if I drive right to the gate and we walk around, and then we go home?"

"Umm. Okay."

I hold on to Al as I unlock the ornate garden gate. I want to unlock his old personality as well, to make him come alive again, to hear him comment on how beautiful everything is: row upon row of gorgeous plots filled with zinnias and cosmos, lupines and digitalis, tomatoes and eggplants. Alan used to spend hours at our own plot and lots of time going obsessively around the garden, seeing what others were planting, kibbitzing, exchanging plants and seeds, looking for tips on how to do things.

Today he might as well be standing at a garbage dump. He looks at nothing. With my hand on his arm, I lead him toward our plot. Some of the other gardeners have pitched in to weed our space, but it still looks pretty bad except for the few annuals Alan planted before we left on vacation, and our old reliable perennials such as Queen Anne's lace and flaming red bee balm. The tomatoes Al put in at the end of

May have that stringy, stressed look of plants that haven't been watered often, and the lettuces and greens are all reaching toward the sky, gone to seed.

"Look how big and overgrown everything is getting. But it's still nice to see it, isn't it?" I say.

Al pokes his cane into some loose dirt at the edge of the plot. "I'm tired," he says. We've been at the garden for about four minutes.

Back at the house, he can't seem to settle in. We go into our living room/dining area, a big pleasant room with exposed brick and high ceilings. I keep smiling like a fool. I have that cheery, patronizing tone in my voice that one so often hears in preschool teachers. Well now! Here we are! I ask him if he wants to sit down and have a soda, look at some mail or pictures. I figure he'll want to relax, pet the cats, read the sports page.

"I'm tired. I need to go to sleep."

I suggest that he stretch out on the couch. I really don't want him doing those stairs without a railing, and they have a wicked turn in them. (High ceilings are great, but they make for treacherous, high stairs as well.)

"No. Gotta go to bed. I want to go up to bed."

Alan looks at a loss. He seems to remember that he has to go up somewhere to find our bedroom, but he can't remember where the stairs are. I'd be really alarmed if we hadn't moved the staircase once during our time here, but, even so, that was seven years ago, when Kelly was born. We used to have a metal spiral staircase that came down into our living room, and after we annexed another apartment we had the space to move the stairs around the corner. Now it's a more conventional staircase complete with carpeting. It still has no railing, but I've been making plans to install one.

Should I tell him where the "new" stairs are? In the few seconds it takes me to decide, he looks very unhappy. I guide him around the corner, and he immediately goes up the stairs, crouched, crablike, clutching the wall. Damn, he's fast for a brain-injured guy. Al has always been athletic, and it shows in his sheer strength. When we first met, he didn't know how to swim, but he didn't want to admit it. Swimming with me in ponds in New Hampshire and Maine, he could get by just pulling himself through the water with his strong arms, even though he didn't know the strokes or how to kick or breathe. Now I watch as he wraps his hand around the wall right at the dangerous turn in the stairs to get the leverage to hoist himself up.

In our bedroom, more disorientation. A few weeks before taking off for Canada we moved our antique oak bed, and that throws Al for a loop. Instead of coming out from the wall on the side of the room, it's now smack dab in the middle, in the bay window space, freestanding. It looks rather stupid, actually. Just a little experiment in decorating, unfinished of course. We never got the curtains to go with it or any new bedding. We're not very good in that department.

He finally gets into the bed, but on the wrong side. We've been sleeping together for eighteen years, and in all that time he's always slept on the left side. Now he's on the right. I ask him about it, and he says he doesn't know it's not his side. Of course he doesn't—the effects of the damage to the left side of his brain seem to include his perception of left and right. This is just another version of those scenes at HUP when he didn't know he was leaning way over to the right. I know that Al's inability to remember his favorite side of the bed is trivial compared to his more obvious deficits, but it disturbs me a great deal.

I climb into bed next to him and wonder, why? Why does this stupid little thing bother me so much? For the first time, the Pod Person theory crosses my mind. I've brought my husband home from the hospital. At least, I think he's my husband. He looks like him, if somewhat thinner. But now that my husband is in his home environment, I can see even more how the alien who is inhabiting his body just can't get everything exactly right. Al is "off," like one of those humans in bad sci-fi movies whose brains have been devoured by creatures from another planet. The brain is gone, but the body stays on, acting as a host for the intergalactic parasite. There was a TV show when I was little, *The Invaders,* featuring space monsters who would inhabit human beings. The only way you could tell if the people weren't their old selves was by checking their pinky fingers, which stuck up at a right angle after they had been subsumed by the aliens.

Al's pinkies seem the same.

I'm tired. I thought I could take a nap with him, but I can't sleep. Al is out like a light. I go downstairs, lonely and alone in our own house. I putter around aimlessly, read the paper for a while, and suddenly it comes to me, one of the stupidest ideas of my life: I will make love to Al. I will *make* him connect. There he is, up in our bed. Every good home visit should include sex, shouldn't it?

He's been asleep for more than an hour when I go upstairs to see if he's all right. I busy myself with folding laundry, arranging things in Kelly's room and ours. Eventually he wakes up. He looks very confused about where he is.

"Hi. Have a good sleep?"

"Unh."

I let him come to fuller consciousness, although these days his full consciousness is not exactly that distinguishable from other states.

"Hey, Alan, have any desire to make love?"

Pause.

"You know, have sex?"

"Oh, I don't know. What do the doctors say?"

"I'm sure it's okay. They didn't say you couldn't."

"Well, I don't know. I mean, I think we should ask the doctors. The doctors would know."

"I think it's okay."

"You sure?"

"Yeah. It's okay."

I wait for a moment, and then I realize how dumb that approach is. I kiss him. Nothing. This is a dramatic demonstration of initiation deficit. I reach down into his shorts, put my hand on his penis, and begin stroking. It springs up immediately, but when I look up to his face, there is no expression. He stares straight ahead, and I loosen his shorts and pull them down. I'm embarrassing myself, but at least Alan will probably never remember. What am I doing? Now Al's fully erect, but if you look at his face, you think nothing is happening.

I should stop. But now I feel as if what I've done is cruel. He's lying there with an erection. I'm sexually harrassing a brain-injured guy. I feel terrible, not in the least like making love. But I still hold a dim hope that it will spur some deep emotion within him, that it will help him reconnect.

Hurriedly, I strip off my underpants and climb on top. Al doesn't even put his hands on my back. I thrust my pelvis up and down on his penis, which seems disconnected from the rest of his body—he comes in about two minutes, like a fourteen-year-old. I try to look into his eyes, but there's nothing there.

Months later, I meet a woman on-line who becomes a fast cyberfriend. By then, Alan's ability to initiate tasks, including sex, has returned, somewhat. This woman's husband, injured in a truck crash four years before Alan's accident, never learned how to initiate emotional or sexual encounters again. "I tried," my honest friend types into an instant message box on her computer late one night. "But I gave up. When I tried to have sex with him, it felt like I was raping a little boy."

There's a pretty woman with long, straight, blond-streaked hair, in her late thirties, waiting for the elevator at Magee.

She looks as though she's been crying. With her is a scrawny four-year-old boy who's butting his buzz-cut head into her thigh and whining to go home. The elevator comes and we step in, following protocol and not looking at each other. I stare at the floor numbers above the door and listen to the buzzer for the blind; the boy continues whining and fidgeting and trying to hurt her as we ascend. I try not to notice that he's now pinching his mother. "Stop it! Stop it, damn it!" she yells in the voice of a person who's reached the end of her rope. She gets off at the fourth floor, too, but I walk quickly ahead, thinking how stressed she looks. I pity her and the kid she's dragging along. I see myself in her. But then I think: Do I look that bad? So out of control and stressed? And who is pitying me?

I arrive at Alan's new room, where he's graduated to a real bed, no safety net. He's already in trouble with the nurses because he is getting up unassisted to go to the bathroom. They've written a note about it on his chart and asked to have a special meeting with me to discuss what we can do about it. He has a new roommate, a Temple University professor also named Al, a tall, stately man confined to a wheelchair. Pretty soon people on the ward are referring to them as Big Al and Little Al. Turns out that my Alan (Little Al) and Big Al were both teaching in Temple University's English department at the same time, in the early 1980s, but they never ran into each other. Big Al is in his sixties, suffering from brain injury brought on by . . . well, my Alan never gets the story, and I am too shy to ask his young wife, who turns out to be the stressed-out thirtysomething mother I saw on the elevator. She shows up only a few minutes after I come into the room. I suspect that Big Al had a heart attack and suffered a lack of oxygen to the brain. Oh, his poor trophy wife.

Big Al has severe motor deficits; he just doesn't seem able to learn to walk again. Perhaps it is because his motor centers were more damaged or because he is about twenty years older than Alan, who is beginning to develop some context for how rapidly he regained his mobility. Alan tells me that during a group therapy session, when they were asked to discuss their goals, "one woman said, 'I just want to learn to walk as well as Al Forman.' Can you imagine that? I didn't know I was so good."

I am fascinated by Big Al the professor, since I figure that he is the closest in background to Alan of anyone on the ward: a smart humanities Ph.D. Like Alan, he has a young child and clusters of concerned, well-educated visitors who are trying to hide their horror. Brain injury is a tragedy for everyone but a special nightmare for people with intellectual lives and jobs. Our intelligence is our greatest pride; I think of athletes who dread losing a leg, artists who say they would not be able to live if they lost their sight. I fear, more than anything, losing my mind. Not being able to remember things. Not being able to write or teach or have into-the-night discussions about ideas. In the same way that I focused on Kelly learning to read, I now focus on knowing that Alan will be able to do so again some day; the alternative is just too frightening. I once had a husband who was doing a dissertation on Samuel Beckett, who had a thing for obscure Japanese cinema. Have I lost him entirely? I can't imagine being married to a new man who won't be able to discuss books or go to the theater with me.

I can't say if knowing Big Al comforts or disturbs me. He acts, in many ways, like my Alan at this point: brain-injured. I can see the shock on his visitors' faces as he struggles to keep up with conversations. Big Al has the same glazed look in his eyes as Alan and often shouts inappropriate comments that are meant to be jokes.

. . .

I've been in contact with Dr. Andy periodically, and he says we should get Alan tested as soon as possible. A neuropsychiatric evaluation, as it's called. I tell him that I think, at this point, Al wouldn't do that well.

"Good," says Andy. "You don't want him to do well. You want to get a baseline. You want to demonstrate how impaired he is and then take it from there. Cathy, this could work in your favor for the insurance benefits."

I don't have much time to think about Andy's advice before the final verdict comes down: since the HMO is discontinuing Al's rehab hospital benefits after only twenty-one days, we have to scramble to arrange for the cognitive testing as part of his hospitalization, or we might have to pay thousands of dollars for it later. Because Al's stay is so foreshortened, he ends up undergoing the battery of neuropsychological tests on the very worst day, a Friday, his last day at Magee.

Alan is a test junkie. His greatest pride is that he does well on standardized tests. There's not a test that he hasn't aced—the SATs, the New York Regents Exams (where he won a scholarship), the GREs, the LSAT—you name it, he's made the ninety-ninth percentile. Yet on his neuropsych evaluation, Dr. Kelli Williams writes, "The assessment was abbreviated somewhat due to his reaction to many of the tests. Mr. Forman was very sensitive to failure and a depression inventory administered indicated some degree of depression. Therefore, testing was not pushed beyond Mr. Forman's endurance level."

Al tests with an average IQ. Great, except that he was way above average before the accident. The neuropsychologist concludes that Alan "would be an excellent day hospital candidate" and that his "primary deficits are in motor coordination and strength/speed, verbal memory for complex and contextually unrelated material, and recall of visual information."

I've already arranged for Alan to attend Magee's day hospital program. I know he needs a lot more therapy, and Lisa Gordon has been able to get the HMO to agree to pay for day sessions for a total of sixty hours, although I misunderstand and believe we are covered for sixty days.

On his final day at the hospital Al is exhausted, mostly because of the hours of tests. I come to collect him around three o'clock, hoping I will be able to get through the scene without tears.

Not to be. The idea that Alan came into Magee strapped onto a stretcher, unable to walk, not knowing where he was, and now is leaving under his own power overwhelms me. I begin crying and cannot stop. It's a repeat of our departure from Kingston—I want to thank everyone and be gracious, but instead I blubber uncontrollably.

"Don't worry about it," says Lisa, as I try to thank her through embarrassing, wracking sobs.

I load the car with get-well mugs and now-straggly floral arrangements before we take our final leave. Alan and I walk out the automatic door of the hospital, into the enclosed parking lot. We're taking a short twenty-block ride home but a much longer journey into the strange land of TBI.

8

The patient will be discharged home with his wife. It was recommended to the family that he would require 24 hour supervision, secondary to safety and decreased cognition.

—Alan's discharge summary, Magee Rehabilitation Hospital

Leaning on his cane, Al laboriously hauls himself up the concrete stairs to the pool level at the Lombard Swim Club. He's been home more than a week, and my mother has taken Kelly to Seattle to visit my sister's family, so we've been able to go through this first period of adjustment alone.

In the late August sunshine, Al looks odd, like a little frail bird. He's lost more than thirty pounds since the accident seven weeks ago. The Coma Diet. With his dull eyes and staggering gait, you might mistake him for a drunk or a lobotomy patient.

"Oh my God, what happened to him?" gasps an elderly woman who has always talked to us poolside.

We've been familiar fixtures at this urban swimming pool for more than a decade. Now everyone stares at us and many ask directly what is wrong with Al, so I must tell the story constantly, and without breaking down emotionally. Alan's enjoying the attention and talking to people he's never spoken with before, but he's unable to really relate what has happened. The worst thing, I think, is the pity in people's eyes. Some of them, at least, make jokes about it, in keeping with how we've always bantered in the past. "Damn, there's a lot of people at this swim club I'd love to see get hit on the head. Al Forman is not one of them," says Brenda, one of the lifeguards who's worked at the pool for years.

The whole issue of Alan's dependency is tricky. I don't want him to go down to the men's locker room alone, but I know he will bristle if I suggest that he be accompanied. So I deputize guys we know to go down and check to see if he's okay changing into his swimsuit, or later, when he decides he has to go to the bathroom. I ask them to be casual about it. The words catch in my throat as I explain that Alan is not really supposed to be left on his own. "Gee, he doesn't look that bad," says one guy. Brain injury is so hard to explain, and I'm not in the mood to give a dissertation on the aftereffects of TBI. For the first time, too, I face the dilemma of how much I *should* tell people publicly. Alan has written wills and managed trusts for some of our pool friends—do I want them to think that their lawyer is now an imbecile who can't be left alone in the bathroom? Even those who work with the brain-injured say they find it difficult to get outsiders to understand that the behavior of the TBI patient during recovery is the result of physiological changes in the damaged organ. TBIers are not mentally ill, even though some of their symptoms might appear similar. All in all, I wish that Magee had been able to keep Alan for a few more weeks, until his judgment skills began to return a little more.

Men seem to have particular problems with Alan's accident and sudden disability. One of Al's close friends, Bruce, a newspaper editor, kept in touch with others through e-mail until Al was recovered to a certain extent. "I was just so freaked out," he says. "I wanted to know that Al was still in there, that there was still an Al."

"Men just can't handle seeing another guy laid low. It makes them think it could happen to them," says my mother, and maybe she's right. In our culture we put so much emphasis on masculine strength, independence, and bread-winning skills, it terrifies guys just to contemplate being help-less even briefly. The men who visit Al or call me about him seem to have two concerns: his cock and his job.

"Does his dick still work?" asks Nick. He's a writer, prone to the outrageous, and since it's the first week we are back from Canada, I just say, "Gosh, I don't know—he's still wear-ing a diaper!"

When Bruce finally does visit Alan, he takes me out to a nice dinner afterward and asks, "So, tell me, has he gotten laid yet?" A lawyer friend, John, visits with his wife, and when we are describing Alan's therapies, John pipes up, "Hey, when's the sex therapy session?"

John also tells Al, repeatedly, that he better get back to work before the Family Leave Act runs out, or he's in trouble. Right after Al gets out of Magee, while he is still in outpa-tient therapy, Bruce says to him, "Hey, you should go back to work. You seem like you could do it just fine!" It's striking: all of Alan's male visitors ask him when he'll return to his job; female visitors ask how he is feeling and if he would like more of the candies they've brought.

The men have no idea. You can't blame them, really. Al's cognitive disabilities are now hidden to the casual visitor, and most have no desire to delve any deeper than necessary. Besides, even if they sense that Al is more damaged than he looks, it is threatening to contemplate. If Al cannot fuck or work, then how can he be a man?

It's hot, that first day back at the swim club, and I keep ask-ing Alan if he wants to get into the water. The old Alan could not wait for more than three minutes before diving in. Yet now Al seems scared of the pool. Finally, he agrees to go down the steps with me holding on to him. Standing in three feet of water, he panics and starts back slowly for the stairs, leaning heavily to his right side on his weaker leg.

"What's the matter, Al?"

"I'm cold."

I paddle over to him and take both his hands. "Well, get all the way under. Duck down. Get your head wet. It feels nice."

"No." He pulls away from me. A look of sheer panic crosses his face. "I gotta get out."

In a logbook entry, Al writes, "Went down to Lombard Swim Club but couldn't get all wet. Afraid of drowning."

Alan is now attending day hospital and, if possible, he hates it even more than the inpatient rehab experience at Magee. The facility, Riverfront, is all the way across town from our house, down on the Delaware River, at the beginning of South Philadelphia. Each morning, they send a car for Al.

He's normally an early riser, a morning person. But the first few weeks he is home, I have to shake him to get him up by eight o'clock. I help him dress, too—he's totally out of it. I guide him into the shower, put on his underpants, his Bermuda shorts, his socks, pull his T-shirt over his head. During his last days at the rehab hospital, he was doing these things for himself. Later I will learn that any change in a brain-injured person's surroundings or routine often causes regression. Right now Al's behavior just scares me. He's like a zombie child.

Mornings in general are intensely stressful. Kelly, now home from Seattle, has to get out the door to her Girl Scout camp bus and Alan to his day hospital car at about the same time. They both wear backpacks, Kelly's stuffed with her swimsuit and lunch, Alan's with the logbook he loathes so much. I give him money for his lunch (ordering lunch is part of the therapy). At first I'm in a quandary: Who needs supervision more, Al or Kelly? In the end I opt to stand outside with Alan, since there are other parents at the camp bus stop a mere block away. This upsets Kelly, who is still scared to be anywhere in our house or neighborhood without me. But the Magee therapists have stressed that Alan is not to be left unattended, and I worry that after coming so far, he will be killed in a senseless accident. I have more confidence in Kelly's ability to walk the short block to catch the camp bus.

Some mornings Kelly starts to cry, "guilting" me into going with her to the bus stop. But I feel as though I'm no good to her anyway. I am distracted, worried that Alan is in peril, and I also end up having to talk to the other parents about how Al is doing, a question to which there is no easy answer. Kelly resents that I stand with her and yet talk only about Alan. She wants to be the focus of attention. Since she came home, she has seemed embarrassed by her father. She's acutely aware that people stare at him leaning on his cane, and she frequently makes impossible demands while I am helping Alan get dressed or showered. She's lost interest in the idea of Daddy getting better someday; she wants it to happen *now*. I'm having a lousy time trying to balance being a caregiver and a mom, and she senses that. It's almost as if there's a sibling rivalry between Kelly and Alan, as if I've brought home a forty-four-year-old baby whom she resents.

What's the first thing Al has to do at the day hospital? Bake a cake, of course. He's furious, insulted: "I'm a lawyer. I don't want to bake fucking cakes!"

Two years later I think about Al's postinjury aversion to baking when I hear an occupational therapist give a talk on taking a person's previous lifestyle into consideration while planning tasks after brain injury. At her facility they spent weeks trying to teach a woman with TBI how to make her own bed, with no success. Eventually they discovered that the woman was obscenely wealthy and had never made her own bed in her life and would never have to, so they switched therapies and helped her relearn how to apply makeup. Then she did fine.

Al is now happiest in physical therapy, where he's doing some sports-related things. At first his hand-to-eye coordination is so bad he can't catch or throw a ball. But at the day hospital he's been placed in a sensorimotor group, where they play a form of hockey sans skates and toss around large inflatable physioballs. He's getting better at riding a stationary bike, too, a skill that eluded him at Magee. In his logbook at the end of his first week, Al writes, "Peggy says I can ride a bike on West River Drive with Kelly when there is no traffic." (The city periodically closes this scenic drive to cars, making it a haven for cyclists and in-line skaters.)

Avoiding traffic is a good idea for someone with TBI. Alan's not aware of how little control he still has over outside stimulation. Whenever I drive him anywhere, he jumps and screams in the passenger seat. "Watch out!" he yells as I go through green lights and he sees cars stopped at the intersection. As cars pass in the opposite lane, his head turns back and forth frantically—he doesn't know where to look, and it reminds me of the trouble he had back at HUP when people made noises in the hallway. His intense distractability emphasizes what a complex task driving is, especially in a large city: you're hurtling through space, operating a gas pedal, a steering wheel, turn signals, lights, sometimes a clutch; you're making judgments about when and where to stop and how far to leave between yourself and other cars; you're remaining alert for hazards and possible mistakes of other drivers and pedestrians; and you're often thinking, talking, or listening to music as you proceed. Basically, your brain is going a mile a minute even when you're not. Alan's anxiety gives me a kind of existential panic about the process of getting around. "You're driving, you're driving, you're driving," I repeat to myself like a mantra, while aloud I am saying, "Al, everything is fine. Those cars are *not* going to hit us."

He hasn't stopped complaining about the schoolmarmish ways of his therapists. They're idiots, he says. They don't really understand what he needs. Fortunately, at the day hospital there is a recreational therapist, Asher Kemp, whom Al responds to in a different way. Tall and handsome, Asher is a refreshing change for Al: a young black man in a feminized, white environment. Al is sick of having a lot of women fussing over him and making him obey rules. He and Asher bond instantly, playing games and talking sports. Asher has just the right knack for cajoling Al into ignoring his fatigue and finishing a task—sometimes, I suspect, by appealing to Al's competitive spirit.

"Played Concentration w/Asher—he was 10 matches to 6—regular deck of cards. It was difficult," writes Al in his logbook. That tells me a lot about his current deficits, because unlike with other activities, I know exactly how good Alan was at Concentration before the accident, since over the last few years we've been forced to play it again and again with Kelly. But the idea that Alan's short-term memory has improved enough to make six matches is encouraging. A few days later he notes that he "lost to girl named ? in matching cards—17–9. Better luck next time." The next day he "lost in chess twice—very quickly." The old Al was good at that game, too. At the beginning of his second week at day hospital, he plays Uno with Asher. "It was hard to play for almost an hour," he writes. "I am tired already," he notes on another day at ten-thirty in the morning.

Fatigue is still one of Alan's major problems. Exhaustion is the most common symptom of brain injury, even after a mild concussion. Friends of ours, a married couple in their early forties, were in a train crash. Both suffered concussions, and for months afterward, they struggled just to get through the day. They thought they were going crazy, that it was psychosomatic or a symptom of depression, until they found out it is physically normal to experience intense fatigue after *any* closed-head injury, even if one has not lost consciousness.

Fatigue is not a very sexy or impressive side effect, but you would think it would be the easiest one to explain since everyone has experienced being tired. But being tired when you have TBI is a far more global experience than occasional exhaustion due to stress or sleeplessness. Think of cognitive fatigue as the head domino of TBI symptoms. Once intense fatigue begins (and it can happen very quickly), it tumbles onto all of the other bad dominoes on the TBI game board, knocking them over and terrifying everyone around. First Alan gets extremely tired, and then everything else goes wrong: he loses his motor functionality, his impulse control, and his ability to pick up on social cues and make simple judgments. When tired, Al knocks into walls as he walks. He drops things, and when he does, it makes him angrier, he says, than he has ever felt before. He takes a stack of magazines or a carton of leftover Chinese food and throws them on the floor, screaming. He yells, "You stupid bitch!" at Kelly or me or sometimes sobs uncontrollably. In my new role as a TBI caregiver I've invented a term for this, one that all my friends understand immediately: "Alan is going kablooey again."

Since his injury, Alan's eyes look weird. He still looks perpetually stoned. Yet when his cognitive fatigue level reaches a dangerous point, his eyes get wild. They almost seem to change from their natural light hazel to a dark, stormy brown. I can tell just by looking at him that he will detonate at any moment. Like a child, he needs to take naps, and he needs to be told when to take them. At this day-hospital stage, he comes home at around three-thirty and goes to bed immediately, sometimes for three hours or more. Only then can he even sit up for dinner.

What is Alan's TBI doing to us, and especially to Kelly? He's been home only a few short weeks, and already I worry. In the parlance of social workers or psychotherapists, we are in transition from the acute to the chronic phase of traumatic brain injury. It's a frustrating phase. Al's progress was so dramatic in the first few weeks: awakening from coma, speaking, walking. All these events seemed like miracles. But now the progress is gradual, difficult to see. I feel like a fish in water, or in a big TBI pond. Is anything happening? I cling to the evidence, brought to me by friends, that Alan is getting better. They say they can see subtle improvements, even if I cannot.

It's 1996, the summer of the presidential nominating party conventions. I can't get the Democratic shindig out of my head, and not for political reasons. On two separate nights, Christopher Reeve and James Brady appear, making it the Summer of the Disabled. Reeve's accident has been in my mind as a reference point for Alan's—as Reeve describes it, it was a fluke, something that shouldn't have happened yet did. I suppose that is the very definition of "accident." Christopher Reeve's fall from a horse was, like Alan's boating accident, unbelievable and horrible, and Reeve also has a small child whose life will be dramatically altered by his injury. As I watch James Brady up there on the podium, making a brief speech for gun control, it is his son, in the background, who fascinates me. Now a sturdy teenager, he was only two and a half years old when his father took a bullet in his head from John Hinckley's gun. It dawns on me that Brady's son has spent his entire childhood in the shadow of TBI. What has that been like? Has his mother told him about who his father was before he suffered a brain injury? Is it better that Kelly will remember what Alan was like before the accident, or is it worse?

The unrelenting action of events, the daily worries that Alan is getting the right treatment have slowed to the point where I now have the leisure to torture myself about the accident. With Al out of the woods and into day hospital, my own mind goes kablooey with "what-if"s. Thinking about how the accident might not have happened is a draining, meaningless exercise but one that I hear all people go through after traumatic events. What if we hadn't attended that school auction, so we wouldn't have gone on that vacation? What if, in fact, Kelly had gone to another school, so we never would have been at the auction in the first place? What if I hadn't miscarried the year before? Then we would have had a small baby, and we never would have taken that faraway country vacation in a place with seventy-eight steps. What if we hadn't gotten a new car two months before, that made us think we could drive all the way to Canada? Our eleven-year-old Toyota would never have been able to make the trip. What if I hadn't had those four glasses of wine at the auction, leading me to think it would be goddamned fun to go to a lake in Canada? (Most brain injuries are alcohol-related, meaning that the people in the accident are drunk. I kid, for months after the accident, that ours is alcohol-related, too, because the wine I was drinking made me want that damned cabin. What was I thinking?) And worst of all, what if I had left Alan the time I thought I might, after a terrible argument six months before the accident? I had been so mad that I had flown to a friend's house for the weekend. What if I had never come back? We'd be divorced now, but he would still have his brain—his original-issue brain. Sure, I know all these thoughts are pointless. But they constantly flit through my mind.

I start to understand Kelly's fear of our house. I develop an overwhelming feeling that I will be murdered. I imagine my demise down to the greatest detail. Every time I turn the key in the front-door lock, I expect an intruder to jump out. Every time I get out of the car, I expect a gun to my back. Worse, I have flashbacks to the moment I arrived to see Al's twitching body in the boat. The flashbacks can happen anywhere. I can be standing in line at an ATM machine or buying a head of lettuce, when suddenly I begin to weep.

Arriving home one night, I pull into the tiny parking space behind our brownstone building only to be surprised by the sight of two half-naked men using the area as a trysting spot. They're startled too—I see their eyes in the headlights for a second, like deer at the roadside. As if in a dream, they hitch up their pants and run in opposite directions. They're like an image of love and life interrupted. Everything seems like a portent these days, and I brood on strange moments such as this one far too long.

Right before Alan was released from Magee, I rode from the hospital to our house with my mother. A crew of more than a dozen young in-line skaters was flying down Arch Street, breathless and graceful. I rolled down my window. "Wear helmets, you assholes!" I yelled. God, don't they know? Do they want me to show them the zipped beds, the ties on the wheelchair?

What does Alan consider *really* stupid about day hospital? The field trips. Each week he and his fellow patients must organize and follow through on an expedition to a place where they will be able to use their social and cognitive skills. One week it's a Wal-Mart, another week an antique fire engine museum. One time the group goes to the movies around the corner. Other trips include a public television station, a supermarket, the Cherry Hill Mall across the bridge in south Jersey, and Dave and Buster's, a huge cacophonous theme restaurant on the Delaware River with a busy video-game arcade inside. (Joellen is amazed by this: "I'm not brain-injured, and Dave and Buster's is too many stimuli for me!")

The patients take charge of each trip. In a memo he writes to Dana Trainor, the director of the day hospital, Alan figures out the cost per patient for going to lunch at Dave and Buster's. He's also in charge of writing a letter to the studios of WHYY, the public television station, to find out when they can take a tour. His memos and letters look normal; you would never know a brain-injured man is writing them. But you would also never know how much time and coaching it takes to get him to finish them.

On my birthday, he goes on a supermarket trip with his classmates and buys me a card, bright pink with a knight and a damsel in distress. It's strange, corny, the kind of card he used to get and give to me ironically, winking all the way. This time I can tell that this pink monstrosity is meant sincerely, and I am delighted to receive it. I'm happy to have a husband who can even be at all aware that it is my birthday. It's funny how one's expectations can change: I cherish the amount of initiation it took for him to remember me and set aside a moment on his supermarket field trip to buy the card. Oddly, in the same way he added a year to Kelly's age, he has shaved one off from mine. In notes all over the inside of the card, he marvels at how I am now forty. "No, you're forty," he tells me, when I mention that I am actually forty-one.

Joellen, Sarah, and I have a tradition of going to a fancy restaurant on our birthdays. This year my friends have chosen Tony Clark's, the hottest restaurant in town. It's usually a girls-only event. But what to do with Al? Kelly is with my mother, and I haven't gotten a baby-sitter for Al. He must come along. It will be his first postinjury foray to an elegant restaurant.

In preparation for our outing, Al takes a long nap. He puts on long pants for the first time in a while, and I can tell he is excited to be included. Rationally, the way he is acting at our table is not that bad, but he begins heckling our hapless young waiter the moment we sit down. He asks a barrage of questions about the menu and makes strange jokes that have no point. The waiter takes it stoically, but I can tell he wants to get away. Alan cannot tell. He thinks he is being charming.

Al goes into the bathroom and returns amazed by the high-quality paper towels there. Each has the logo of the restaurant, the chef's signature. He brings a pile of the towels out to the table. "Look, he signed every single one!"

It's a lousy birthday for me. I hate this new strange husband. I feel, at various times during the meal, as if I am with a precocious five-year-old or a senile man of eighty. At one point I begin to cry, although I try to hide it from Al and the others. I can't believe that my friends are paying seventy bucks for me to eat here and all I can taste is snot in my crème brûlée.

On the day I accompany Alan during his therapies at the day hospital, he's loopy, giggling a lot and showing more symptoms of disinhibition. The scenes in the restaurant were just a warm-up. Al is getting progressively more garrulous and can hardly pass a stranger without making what he thinks are witty or hilarious comments. Like a child, he goes through several periods a day of being "wound up." I find it very hard to take.

Yet, despite my discomfort, I'm also proud of him during my visit. He has a community here at the day hospital, and a sense of belonging. He seems totally at ease, however much he complains about the place when he is home. I can tell that he is already a beloved character, whether he is hanging around in director Dana Trainor's office cracking bad, impenetrable jokes or wandering the huge open space, talking to people as they exercise. What I can't tell is if he is making much progress. In occupational therapy, I watch as he spends a half hour trying to arrange a schedule of household chores in descending order of priority. He has no idea how to begin. Everything seems equal to him.

Al's problems are still the same: initiation and organization of tasks and ideas. He's also lost his sense of time altogether. Everything at the day hospital is in the open, so I get a better perspective on the other patients' problems. Initiation and planning are major bugaboos for most. The day I visit, a patient who was a short-order cook before his stroke is trying to make potato salad, but he screws up all the timing, gets exhausted midway through, and has to leave the potatoes on the stove until the next day.

I once saw a presentation by a neuropsychologist who described what happens in the brain after frontal lobe damage: "Imagine a world where the library is intact but the librarian has gone insane." Experts call this librarian role "executive functions," which are performed by the part of our frontal lobes that allows us to make decisions and judgments, prioritize information, and organize information into categories. A TBI patient might never be able to totally recover those executive functions, but he can learn strategies to cope with his deficits in that area. However, he must be aware of the deficits before he can create successful coping strategies.

Al is not at all aware that he is having problems. He thinks his therapists are picking on him. He believes, fervently, that if I would just let him quit the day hospital, he could go back to work and everything would be fine. One day he tells me that the assholes want him to buy a book and write everything down in it. They say his old logbook from the hospital is too big; he needs a Day-Timer or some sort of small calendar/planner to carry around with him.

"I don't know where to get that," he says.

"Al, you can get one of those in any stationery store."

"No, you can't. This is a special book."

Then he comes home from the day hospital with a written note asking that he get a Day-Timer by next week.

"Al, most people use books like this. We never have, but we're in the minority. It's perfectly natural." He looks at me as if I am insane or in cahoots with the therapists who are torturing him.

We go to a Staples store, where I guide him to a whole aisle of planners, calendars, and other mnemonic aids. After a lot of deliberation, we choose one that is small and portable yet has enough space for him to write notes to himself.

"Wow, there must be a lot of brain-injured people," he says, looking again at the sweep of calendar displays.

Our HMO rears its ugly head again. I don't have to talk to the people there anymore, thank goodness. All they want to do is deny benefits, and I'm afraid I will burst blood vessels in my rage. At the beginning of this ordeal I used to imagine murdering the wealthy HMO executives who make their money from denying benefits to people who have worked hard their whole lives; now I fantasize about roasting the executives slowly on a spit, then taking them down and throwing a few Band-Aids and a jar of Vaseline at them: "Here's the treatment—this is what we've authorized for first-degree burns under your plan!" I understand that I will never again be able to speak rationally about the state of managed health care in this country.

At Magee, Lisa Gordon bore the brunt of the HMO's machinations, and now at the day hospital it is Dana Trainor's turn to fight for Alan's right to be treated. But she is up against the wall. It turns out that the HMO will authorize only sixty consecutive hours of treatment, which is used up in less than three weeks. I know, though, that Alan needs this structure if he is to make it in the outside world. He is just beginning to regain some of his memory. He comes home each day and can recite what he did, although not in elaborate detail. The specific details of his three weeks at Magee are hazy, and he cannot recall a single visit from anyone. But if someone calls, he can often remember for up to an hour afterward that he spoke to them. He knows, too, what he will be doing the next day, which I find encouraging. He even tells me about some of his fellow patients. Yet he still cannot initiate tasks. All the trips and the therapy sessions, which are now more focused on enabling him to live independently, are important for his future. If he leaves the day hospital now, what will he do all day long? How will he possibly get to the point where he can work again?

Al has only one brain, and I don't want to miss this window of opportunity to have him rehabilitated. They already kicked him out of the rehab hospital weeks too soon. Alan will stay in day hospital, even if I have to pay for it, gradually, for the rest of my life. ("When the bill comes, just say you can send five dollars a week," says my mother. "What can they do as long as you're *trying* to pay it?") Dana Trainor suggests that we can cut down on expenses by canceling the special transportation and having Al take cabs to and from the facility or having me drive him when I can. Amazingly, even taking a cab is about one-fifth the cost of the "official" transportation.

At night, when Alan is alert enough, we fight about his therapies. He doesn't understand why I am so adamant that he stay in a place he hates. He thinks he will get better on his own. He is sick of all the namby-pamby therapists making him do things he doesn't want to do, he says. He acts like a defiant teenager, even hinting that he will just not go to day hospital and not tell me about it.

What can I do? It's becoming much more difficult to control Alan. Now that his transportation has been discontinued, new problems crop up. A lot of times I can drive him in the morning, but when I am working in the afternoon, Al is supposed to call a cab from the day hospital and wait for it to arrive to take him home.

After a few days I find out that he never calls for a taxi from the day hospital. Instead, he goes out on the busy street—a four-lane semi-expressway—to hail a cab. I know how he does that, with his New Yorker ways; I can imagine him, standing in the middle of the street, ready to tip over, face flushed, arm raised, suddenly caught and dragged for yards by a tractor-trailer. Sometimes he wanders around South Philadelphia or walks for blocks and blocks. He gets home later and later in the afternoon, and I find that I can't work anyway because I am always subliminally waiting for the call saying he's been run over by a bus. He is still suffering from mild confusion and is distractable, impulsive. City streets are no place for a brain-injured man. He has stopped using his cane because he "doesn't need it." I explain that although his mobility is good, the cane sends a message to people on the street to keep their distance and not jostle him. Also, his balance is still very bad, especially when he is tired. I often talk to him about his wanderings. I even take his face in my two hands and *force* him to look at me, to focus on what I am saying. "You *must call a cab*. It is dangerous for you to be wandering around. Okay?"

"Okay," he says, and then he gets a mischievous grin on his face. I know tomorrow he will be wandering again.

He is not even supposed to be left alone in our home. On the few occasions when I must go out for business, I invite friends over and make it seem as if they just want to visit. One night Tom and I do a reading from one of our books in a bookstore out in Bryn Mawr, and I enlist Kay to come over bearing a pizza. She's there to watch Kelly, I tell Al.

So this is "parentification." I've read about it, and now I am living it. Is Alan my spouse or my child? I have to tell him when to eat, when to wipe his mouth, when to take a nap. I am making all the decisions for him, too, and like a child, he doesn't appreciate or even like most of them. He's surly and has temper tantrums. At times I become a maternal tyrant, bossing him around, screaming, telling him he will die if he gets himself into dangerous situations. It's not a good role for me. I've always been a kind of hands-off wife, not the kind who nags and interferes. But he now seems to have the judgment of an eight-year-old, with about the same emotional range. He defies me in mischievous ways, but sometimes, when he sees how angry he's making me, he breaks down and cries.

"I'm your son. I'm your little boy," he says.

At around this time, Al also gets into crying jags that have nothing to do with our arguments. He is entering what the brain injury experts call "an emotionally labile phase," in which he is often overtaken by sadness. He weeps and tries to apologize for the accident. "I am so sorry. I fucked up," he says between sobs, and I tell him all the time that it isn't his fault. He did nothing wrong. It was just bad luck. It wrenches my heart to know that he would think I'd ever blame him for the accident. Yet it is a good sign, all the therapists tell me. Alan recognizes that things have changed and that his role and mine are reversed right now. Acknowledging one's own loss and another's stress is a significant step toward cognitive recovery.

During this phase, Alan is also extremely vulnerable to suggestion. Products start arriving in the mail: CD-ROM encyclopedias, trial books from book clubs. Before his injury Al hated talking on the phone, but now he seems to love yakking to anyone, even people selling useless items. I want to kill the telemarketers for preying on a brain-injured mark, but then, how can they know? Al's behavior is well within the norm—we've all bought something we don't need now and then—but he is out of control and no longer the frugal man I remember.

Alan circles and then spots his victims. At the pool, it's a local restaurateur and his wife. We didn't know them very well before the accident, but now Al fixates on them. In the few days left of the season, he becomes a relentless socializer. He usually makes a beeline for the wife, Sheila, and plunks himself down next to her. He tells her lengthy, obtuse stories, and she's polite enough to actually listen. He talks about his accident, but in a garbled, random way, mixing up time sequences and going into routines where his doctor is always saying stuff like, "Son, you got run over by a boat." How should I deal with these scenes? I sometimes try to get him away, but he doesn't pick up any of my cues. He "teases," as he says, her husband, Dmitri, relentlessly and for no reason. Sometimes I think he focuses on him because he can always say something about his restaurant at the start of the conversation. Alan sees him as "Dmitri the restaurant owner." I notice that Alan now has labels for everyone, including himself. He is a Jew, a boy from Brooklyn, he has told people since his injury. He is a lawyer. Our veterinarian, another person with a very defined but distant role in Alan's life, is also the object of his attention. When she comes to the swimming pool with her husband and toddler son, Al nabs her, telling her jokes or long stories about our cats. Once when Alan is not around, I apologize to the vet and try to explain that he is more garrulous since his injury. "Oh, it's okay," she says in her slight drawl, "really it is. He's such a nice man."

We're at Dr. Eric Zagar's office for a follow-up exam, and he's asking why Alan is not doing the exercises to rehabilitate his torn rotator cuff.

"Alan, you are a young man. Do you really want to lose the use of your right shoulder forever?"

"I just don't remember to do the exercises," says Al, who, on his own, is having a tough time following any schedule. You'd have to know the "premorbid" Al to realize how different this behavior is: He used to be jock obsessed by his joints and muscles. In his early thirties, he lost most of the meniscus in his knee after a squash accident and spent months doing physical therapy to the point where he could still play touch football. He rehabilitated his back, too, after he discovered that he had possible herniated disks. Being able to play sports once meant everything to him.

Dr. Zagar looks as though he's had experience with this problem before. He knows what I am just beginning to learn: there is no point being subtle with the brain-injured. The doctor raises his voice: "You *must* do your exercises, Alan. You have to do them. Promise me you will do them. Otherwise, your arm will stop working."

"Okay," says Al meekly.

And it works. He's scared of the mean doctor who has told him he must do something, so he does it. By the end of two weeks, his shoulder begins to feel better. He no longer cries out in pain whenever he turns over in his sleep. He will forget, it turns out, that he ever saw Dr. Zagar, but emotionally he retains and internalizes the threat by the Doctor in Charge.

. . .

It is Labor Day weekend, the end of this strange summer, and Al, Kelly, and I are going to drive down to Cape May on Labor Day itself to spend the night.

I'm setting myself up for disappointment, I guess, with all these "milestones" I want to create. The first visit home was a bust. The first time out in a restaurant was pretty much a disaster. So what makes me think that an overnight trip to the Jersey shore is going to be celebratory?

But what else can I do? If I admit that we should just sit at home for the next few months or years or decades, I am accepting the loss, and I am not ready to do that yet. I couch it in family terms: I say I think it would be nice to do something with Kelly.

All in all, the trip is uneventful, especially for Al, who seems not to notice or care that we are in Cape May, one of his favorite places. Located at the southern tip of New Jersey, below the Mason-Dixon line, it's unlike any other shore town in the world, with a wonderful street life, sophisticated restaurants, and Victorian houses covered with gingerbread and surrounded by picket fences. You can arrive in Cape May, park your car, and never use it again. When we were in our twenties, we used to stay in a cheap guest house in the swanky section of Victorian bed-and-breakfast inns. We'd walk the four blocks to the nice little beach, where we would linger until well after six o'clock, then go back to our crappy little room and make love, waking up at about nine or ten o'clock, in time to catch the restaurants before they closed but after the big crowds had disappeared. After Kelly was born we reluctantly switched to staying in motels, more practical for a sandy, noisy toddler.

When we arrive at Cape May this time, we walk the half block from our motel to the beach, where Kelly frolics by the water and Alan stands and stabs randomly at shells and rocks with his cane. If the waves come up too quickly, he scurries backward, like a sandpiper. He seems as terrified of the water here as he was at the swim club.

A hurricane a few days ago has left the surf wild and brought up amazing things from the ocean's bottom, the types of shells and driftwood you usually don't see in this tame resort town. I'm in the water swimming when I hear Al screaming. "A conch!" he says. "Look, a conch!" He's flailing a foot-long shell with his cane. Kelly runs over and dives for it, coming up with the precious shell and a face full of sand.

"I can't believe we found a conch here!" says Al, taking it from her, and for a moment he seems like the old Al, obsessed with wildlife and the natural castoffs of planet Earth. Some of our friends have a silly nickname for him: Mic Mac Al, from a trip we took to Nova Scotia, where he was always foraging for berries and driftwood like a noble Indian warrior. But the glimpse into his old personality doesn't last long—a few seconds later he looks as if he is collapsing from within, like the picture of the elephant king who eats the bad mushroom in the original *Babar* books.

"Al, are you okay?"

"Tired."

Kelly and I drop him off at the motel room, where he sleeps for hours while we go to the arcade and roam about town. Dinner is a truncated affair without conversation, and then it's back to the room again so that Alan can sleep some more. I don't sleep much, and Kelly wakes up screaming, as she has done fairly regularly since the accident.

We leave the next day with the conch shell in the trunk. No one has drowned or been hit by a boat. I suppose that is a start.

9

Level 6—Confused but appropriate. The patient's speech makes sense, and he or she is able to do simple things such as getting dressed, eating, and teeth brushing. Although patients know how to perform a specific activity, they need help in discerning when to start and stop. Learning new things may be difficult.
Level 7—Automatic, appropriate. Patients can perform all self-care activities and are usually coherent. They have difficulty remembering recent events and discussions. Rational judgments, calculations, and solving multi-step problems present difficulties, yet patients may not seem to realize this.

—Rancho Los Amigos Hospital Scale
of Cognitive Functioning

In the summer of 1848, Phineas Gage, a twenty-five-year-old construction foreman for Vermont's Rutland and Burlington Railroad, had a very bad day at work. Maybe he was day-dreaming about sex or dinner. Maybe he had a cold, or one of the men he was supervising was telling a good joke. Whatever the reason, while engaged in a fairly routine task he'd performed hundreds of times before, Phineas zigged when he should have zagged. Bending over the track bed, he drove a tamping iron directly into some gunpowder instead of waiting for one of his workers to add a buffering layer of sand. Boom! The three-foot-long, inch-round piece of iron took off like a slender cannonball, entering under Gage's eye and exiting out the top of his skull.

Bystanders were stunned, especially when Phineas struggled to his feet and tried to walk away. He was taken by oxcart to a physician's office, where he reportedly asked how soon it would be before he could return to work. And return he did, although missing one eye and, apparently, much of his former personality. Before firing him, his employer stated that Phineas Gage, once a responsible, level-headed, friendly man, had turned into a belligerent jerk prone to inappropriate displays of rage. Whereas Gage had been evaluated as "the most efficient and capable foreman in their employ previous to his injury," now his boss labeled him as "irreverent, indulging at times in the grossest profanity (which was not previously his custom), manifesting but little deference for his fellows, impatient of restraint or advice . . . obstinate, yet capricious and vacillating." Historical accounts say that Phineas's horrified friends and coworkers put it this way: Gage, quite simply, was no longer Gage. Yet until well after his death, Phineas Gage was held up as a medical success, a man who had survived the most terrible head injury imaginable and could still walk and talk. Only decades later did neurologists identify Phineas Gage as the first recorded case of "characterological change" brought on by frontal lobe damage. In effect, Gage gave himself a lobotomy. By examining Gage's skull (it now rests in a case, along with the infamous tamping rod, at the Warren Medical Museum at Harvard) and looking at the position of the entrance and exit holes, nineteenth-century neurologists posited that the tamping rod had damaged only the part of his brain affecting his personality and left intact his motor and speech. Years later, around the one hundred fiftieth anniversary of Gage's unfortunate accident, neuroscientists reconstructed the trajectory of the rod by using computer imagery and concluded that the iron staff had made a significant dent in Phineas Gage's orbital frontal cortex, a part of the frontal lobes responsible for our emotions and personality traits.

I often think of poor Phineas. I wonder how he lived after he got fired (history says, rather cryptically, that he became a

vagrant) and how his brain injury affected his closest relationships. I'm not surprised that early accounts focused on
his amazing physical recovery and the way in which he could
still remember facts and do calculations. That's where most
stories of severe brain injury stop even today. Survival at a
certain functional level seems miraculous, but it's the part
that comes afterward that's hardest for the patient and his
friends and family—the process of adjusting to the chronic,
long-term cognitive side effects of TBI and carving out a life
for oneself after significant personality changes.

Many of the changes Phineas underwent are classic symptoms of frontal lobe damage. With his brain's executive functions impaired, he found it difficult to make decisions,
"devising many plans of future operation which are not
sooner arranged than they are abandoned in turn for others." His overuse of profanity was typical—ask anyone who
works on a brain injury ward, where they are frequently
accosted by disinhibited patients who swear or expose themselves. Parents of TBI teenagers report that an obscenity is
often the first word out of their kids' mouths when they learn
to speak again. "Fuck" and "shit" occupied, in those first few
postinjury months, a prominent place in Alan's discourse.
Even now, we have one friend who will do impressions of
Al's everyday frustrated talk: "Well, *fuck,* I don't know *what the
fuck, fucking shit. Al, what the fuck do you think?*" Al laughs uproar-
iously. Obscene gestures, too, abound among those with
frontal lobe damage. Alan will often "give the finger" to
Kelly without thinking.

What the historical accounts don't mention about Phineas
Gage is whether there was any change in his sense of humor.
I would bet anything that after his accident he laughed more
often and more loudly than before. Most TBIers with frontal
lobe damage have a tendency to do that. One friend with
a TBI wife describes it as a maniacal cackle. Another,
whose husband is brain-injured, says, "He sure finds almost

everything hilarious, not like before." Alan, when confronted with anything in the slightest bit amusing, throws back his head and guffaws. When we attend movies or plays together, people in the aisles around us turn and look to see who is laughing so much and sometimes so inappropriately. Al could now get a job making laugh tracks for sitcoms. Neurologists have done studies that show that a probe placed in the right place in the frontal lobes will cause spontaneous laughter (an intimidating idea for those who think humor is a craft!). Also, according to a University of Toronto study, people with frontal lobe damage tend to laugh hardest at inappropriate punch lines to jokes. Who we are, even right down to what we find funny, is locked away in that front part of our brain, right above our eyebrows.

Phineas Gage, the nineteenth-century poster boy for frontal lobe damage, haunts me. Perhaps if he lived today, an MRI could tell us exactly what happened to his brain, but even with such sophisticated tests, doctors cannot predict with much accuracy what the effects of specific damage will be. Like doctors in the nineteenth century, they must treat each brain as dysfunctionality manifests itself through inappropriate or disturbing behavior. Yet if Gage had lived at the turn of the twenty-first century, he would definitely have the benefit of a modern pharmaceutical approach, which is making great strides toward helping persons with TBI function in the everyday world. Drugs might have been able to control his terrible rages.

After Alan is discharged from Magee Rehabilitation Hospital but before he becomes involved in a serious back-to-work effort, his rehabilitation doctor, Dan Weinstein, starts exploring using medications to control Alan's outbursts of anger and possibly to give him more energy. Doctors know that a damaged brain suffers from severe chemical imbalances, and it seems that seratonin, the substance responsible for good sleep and good moods, is involved. So in the last few years they've begun using antidepressants such as Prozac, Zoloft, and other seratonin-based drugs on people with TBI. No one knows exactly how to medicate a damaged brain. Dan Weinstein freely admits that Alan is a guinea pig, and he adjusts Alan's dosage frequently. The antidepressants seem to help. Instead of having, say, three fits a day in which he will rage and throw things around the kitchen or smash the cellular phone because it gets stuck under the car seat, Alan on seratonin-based antidepressants might have one such episode daily. It turns out that Ritalin, used to focus children with attention deficit disorder, makes Alan crazy. Yet many people with TBI respond well to the drug. The doctor had hoped that Ritalin would give Alan more energy and lessen his fatigue, but instead it makes him a slave to raging anger attacks and episodes of wanton impulses.

I realize the benefit of seratonin-based antidepressants for TBI a little over a year after Alan's accident, when we visit his brother, Gary, in California. I know something's wrong: Al is acting loonier than usual. Gary's two-year-old son, Joey, is prone to hitting and biting people, as many two-year-olds are. One day I walk into a strange scene where Joey is trying to get Alan's attention by hitting him playfully on the face. Instead of reacting as a normal adult, Al just hits Joey hard right back. A few days later, when Alan and Kelly and I are in Yosemite National Park, Al begins having multiple anger attacks. Kelly is frequently in tears because Al has screamed at her for minutes about nothing at all. Finally, when he fumbles and drops a paper bag onto the floor of the car by mistake and reacts by picking it up and smashing it repeatedly against the windshield and screaming *"Fuck fuck fuck!"* I pull over to the side of the road and stop the car. A revelation comes to me: "You're not taking your medication, are you, Alan?"

"No," he says, sheepish but proud. "I wanted to be able to satisfy you on vacation. I wanted to be able to come, so I stopped taking the pills." I feel awful, because Kelly is in the backseat witnessing this scene.

As soon as we get back to Philadelphia, I send notes with Al and he goes to see Dr. Weinstein—working together, through trial and error, they find an antidepressant, Serazone, that will keep Al's angry impulses in check but not cause sexual dysfunction.

If Phineas Gage lived today, and especially if he lived near a major city, he would never have just waltzed back into his old job as a construction foreman. Nowadays professionals who work with the severely brain-injured know that they need extra help to reenter the workforce. Like Phineas, Alan is constantly asking when he can go back to work. He tells a lot of his friends that he is going back sometime in late October or early November; he seems to have no idea that he is far from ready to return yet. He's going to be discharged from day hospital soon—we can't keep him there forever— and I must start looking into the next phase. In the TBI professionals' jargon, the next step is called "community reentry."

Community reentry can involve anything from learning how to live on one's own to actually going back to a former job. We've been told that Alan has a chance of being able to work again as an attorney and bank trust officer. Lisa Gordon at Magee said, "I don't usually make such statements because I don't want to get hopes too high, but I do believe that Alan has the potential to do his job again."

So I start to look around. What is the perfect community reentry program like? It turns out that community reentry is a diverse network of services, highly individualized. You don't "go" anywhere for the therapy—the therapy comes to you. A good community reentry program consists of individualized counseling and later, if you are lucky, on-the-job coaching at your former position or, if that's not possible, in a new job you and your reentry counselor find together.

Alan is in a great position to attempt reentry because he has few long-term memory deficits (meaning that he retains all that he knew about law and banking) and because, according to his therapists, he has fewer social deficits than many TBI survivors.

Social deficits? Lisa Gordon has already said that Al is less self-centered than many persons with TBI and is fairly good at picking up on social cues. His neuropsychologist at the day hospital, Barbara Watson, is impressed by Alan's sense of self this early after injury. He is socially at ease. I'm proud of him, as a parent would be proud of a kid with a good report card.

Other factors working in Al's favor are his years of education and job experience, an advantage the majority of TBI survivors, men in their teens and twenties just starting out in their educational or work trajectories, do not have. In addition to working as a trust officer for the bank, Alan has a small law practice serving a few clients he brought with him from his last law firm. One of them, Dan Sargent, who manages the development program for the Masons of southern New Jersey, calls and makes me cry with his kind words. "So it's going to take a little longer before Al is back?" he says. "Okay, we'll wait. Don't worry. We'll wait for Al. In the meantime, we'll farm it out to other guys, but Al is still our lawyer. He's a great guy, and we want to continue working with him." In fact, Dan is so enthusiastic, he agrees to be a test case for Alan's reentry. The first task Alan will try at home after graduating from day hospital is drafting a simple will for the Masons.

I hope I am not leading Dan on in even suggesting that Al could do legal work again. I've noticed a lot of positive changes since he began day hospital six weeks ago. He seems more together and a bit more willing to listen to suggestions.

He's having fewer crying jags, and his angry fits are not lasting as long. Perhaps, with a one-on-one counselor, he really could practice law again.

At least I can leave him alone for a few hours at a time again, and I've become less worried about having him take care of Kelly for a half hour here and there. Often, though, I will return from a brief errand to find them at each other's throats. The normal childish things Kelly does, such as forgetting where she put her sneakers, yelling with excitement, or turning up the volume on the television, irritate Alan all out of proportion. He calls her "stupid" or "an idiot," and when I confront him about it, he claims not to have said it. He reminds me of a seven-year-old himself, since he'll deny yelling or breaking something even when I've heard or seen him do it.

Recovery from brain injury is a long process, I tell myself every day. I try to dwell on the positive and the potential for improvement. For example, Alan is beginning to participate in household chores again, emptying the dishwasher and worrying about whether the cats have food and litter. He talks to his family for a long time on the phone and can relate a few details of the conversation to me immediately afterward. And in between the fits of anger, there are fits of loving, too, when Alan tells me and Kelly how terrific we are and how he never could have survived the accident without us.

But I am still making all the decisions, and often Al seems not to understand what is going on or exactly where he is in his recovery. He knows a boat hit him, yet he still has moments when he totally denies that he had a brain injury. His demeanor is consistent with everything I've read about the trajectory of TBI: although a person typically passes through distinct stages, explained by the Rancho Los Amigos

Hospital Scale of Cognitive Functioning, the phases often overlap, and when it comes to the finer nuances of cognitive recovery, such as making decisions or always clearly recognizing cause and effect, a person with a severe brain injury may lapse in and out of several stages at once.

As Alan's caregiver, I have to select an appropriate community reentry program before he graduates from day hospital. Al can't participate because he's still incapable of weighing different factors or seeing why he would ever need such services. I comfort myself by clinging to the flashes of insight he *is* showing these days. "You know how you told me rehab would be the hardest thing I would ever do?" he says to me one day as we drive home from Riverfront. "I thought you were just bullshitting me, but now I think you're right."

We have the option of staying for the next phase with Magee, which is rather new at the reentry game, but I have a gut feeling that it is time for a change. We could go to Moss Rehabilitation up in North Philadelphia. It is an excellent hospital with a wonderful reputation, but it requires that Al be evaluated thoroughly again to join its reentry program, and I think he has had it with testing. When I even mention that he'd need to go up there for a complete battery of day-long tests, he starts screaming, saying he doesn't want to go. Then I consider a smaller, more freewheeling organization, Community Skills Program, which has close ties to Moss (many of its counselors were trained there) but which will accept Magee's evaluations of Alan's deficits and strengths and would be able to start his individualized reentry program immediately.

In the meantime, the people at Magee keep advising us to look into the benefits available from the state of Pennsylvania's Office of Vocational Rehabilitation (OVR). The OVR assists people with disabilities in getting back into the workforce—the agency was funded in a rider to the Voter Registration Act, and I guess the thinking was that the more people working, the more tax revenues. There's a possibility, we find out, that the state might actually fund some of the therapy Alan will need to adjust to work again.

Even before we go for our interview at OVR, I've heard from many people about Crystal Mangir's dedication to her clients and her intense interest in TBI. "She is *the* best person to get, an incredible advocate," says Drew Nagele, a neuropsychologist at Moss Rehab. "She knows everything about brain injury." Crystal, a small, cheery woman with a pleasant round face, has worked for OVR for nearly twenty years. She's optimistic but also blunt and honest about the realities of life after brain injury. In all the time she has been helping people reenter the workforce, she tells me on the phone one day, fifteen lawyers have come to her office seeking help. Only five have returned to work successfully. "Law is a profession requiring high cognitive functioning," she says, "but Alan seems like a good candidate for reentry." The goal of reentry, she reminds us many times in the next few months, is not necessarily to return to one's old job but rather to find a way to contribute to society, some position that will enable one to live up to what might turn out to be a drastically altered potential. Sometimes it can be more a curse than a blessing to go back to your old job, says Crystal: you will always be compared to what you were like before your brain injury.

At her office, Crystal laughs as she helps Al fill out the application. There's not enough room on the form for all his educational information. "We've never seen anyone go above twenty years of schooling," she says. She looks at Al's long résumé and tells him she's impressed. I've been worried that our income will disqualify us for state help, but Crystal takes us through the steps where we list all of our out-of-pocket medical expenses and additional child care costs, which so far have been astronomical, including the bill for the Canadian government helicopter, which was thousands of dollars and not covered by any insurance. I don't know why I am so surprised at all of this—of course we are going broke. And this is just the beginning. Alan is still being paid his full salary under his six-month disability plan at the bank, but that will end soon and we will be facing the reality of a serious reduction in income. He's covered by a private disability policy, but only for up to 60 percent of what he was making. Later I discover, unsurprisingly, that the bankruptcy rate among brain injury families is sky high.

After we work out the financial side with Crystal, we sign a paper saying that we'll be responsible for the first two thousand dollars or so of the reentry counseling fees. Then the state funds will kick in. It's the first time I feel as if we've ever gotten anything out of the state of Pennsylvania, and it seems so lucky—the cost of getting Al back to work through one-on-one counseling could well exceed thirty thousand dollars. I didn't know how we were going to afford it.

Crystal says OVR will fund either Moss or Community Skills Program, so the next day I call Community Skills. Cheryl Boyd, a young, friendly social worker who will manage Alan's case as his "team leader," meets with us one afternoon at our house, asking questions about his injury, his previous employment, and his goals. She says she has someone in mind as Al's rehabilitation counselor, a young man who is finishing up his Ph.D. in neuropsychology at Drexel University, just across the river from our house. I like the idea of a young man—I figure they can be more like pals and Al will get away from the idea that he is being smothered by protective females.

I meet Bill Gardner, Al's new counselor, a full twenty-four hours before I'm supposed to. He shows up a day early by mistake, and I like him immediately because of it. We joke about how he can have the balls to claim he can help brain-injured people get organized when he can't even keep track of his own schedule. Bill doesn't seem to have the typical profile of those in the "helping professions"—he's dressed way too hip, with one elegant earring, a cool dark-colored shirt and tie, black jeans, and fashionable black boots. His hair is close-cropped, his sideburns outrageously shaped in sharp wedges that reach nearly to the middle of his cheeks. He's twenty-nine, likes alternative music, and eats mostly vegetarian. His live-in girlfriend is a neuropsychologist, too. Bill is very articulate and seems as interested as I am in the ironies and peculiarities of brain injury. He was an intern at the Kessler Institute in East Orange, New Jersey, where Christopher Reeve was rehabilitated. He's doing a dissertation on the high rate—75 percent—of divorce among TBI survivors and spouses. I pretend to grill him on how many "high-functioning" TBIers he's worked with, but really he's a shoo-in for the job. He's like a breath of fresh air.

I naively expect Alan to like the very *idea* of Bill as much as I do. Instead, he bridles at the enforced supervision. "I don't know why I need someone around me all the time, telling me what to do," he says. We go over it again, exposing, for me at least, the incredible imbalance in our current relationship. I'm reading ahead, worrying about all the aftereffects of TBI, while Al is barely acknowledging that anything is wrong with him. On a self-awareness scale of one to ten, he has advanced, maybe, to two, a remarkable achievement for someone with a serious brain injury, since lack of self-awareness is the most pesky of deficits, one that can sometimes stall full recovery indefinitely. Yet Alan's still fairly oblivious to many of his ongoing problems with organization, impulse control, and short-term memory. His lack of concern for how he will make the transition to work and his conviction that he is all better now leave me totally frustrated. When I try to tell him that I've read all about job reentry and its pitfalls, I sound as if I'm a child taunting him on the playground: "I know something you don't know!"

But it's true, I have read ahead, study after study of people who tried to go back to work and failed. They don't usually fail as quickly as Phineas Gage—he's an extreme example. Here's what normally happens: The high-functioning TBI survivor triumphantly returns to the workplace. A sort of "halo effect" is in place, and for a while all are happy that their coworker survived a terrible accident and has now returned. They even cover for him and do extra work to ease his time back. Then, after a few months, the changes in his short-term memory and ability to juggle projects or his weird penchant for cornering them at the coffee machine and telling them long, tedious stories begins to wear on them. Coworkers get tired of mopping up after the returnee's mistakes and doing extra work because he is not up to speed. They have assumed, mistakenly, that he is all better. But after the first year or even sooner, the TBIer begins to get crummy evaluations. Eventually he either quits in frustration or because of intense fatigue, or he is fired. Case studies of brain-injured people who try to return to work without help chronicle how those workers often lose their jobs years down the road, and by that time no one really attributes it to the brain injury because they think all that was over a long time ago.

I explain all this to Alan, but he doesn't care. I have to go ahead pretty much against his will, and I watch uncomfortably as he reacts to Bill Gardner as a symbol of some authority he wants to flout. He tries his best to put Bill down at first. "I hope he isn't going to wear that earring to the bank," he says. "I don't think they'll like that at my bank."

Transitions are not good times for any brain-injured person. Al is graduating from the day hospital, so naturally he will regress for a while.

In spite of all his complaints about the place and especially "the stupid class trips," Al seems genuinely sad when I pick him up on his last day in the outpatient facility. Dana

Trainor and her staff have gotten a cake, and everyone gathers around. His day hospital pals present him with Charles the Brain Child, a little plastic doll with an empty cranium and a brain on a string. The instructions say, "Swing the brainy ball in an upward motion and try to catch it in the hollow of Charles's head." Dana kids Alan that he hasn't really graduated until he can get the plastic brain into the head cup. He does it on the second try—his coordination is getting better and better.

Shortly after Al's graduation, we go on our first movie date together. The old Al had very strange and eclectic tastes in cinema—he liked either deeply depressing, obscure Japanese films, slapsticky French comedies, or crass shoot-em-up boy flicks starring Arnold Schwarzenegger, Bruce Willis, and other action heroes. I figure he's not ready for subtitles yet, so I choose *Independence Day*, the biggest, campiest movie of the summer. I've been dying to see it, although I know from friends' comments that it's the type of movie you should pretend to dislike. There's something odd about seeing a summer blockbuster movie in October, but what the hell? We go to an early show.

As soon as the movie begins, I realize I've made a bad choice. The first half hour is given over to introducing the ensemble cast, the folks we're supposed to care about on planet Earth as the aliens invade. Many actors come and go quickly, and Alan can't really follow what is happening. Things are blowing up. There's noise. He starts muttering under his breath, "This movie sucks. Fuck this piece of shit. Aww man, this is the worst fucking movie I've ever seen." I hiss back, telling him to calm down, it will get better.

"I hate this piece of crap. Goddammit, why does this fucking movie suck so much? I gotta go. I gotta get out of here. Cath, I gotta leave. I gotta go."

I take a deep breath and whisper, "Just stay, okay, Al? Give it a few more minutes?" I hope I can wait him out, as I sometimes can with Kelly when she is whining.

It works. He stays. I think he might even doze, but he makes it through the overly long movie, and when I look over at him during some of the more emotionally expansive, intimate scenes, like the ones between the stereotypical Jewish father, Judd Hirsch, and his nerdy scientist son, Jeff Goldblum, I can tell that Alan is actually following and enjoying them.

Afterward we go to a Vietnamese restaurant where we've known the owners for nearly twenty years. They haven't seen us in a long time, and it feels very celebratory to be stepping out, visiting old haunts. "You know, that was a bad movie for someone with a brain injury," I tell Alan over spring rolls and kimchee. "Sorry I chose it. Way too many people in the cast, and too much going on. I didn't think about that. I'm proud that you made it through."

"Yeah. Gee, that thing made me tired," says Al.

10

One-to-one treatment began with Mr. Forman describing his work responsibilities, with an emphasis placed on his private law practice, as that will be the first job focused on during therapy. Before treatment had started, Mr. Forman reportedly had been reluctant to attempt any legal work, stating that he did not know if he was allowed, or should try, to perform the work. He had created a list of work-related and personal tasks to accomplish, but had little success in initiating or completing many tasks. . . . Mr. Forman required cueing and assistance in selecting and initiating tasks.

—rehabilitation counselor Bill Gardner's initial report for the Community Skills Program, filed on October 15, 1996

Bill comes to our house three days a week for four hours per day. Al and Bill start trying to organize Al's home office. He has an initial assignment to draft a will, and that takes them quite a bit of time; in fact, the drafting of that will stretches over days. The plan is to ease Al into working again with his home law practice and then to aim higher with a return to his regular job at the bank on a part-time basis sometime in the next few months.

Al finds any excuse to come to my office while Bill is there and ask me questions. Bill tries to point out to Al, politely, that he is invading my workspace, but the comments seem to go right over his head. Yet after the first week Alan has finished the will, which feels like a new start for him. He still tells me each night that he can't stand having Bill around, but I think that they are bonding nonetheless.

Alan has another concern, and it turns out that OVR can help with that, too: he wants to drive again. Because driving is almost always necessary for employment, OVR pays to have Alan's driving potential assessed at Moss Rehabilitation Hospital, at its special driving school for the disabled. He passes the assessment with flying colors, which means that he and Bill can start studying for the written driver's test.

Fall, the time of renewal. Although we've never believed in sending form letters for the holidays, I ask Alan if he would like to send a Jewish New Year's letter. It has been nearly three months since the accident, and I want to thank everyone who has helped us so far and let them know how Alan is doing. Alan loves the idea and offers to write the letter. After a few days I realize that he will never start it, so I write it. Al says he will "edit" it, and when we get calls about it later he proudly tells people that he contributed the finishing touches. In actuality, he merely reads it over, which still thrills me. Yet he seems to see it as a story about someone else. When he gets to the part about being in a coma for five days, he stops and says, "Really? I was in a coma?" In keeping with his new goofy outlook on life, he chooses to focus on the few humorous comments I've interlaced with the facts about his injury. He's especially tickled with the line "Everyone will be pleased to know that the accident in no way affected Alan's huge brain reservoir of sports knowledge and early rock lyrics."

Rosh Hashanah and Yom Kippur, the high holy days marking the new year on the Hebrew calendar, are a time of renewal, a time when a person is once again written into the Book of Life. This year, even though I'm not a believer, I feel very emotional. I think of how easily Alan could have missed getting into the book. Just seeing him walking around, talking, trying to work again, seems miraculous. At Thanksgiving a few weeks later, I burst into tears as I stand up in front of our friends and relatives and give a toast of thanks that Alan is still with us.

In November, Alan's right leg starts to bother him again. He says it feels numb. When he gets up, the unruly limb often buckles under him, and he drags his right foot a bit as he walks. He also seems a little more out of it than he's been. I take him to see David Nicklin, his primary care physician, so that we can get a referral to see the HUP neurosurgeon, Eric Zagar. David is alarmed enough to get us an appointment right away, along with the authorization for another set of MRIs to see if there is any renewed bleeding in Alan's brain.

Alan saw Dr. Zagar only a few weeks ago, when Dr. Zagar scared him about the need to rehabilitate his shoulder, but this time he has no memory of ever meeting the doctor. "And you're sure you don't remember being here before?" asks Zagar.

"No, gee, I don't remember you at all," says Al.

I had thought that Alan's posttraumatic amnesia had been easing, but it still shows up in pockets. He never has any trouble recognizing Kelly and me or anyone close to him, but he can't remember anyone he met during his hospitalization or other recent acquaintances, such as the parents at Kelly's school. When we visit Magee for appointments, he does not recognize any of his therapists except for Lisa Gordon, which is strange since he spent more time with his occupational and physical therapists than he did with her. These pockets of amnesia will continue for a long time, very noticeable in the two years after Alan's injury. Even today, nearly three years after the accident, Al has one or two episodes a week in which he has no memory at all of something that happened. In April, nine months out of injury, I throw a surprise party for his forty-fifth birthday at his favorite cheapo

Indian restaurant. About twenty-five people, all close friends he has known for years, attend, and Al talks to them all. Yet the next day he tells me he cannot remember a single person who was there. One day a few months later he walks over to pick up Kelly from school and then goes upstairs for his nap. When he awakes, he comes screaming down the stairs to my office: "Cathy! Oh my God, it's way past school time. I forgot to pick up Kelly! Did anybody get her?"

Today the neurosurgeon says there is good news about the new MRI images—there is no new bleeding visible, and Alan's original injury seems to be healing. He wants to order an electroencephalogram (EEG) to see if there is any unusual activity in Alan's brain. He could be suffering silent seizures, the doctor says. Renewed bouts of paralysis or weakness can be indicators of this problem. I've read that people with TBI frequently suffer seizures months and years after an initial injury, so even the mention of the word terrifies me. But the neurosurgeon is calm. He suspects that the weakness and numbness in Alan's right side are just a strange regression that will eventually right itself.

The doctor's suspicion turns out to be correct, and in the end Alan's physical regression remains a mystery, as do so many of the side effects of TBI. Was his right side acting up because of the new stress of working toward a return to his job? Were the numbness and limping a symptom of scarring on the brain's motor strip from where the major bleed had been? People who care for the brain-injured often refer to the experience as a "roller-coaster ride" of stress, since there are so many ups and downs. Progress, both mental and physical, is rarely measured in a steady, upward curve; instead, the person's abilities might surge ahead for a while, then plateau, and even sometimes get worse, all in the course of a few months, and factors such as stress and fatigue can make a big difference.

"Get your coat, Crimmins, we're going to celebrate!" Al shouts, bursting through the door with Bill following close behind. Bill has driven Al out to the hinterlands of southwest Philadelphia to take the road portion of the state driver's test; Al passed the written a few weeks ago. Now he's been successful at the driving part, too. "I passed! I nailed the sucker!" he yells over and over. It's December 4, only five months after the accident, and he's a fully licensed driver again. Beaming, almost dizzy with his triumph, Al pitches the idea of going out for his favorite food, masala dosa, a lentil crepe stuffed with spiced potatoes, a southern Indian specialty served in only one restaurant, out near Penn's campus.

Lately Alan has been obsessed with masala dosa. As Bill often points out, whatever your traits were premorbidly are exacerbated after a brain injury. Alan has always liked Indian food, but since his injury a large part of his brain seems devoted to seeking masala dosa. He will take a bus to this place to get it, rearranging his schedule. He talks about masala dosa all the time. At this point I welcome any of his obsessions that hearken back to our former life. At Magee he couldn't even remember what masala dosa was, and when I brought him one he refused to eat it.

Luckily, Bill likes Indian food, too, so we go to lunch together. Alan drives, which seems almost as amazing as seeing him walk again. Yet I worry about how he would react in a car under stress. And I am well aware that the responsibility of driving a lot might still be too much for him. He must take it slowly—there are those pockets of amnesia and lapses in judgment to worry about. A year and a half after the accident, he takes our car to his office, parks on the street, and then walks home afterward, not even recalling that he drove or where the car is. He reports it to the police as stolen. I once read an amusing case study of a TBI survivor who would call the police whenever he had misplaced his coffee mug in his kitchen, an instance where lapsed memory and faulty judgment merged to make life particularly difficult.

But today the mood is triumphant. The new driver's license is proof that Al is regaining his independence.While we're wolfing down the curried goat, tandoori chicken, and Al's precious lentil crepes from the buffet, I talk with Bill about what's going on with the status of Alan's job reentry. Yesterday Bill and Alan met with Al's employers at the First Union Bank. All systems seem go for a return to work part-time some time in January, and at this point the folks at the bank say they understand Alan's limitations. Part of Bill's job is to act as an advocate and explain brain injury to Al's bosses and coworkers. He will also go to work with Al every day, functioning as a job coach. The biggest accommodation the bank will have to make is to allow Alan to work part-time, at the beginning only twelve hours a week. Alan looks just fine— that's why TBI is often dubbed "the hidden disability"—but everyone must understand why he has to take it slow. The hardest concept to get across is that brain injury is a *physical* condition. "If Al were in a wheelchair or had a cast on his leg, people would understand that something happened," says Crystal Mangir. "But no one can see a broken brain."

Bill reports that Alan is beginning to use "compensatory strategies and devices," which include his appointment book and "to do" lists. Al says that the aids are starting to feel more natural to him, an important first step toward being able to work again. He simply won't be able to hold as many things in his head at one time as he could before his accident.

Bill's also helping Alan develop strategies for managing his impulse control problems, which might affect his ability to work again. While he can get away with throwing things around or screaming obscenities at home—something that still happens at least once a day and sometimes more—that type of behavior won't cut it at the office. It's Bill's job to help Alan better understand the connection between the fatigue and his emotional outbursts. Al still refuses to see how pushing himself to work for, say, more than an hour or two at a time will lead to bouts of extreme irritability. Since Al has lost his sense of time, Bill must remind him to take frequent breaks before fatigue overwhelms him. When Al begins one of his tantrums, Bill suggests stepping away from the frustrating situation until he calms down. He hopes that Alan will internalize these suggestions before he goes back to his cubicle at First Union.

I hope so, too. I am worried about Al's return to the work world. Will he succeed? Will his coworkers accept him? I've read all of Bill's reports, and I think Alan is making progress. Yet I still feel he needs a safety net, which Bill will provide when he accompanies him back to the office.

11

"Why does Daddy yell at me all the time?"

*"Because he can't help it. Something in his brain makes it hard
for him to stop yelling."*

"Who do you think he yells at more, you or me?"

*"You. Because you're a kid. It's hard for brain-injured people to
be around children, because they make a lot of noise and
move around a lot. But the medicine helps."*

"He doesn't love me."

"Of course he does. Of course. He loves you very much."

"I wish he would be like he was before."

"How is he different?"

*"He yells a lot more. He looks different. Sometimes I think he is
all different—like he has different skin and a head and his
whole body."*

"You're right, Kel, he is different."

"Is he ever going to be better?"

"No, I'm sorry. He isn't."

—conversation with Kelly

We hired a therapist to help Kelly cope with the accident and
the changes in her father. The psychologist, highly recommended, came to our house for a family meeting before she
began treating Kelly. I disliked the woman from the start, but
I thought it was just my natural tendency to distrust therapists. To me, she seemed creepy and condescending, but she
had also caught me on a bad night, when I was feeling overly
exposed. That's the terrible thing about a catastrophe like
brain injury—you go from being a private family with private issues to being a "case" and a "syndrome" and a set of
symptoms that are discussed by professionals. You feel like a
bug caught in a special box with a magnifying lid. I admit
that I was raised to be fairly therapyphobic, so maybe I've
transferred that feeling to my daughter. After a few sessions,
Kelly says she doesn't want to go back to see a psychologist,
even though I later find her a more appropriate therapist.

Kelly is adamant about how stupid the first shrink seems. "She keeps asking me if 'it' bothers me. 'It,' she says. And I finally said to her, 'You mean *the accident?*'" says Kelly, moving her hands in a scary motion and laughing.

But Kelly's fears are no laughing matter. She won't go upstairs by herself. Her sleeping habits have regressed to about the level of a four-year-old's: she can't fall asleep on her own, and she still frequently wakes in the night, screaming. One day she tells me that she knows the accident is all her fault because if she hadn't wanted to go in the boat, Daddy would have been safe. I tell her, of course, that it's not true, she had nothing to do with the accident. I explain that I, too, sometimes get mixed up and think it was my fault, but it was no one's fault—not Daddy's, not hers, not mine. It was bad luck. I have to tell her that again and again: sometimes bad things just happen to people, and there's very little you can do about it. Somehow it's not a comforting message for a girl about to turn eight.

I would do anything—anything—to erase the accident from her childhood. If a genie were to appear and give me only one wish, it would be that my daughter would not have to see her father lying comatose and then later, agitated and confused, zipped into a bed, acting like a raving lunatic. I can never undo that reality, and I hate it. I try to be rational about the whole issue of bad luck in life: my dad dropped dead of a heart attack at forty-seven, and Sarah's mother died in her thirties, when Sarah's sister, Joanne, was only nine. Joellen's father was diagnosed with multiple sclerosis when she was very small; she doesn't really remember him out of a wheelchair. Tom's father died of Parkinson's disease, mute and paralyzed, when Tom was sixteen. When my mother was seven, her father lost a lung and was in the hospital for a year. Terrible things happen, I know, and people get on with their lives. I just never imagined that something this bad would happen to Kelly at such a young age, and it's a horrible, powerless feeling to know that there's nothing I could have done or can do now to protect her. It's like watching a bully torment my kid without being able to leap to her aid: she's being bullied by life.

The rotten-luck issue reaches ridiculous proportions: Kelly tells me one day that she would like to have a big party when she turns thirteen, five years from now.

"I want it to be an unlucky thirteen party," she says very seriously, and I ask her what that would be. We'd have stuffed black cats on the tables, she says, and open ladders for people to walk under. I suggest seating thirteen people at each table, decorated with broken mirrors. She comes up with the idea of guests opening umbrellas indoors. "We're the bad-luck family," she says.

One morning I'm driving her to a friend's house for a play date, and she asks, "Why did you leave me when you went away with Daddy in the helicopter? Why did you? You left me. You never even said good-bye."

"Yes, but your dad needed me. I had to go with him. Somebody had to go with Daddy, because he couldn't talk for himself."

"You should have stayed with me. I was in the accident, too."

"Kel, I couldn't. I knew Sarah and Honey would take care of you. I knew you would be all right."

During that first fall after the accident, the issue of abandonment comes up again and again. I think about her question a lot, and I console myself that she just doesn't really understand how serious Alan's condition was. Or does she? One day she catches me in a stressed moment: "Why, why did you leave me and go in the helicopter with Daddy?" It's become a refrain that I dread, and this time I just snap.

"Because he almost died," I yell at her. As soon as I say it, I feel awful. For a moment Kelly is very still.

"Really?"

"Yes. Your father almost died, and I wanted to be with him. He needed someone to be with him."

"Daddy almost died?"

"Yes."

Interesting. Here I think I've been very open with everyone, including Kelly, but I've withheld the one bit of information from her that could help put together the pieces of the puzzle: her father might have died. The thought had never crossed her mind, even though she'd seen Alan comatose and covered with tubes and wires, hooked up to a ventilator. Kelly stops asking me why I didn't stay with her at the lake, but my revelation opens up a world of unsettling possibilities. Knowing that Alan could have died, she confesses to me tearfully one day, makes her wish that he really had. Then he would be dead and not just weird.

I hold her and tell her I understand, that it's okay to feel that way. I don't tell her that mourning for the man who used to be my husband, who's now been replaced by a very odd stranger, sometimes leaves me so weak with anguish I can barely get out of bed in the morning.

On Bill's advice, we try the some of the strategies he is using with Al in the office in the home environment. For example, as soon as Al starts ranting or smashing stuff on the kitchen counter, I ask him to leave the room. Sometimes it works, but most times it doesn't. Unfortunately, I also have to ask him to go away when he's yelling at the top of his lungs at Kelly for small offenses, such as not putting her sneakers on fast enough. Because the new, disinhibited Alan will just say anything that pops into his head, he uses words around her that no child should hear from a parent. "*Fuck* her. Why is she so *fucking* annoying? She's a stupid little lazy *bitch*." We have many scenes where Kelly runs away crying, Al stomps away, smashing into walls and doors, and I sit stunned at the dining room table, wondering if I will ever have a family again. In the same way that I longed for a recording to tell Alan about his accident in the early days, I now would like to just flip a switch for the talk I must give Kelly after each of these terrible episodes:

Daddy doesn't really mean what he is saying. His brain has been hurt. The part of his brain that helped him think before he yelled has been damaged. He can't control his anger.

Kelly never seems convinced by my explanations. In fact, I'm sure she's not. She's beginning to internalize all the scenes, to think that they're her fault. Afterward, Alan will deny that he was out of control, or he'll say that she deserved it. He'll never admit that his anger was out of proportion to the situation, and even with his use of antidepressives we have at least one but usually more of these scenes daily. Rage is such a part of our household that there is no space for regular discipline. I become Kelly's ally and protector, my role as authority figure shrinking daily.

How can Kelly make any sense of this new father of hers? One moment he is screaming, and then only minutes later he will show her the latest stuffed animal he has bought her or give her five packages of bubble gum he picked up at the drugstore on his way home from the gym. Neither Kelly nor I can get a handle on what will set him off, and while his fits are happening they seem almost as surreal as they are scary.

The worst incident of Al's irrational anger occurs about nine months out of injury, when I ask if he can take Kelly and her friend Jen to the movies one Saturday because I have a deadline. When they come back, the girls look strained. I know from their faces that there's something wrong. Alan brushes by me and goes right up to our bedroom, where he frequently ends up these days, lounging in a half stupor.

"Daddy kicked me," says Kelly. Her cheeks turn almost red enough to hide her freckles. Jennifer, her best friend, adds hastily, "Yeah. He kicked her in the *butt*."

Kelly had decided she and Jen should get candy from a self-vending machine with expensive gourmet jelly beans and the like, sold by the pound, and had asked Al if she could do it. But when the bill came, she and Jen had bought more than seven dollars' worth of candy, which enraged Al. Kelly started getting nervous and dropped the bag, scattering some candy on the floor. While she was bending over to pick it up, Al booted her smack on the rear end, hard, in front of everyone and, most humiliatingly, in front of her best friend. Even telling me about it a few hours later, Kelly seems stunned.

After Alan emerges from his nap, I confront him, and he readily admits to the kick: "She dropped the *fucking candy*. And it cost a lot of money!"

This moment is a turning point for me. Until now, I'd thought I could modify Alan's behavior by giving him "feedback," and talking to him about strategies for controlling his violent impulses. Now I want to kill him. "If you ever, ever harm our child physically again—*ever*—or if I even hear about it second- or thirdhand, I will take her so far away you will never see her again."

Alan stops dead in his tracks. He can tell I am serious. Like a deaf man reading lips, he can read my face, and only by doing so does he know that he has behaved inappropriately. He cannot process an incident by himself but needs the aid of my reaction. "Okay," he says meekly.

I should have given up on subtle hints a long time ago, I guess, but how can I describe how odd it is to have a husband who needs to be bullied to be fairly normal? Dr. Zagar the neurosurgeon knew he had to threaten Al to get him to take care of his shoulder. Bill, also, is very blunt with Al sometimes. I learn after a while that you really can't hurt a severely brain-injured person's feelings by just coming out and telling him what to do or how to act. Or at least not Al's feelings. He needs crutches. You wouldn't think twice about driving a car right up to a door for a person without the use of his legs. Suggesting things, indeed, even forcing things on a high-functioning brain-injured person is like offering a type of mental crutch. A person with TBI needs normative grounding and constant reality checks. Often Alan will say he was not yelling or being abusive at all. Bill suggests that I videotape Al as he rages or write down every single incident of when he yells at Kelly needlessly. I find that approach impossible, both because these are not home movies I want to make and because I'm so sick of living this nightmare and then having to talk about it. Do talk therapy and reasoning ever work with the brain-injured? Al forgets our talks by the next day, anyway. This is ironic, since one of the reasons I married Alan was his ability to really talk out problems and to try to understand my feelings. Before the accident, he was a model husband in that sense and was always quick with an apology when feelings had been hurt.

Around the time of the butt kicking, Bill senses I am at the end of my rope. In our meetings with Crystal Mangir and Cheryl Boyd, and in private meetings with Bill, I describe how Al's inappropriate behavior is driving me crazy, how it keeps me on edge all the time, since I never know when he will blow up or start destroying property.

Bill tells Alan that he must start to respect my sense of reality in a situation and not just deny that it is happening. Since his self-awareness is not increasing dramatically, he will have to borrow mine. Otherwise, his relationship with me, and his bond with Kelly, will suffer. If I tell him he is yelling, he is. If I tell him that he's ridiculously tired and needs a nap, he should listen. If I say he's being crazy or out of control, he must try to stop that behavior. Otherwise, Bill says, he will lose me. He will lose his wife and child. Does he want that?

Al broods on this for a while. He comes to me, crying, "I don't want you to leave me. Please don't leave me." He knows that Bill is working on a dissertation about how few couples—under 25 percent—are able to stay married after a traumatic brain injury. Alan wants to stay married, no matter what.

"I won't leave you," I say, and I hope that it's true.

12

As individuals with TBI attempt to resume their usual daily activities, the environment places increasing demands on them, uncovering additional psychosocial consequences. For example, executive dysfunction may become obvious only in the workplace; behavioral changes affecting interpersonal relationships may appear after leaving inpatient care. Spiraling adverse consequences of TBI may become apparent not only for persons with TBI but also for their significant others. Family members report depression, social isolation, and anger. Overall family functioning and relationships are disrupted. Such consequences may continue and, in some instances, worsen with age.

—"Rehabilitation of Persons with Traumatic Brain Injury," National Institutes of Health Consensus Development Conference Statement

We've decided to go to Mexico, which in retrospect will seem like a very stupid idea.

I'm burned out almost beyond recognition. It's six months after the accident. My health feels wrecked. The look of shock in people's eyes when they see me is painful. I know I need a rest, but of course Alan can't be left alone, and especially not with Kelly. Also, Al is totally hepped up to go back to work at the bank as soon as the holidays end, and that sounds dangerous. He needs a little more time, or at least a week or two, to recover from the overstimulating round of parties and holiday obligations. Everyone has been wanting to see us, to celebrate that Al is still alive and kicking, so our holidays have been wonderfully significant but extremely hectic. And that's not good for the brain-injured—the newsletters and magazines about TBI all give hints for keeping the brain-injured from freaking out at this time of year. Bill has even noted the effect of Christmas on Alan in his

Community Skills report: "[D]uring this month, he faced the additional stress of the winter holidays. Mr. Forman and his wife hosted several holiday gatherings and attended numerous others. He reported that such events can be 'over-stimulating,' which leads to both fatigue and irritability."

So I ask Sarah, who's something of an island expert, if she can find us an inexpensive trip to a beach where we can relax and I can keep Al from going back to work until the very end of January. Joellen decides to come along, too. Sarah does the research, runs all the numbers, and finds that the only place we can really afford in the height of the winter season is Mexico—a package deal in Cancún. We think of it only as a short beach vacation, like Florida or the Caribbean. We don't really grasp that it's a junket to a foreign country.

Duh, as Kelly would say.

I see how stressful travel is for the recently brain-injured when we reach Mexican customs and Alan starts screaming. He's exhausted from the flight. (Any sort of change in environment still does him in.) There's a long line, and he can't tolerate waiting. He lets out a string of obscenities, becoming louder and louder. He makes threatening gestures at customs officers. His mouth contorts, and his lips seem to be getting bigger. He looks like a teenager standing on a city corner, hurling taunts at an opposing gang. Shhhh! we say. Joellen, Sarah, and I have visions of ending up in a Mexican prison. By the time we get on the bus to the hotel, I am in tears. Kelly is pressed up against me, tired of hearing her father scream swearwords.

Because the tacky resort is a self-contained compound, I keep thinking Alan will be safe. There's a big pool with a swim-up bar and tennis courts—not many places where he can get into trouble, I think. Yet at first I don't realize that even the athletic contests—water volleyball, for example— involve copious amounts of liquor. When players miss or make important shots, they are expected to atone or celebrate by slugging down tequila. The Mexican bartenders, interpreting Al's disinhibited behavior as the typical party animal personality, keep pouring cherry tequila poppers down his throat. Every time Al throws back his head to laugh, they pour in another shot. Al never drank much before his accident, and now he has even less tolerance for alcohol. In fact, he's not really supposed to drink at all because alcohol increases the effects of TBI. I can't talk to the bartenders, who know very little English. I try to get Alan to stop, but it's impossible to watch him all the time. Then I try to relax. I'm sick of telling him what to do, and he must be sick of it, too. He's on vacation, not driving, so what could happen?

Then Al discovers the ocean. The resort is perched on a ridge about fifty feet above a narrow beach, a short climb down some stairs. There's no lifeguard at the beach, only some red flags that I guess are supposed to mean "Watch out, you crazy swimming gringoes!" At first I don't worry, remembering how scared of water Alan was just a few months back. But now his brain seems to have done an about-face: he swims way out into the waves, much farther than I've ever seen him swim before. All judgment appears to be gone. I stand at the shore and call to him. I go into the water to a reasonable distance, hoping he will swim back in and float next to me. He gets so far out, he can't make it back. There's a terribly strong undertow. I see him float to my right, way down the beach. Eventually he makes it in to shore, about a hundred yards away from where we've left our beach towels.

"Al! That's too far out! Don't swim that far out again. You're not that strong, remember? See those flags? There's a bad undertow. Maybe even a riptide."

"What? Aw, come on. I wasn't far out. Nah. You're just a worrywart."

"Al, please."

He smiles his goofy smile, and the next time he goes into the ocean, he swims even farther out. "That's just so *not like* Al," says Sarah. "What is he doing?"

"Where is Daddy?" Kelly keeps asking me, and I have a panicky moment each time before I spot the top of Al's head out in the waves. At one point I try to persuade Al not to swim in the ocean at all. I stay up on the pool deck, inviting him to sit with me, but within minutes he tells me he's going down to the beach again. I follow, reluctantly, thinking, "Do I really want to be there when his lungs fill up with water?" A strong swimmer myself, I'm stunned each time I assay the surf—the undertow is wicked. One time Al is out there for more than a half hour until he floats, again, way down the beach. I think of one of my students who wrote an essay about nearly drowning in Mexico.

"That boy has a death wish," says Joellen.

"Where's Daddy?" asks Kelly as she takes off again for the shore to scan the waves. I mumble bitterly to myself, "Oh, he's drowned. Sorry. We just went through these last six months of *hell* to have him drown."

Long after a baby is born, the brain continues developing. Two of the last faculties to kick in, around age nine to twelve, are self-awareness and judgment. Last to develop, first to go—a lack of judgment is one of the most common side effects of getting knocked on the head. The damage to Al's frontal lobes has quashed whatever common sense he had before the accident, and even he admits (now, three years after the accident) that judgment was never his strong suit. During the first year postinjury, we travel with my mother to meet my sister and her family at a Charlottesville, Virginia, hotel. My mother comes back from the hotel pool to tell me that Al has been encouraging Kelly to dive into two feet of water—she stopped her just in the nick of time. "His judgment is all off now, Cathy," she says fretfully.

I once read an interesting interview with a neuropsychologist who studies brain injury and its subtle social effects. After she had been looking at TBI sequelae for a while, she discovered that brain injury had played a major role in her own family's history. Her grandfather had been a self-made millionaire—the family had owned several mansions—who had lost all his money in the thirties. She just assumed he had lost it in the stock market crash until she found out he had sustained a head injury in an auto accident. After the accident, he made only foolish, reckless investments, dipping into vast amounts of capital and refusing to listen to advisers who told him he could live comfortably for the rest of his life if he would stop making such rash decisions. The neuropsychologist realized that it had in fact been brain injury, with its tendency to cause judgment deficits, that had ruined her family financially, not the vicissitudes of the American economy.

Alan will not take my word for it that he's taking too many risks. To get him away from the ocean, I suggest that we rent a jeep one day and explore a Mayan ruin, Cobá, about three hours away.

At least Kelly is having a lot of fun at the resort. She loves the organized activities, including the sexist, silly Miss Royal Solaris contest. She pals around with the activity director, a young American woman named Laura, and we go together to a show given by Laura and the staff every night. On the day Alan and I go touring, Kelly has planned to get her hair braided in cornrows all over her head, a service provided by older women who sit on the pool deck from nine to five, their fingers flying over the scalps of female tourists. So Kelly stays at the hotel with Joellen and Sarah. I am happy that she can have a one-day vacation from worrying about her dad.

Alan and I take off early in the morning, with me driving. He's brought some snorkeling gear because he looked in the guidebook and found that there is a particularly good, calm spot with coral reefs off the road on the way, near a restaurant where we could have lunch. I'm seduced into thinking this is a good idea. He seems a lot like the old Al, reading ahead, getting excited about esoteric travel jaunts.

We find the snorkeling beach and park the jeep. The ocean here is beautiful and shallow, the floor covered with mostly dead, pockmarked coral. We decide to go in the water for a little while and then have lunch at the open-shack restaurant before we go on to Cobá.

Alan looks a sight. He's got all sorts of stuff hanging from him, including a waterproof disposable camera that he's been obsessing about. The only thing he *doesn't* have on is a lifejacket. I've been swimming in the shallow water with my mask down, looking at a rather paltry selection of fish, for maybe five minutes when I pop up and can't see Al nearby right away. I'm not worried, because it's only about four and a half feet deep here.

But Al left this dimpled coral area long ago. He's swum about fifty yards out, where he has no business being. I go after him quickly, getting sucked into a current I can't fight. In all my years of swimming, I've never felt anything quite so strong. I can't get anywhere doing my strongest stroke, the crawl, and so I retreat. With great effort I finally find a patch of coral where I can stand. I'm halfway between Alan and the shore.

Standing on the coral reef, I bend my flippers as best I can to try to stay in one place. The current is still pushing at me relentlessly. Even from a distance of about twenty yards away, I can see that Al is in trouble and that he's thrashing.

"I can't get the fuck back!" he's grunting. His mask and snorkel are perched on the very top of his head. The disposable camera hangs from his wrist by an elastic band—he keeps bringing it up to his face frantically, each time slamming himself in the mouth and screaming.

"Al, Al, calm down. Keep calm. Throw away the camera. Forget the damned camera. Drop it in the drink."

He makes another grunt and tries desperately to jump into the current and swim toward me. Like an aquatic boomerang, he ends up back in the same spot. "Fucking this fucking fucking fucking!" he screams, and then I hear him choking as he takes in water. For a moment I see only the very top of his head.

Time freezes. My chest feels as if there's a grapefruit inside trying to work its way out. I can't imagine a more appropriate Hell for caregivers who try to pretend that brain injury isn't really happening to their family. I'm in Denial Purgatory. Isn't it enough for me that he almost died once? Couldn't I just stay home and watch television, like everyone else? I've put a seriously impaired man in danger. Perhaps Alan's right, brain injury *is* contagious. I stand on an uneven rock made up of dead animals, watching my husband begin to drown, and there's nothing I can do about it. Turning slowly so I won't slip, I check to see if there is anyone sitting out on the restaurant deck. Yep, they're there. I try to wave my hands in the air without falling off my coral perch. My voice won't carry that far. This is rich: Al will die, and the people eating their cheeseburgers in Paradise won't even notice.

He coughs and gags, taking in more water. I turn back. There's a real edge to my voice, even though I'm trying my best to sound assured. It's hard, because I have to shout to him this far away: "I know, Al, just calm down. It's a bad current. Don't use up your energy. Don't move."

Our only chance is for me to try to swim to shore and then get others to help. But can I make it in time? He's popped up again, even after swallowing the water. I wonder if they have anything like a life preserver on a rope around here.

I take a leap toward shore and let the current take me sideways. That's what the experts always advise: ride out an undercurrent or riptide horizontally, passively, and eventually you will get to shore. It works. About two minutes later I'm crawling up on my knees on the beach only about twenty yards over from the restaurant. I scan the sea for Al: miraculously, either because he's just too tired to fight anymore or because maybe he, too, remembers the advice about getting caught in currents, he's now free, floating a long way down the beach. I watch him floating so fast, away from where I am, and I think: if he had died, I could never go home. How could I call his parents, again, within six months, from yet another country, and tell them that something was wrong? How could I call his office and say he's not coming in, after all, he's drowned? No, it's starting to look suspicious. Obviously I take my husband on vacation and try to kill him.

Al's exhausted. It takes him a long time to walk back up the beach to where I sit. He never talks about what happened. He seems to forget it within moments, and when we get back to the hotel, he tells Sarah and Joellen that I'm crazy, he was never in any danger.

Monday morning, January 20, 1997. Six months and three weeks after Al's accident, he's standing in front of a mirror, knotting his tie. I watch him, remembering last August, when I brought in one of his ties to Magee for his occupational therapy sessions; despite several tries, he had difficulty executing the knot. I remember standing in our walk-in closet that same month, moving his business suits to the back and his casual clothes to the front, weeping, believing that Al's professional life was over forever. I think back to last October, when the challenge of putting on a suit and tie for the funeral of Sarah and Joanne's beloved Aunt Kay left him exhausted and disoriented.

And now he is going back to work as a trust officer.

He'll start slowly at sixteen hours a week, only twelve of them at the bank, the rest at home, where he can better avoid overstimulation. Bill will accompany him to the office. "Just your luck," I tell him, "to get a job coach who's always going to be better dressed than you are." Bill shows up, natty. The earring has stayed, even though Al has made crude comments about it. But I notice that Bill is wearing his most conservative stud.

Crystal Mangir tells us that many brain-injured people returning to work hide the fact that they have a job coach. We could have chosen that option, introducing Bill as a college intern or an assistant on a special project. Al and I believe that's a stupid strategy, especially since we've been so open about his injury up to this point. Why stop now?

At first, Alan's coworkers think it's strange that he has a hip-looking young man with outrageous sideburns in his cubicle at all times, but within a few weeks they relax and start joking. "Where's your sidekick?" they'll ask if Bill steps out for a moment. They call them Batman and Robin, the Lone Ranger and Tonto.

"What does that guy do all the time with Al at his job?" ask friends, and it's hard to explain without getting into the depressing reality of Alan's deficits. Bill helps him prioritize tasks. They write "to do" lists and organize his files. Bill provides "cues," letting Al know when his behavior is becoming inappropriate or when he thinks Al is getting unduly exhausted. He also educates people around the office about Alan's injury. His greatest value, I think, is simply his presence. He is like the cane I wanted Alan to carry to show people that his balance was unstable. Bill is a walking announcement, living proof that something serious has happened to Alan, that he needs help to get back to work.

No, it's not the greatest position to be in, to have a constant sidekick, to feel as if you have a baby-sitter in your own office, and Alan hates it. I know he feels, in his heart of hearts, that Bill's presence is an unnecessary invasion of his privacy. But the alternative is unmitigated stress and, ultimately, failure. To this day, Alan and I disagree about Bill's importance. Of all the indignities foisted upon him by the brain injury, Al bridles most at being exposed by needing a helper at his job.

But achieving the goal of going back to his old job still has no context for Alan. He has no idea how amazing it is that he's returning to a position requiring so much brainpower, even though I tell him so daily. When he is working with Human Resources, trying to straighten out his benefits, he says casually to the HR director, "But surely you've had other situations like this."

"We had one other employee with a brain injury years ago," she says. "He came back as a janitor."

Some of the stupid things people have said about Alan's brain injury:

"Don't worry. Kelly is young. She won't remember what her father used to be like."

"This could be the best thing that ever happened to the two of you! It's a blessing in disguise!"

"It will get easier for you after you forget the old Al."

"Don't you really think this happened for a reason?"

"At least he didn't break his arms and legs!"

"I like him better since his accident."

No one saying these things understands. TBI is like an incomplete death: you've lost a person, or parts of that person, but he's still here. Do people grasp how precarious and mutable the human personality can be? At first I forgive them their ignorance, but as the years go by, I begin to judge them on their failure of imagination. It all boils down to what makes a person a person, and for some people that seems to entail merely walking and talking. They don't have much interest in the nuances of character. Yet there is so much more to life and so much more to the people we love.

Is Alan still Alan? Yes and no.

"When I'm around Al now," says Joellen, who is close enough to perceive his personality change, "I feel a palpable sense of loss. I find it poignant to always be aware of the doubleness: he's here, and yet there is that other man who once was."

The Ghost of Alan Past. He haunts me even more than Phineas Gage does. The worst thing you can do, says the literature aimed at families, is to remind the brain-injured person of what he was like before, of what he could do back then that he can't do now. But how can you help remembering?

"I wish you could have known the Old Alan," I say to Bill. I know that sounds silly, since he has been hired to get the New Alan back to work. But he says he understands. He's willing to talk to me about grief and how it is a perfectly natural reaction to my husband's severe brain injury. According to Bill, the brain-injured are well described as "the walking wounded"—the outside world has no idea that anything is wrong with them. It is their families who must cope with their cognitive deficits and emotional changes as best they can.

"I feel like I was divorced on the day my wife was injured," says a friend of mine (his wife, whose car was run over by a large truck, now has substantial frontal lobe damage), "and then there was a hastily arranged marriage to a woman I barely know."

This New Alan is a strange version of the one I knew before. I walk into the living room, and he's on the phone, laughing. He throws his head back and chortles. I think to myself, Who *is* this guy? The premorbid Al hated talking on the phone. "I always got the feeling that Al never liked me," confides one of my friends. "But now he just talks and talks. If I call and you're not around, he can stay on for half an hour."

Sometimes the changes surprise even Alan himself. He'll make a comment about the astronomical phone bill, then look at it and see that most of the long-distance calls are his. He makes "guerrilla" phone calls, dialing up to tease our friends.

How can I explain the personality oddities of brain injury to people who think Alan is the same as he was before? I ask for Bill's advice. "Just tell them to imagine the things they hate about their spouses most and then multiply that trait a hundred times," he advises. How true. Anything annoying that Al did before the accident, he now does more, and more intensely. He always had trouble with his temper and with loss of patience, but whereas before he might have blown up once or twice a week, now temper tantrums are a daily occurrence. When I met Alan, in his midtwenties, he showed me a hole in the wall in his apartment, created by his fist. By the time of his accident he'd long stopped that young-buck behavior. But nowadays it's not unusual to hear screaming and come upon Alan in the kitchen with a container of gazpacho or sour cream spread all over the floor. Something goes wrong—say, a stick of butter falls on him out of a bin in the refrigerator—and all hell breaks loose. It is the refrigerator's fault, and it must pay. He smashes things, especially food containers, randomly until the rage subsides. Objects fall off the counter, and he crushes them with his feet.

The old Al did not take to change easily, and once he adjusted to a new situation, he often claimed not to remember his old way of life. When Kelly was about five, he told me he could barely remember a time when we hadn't had a child, even though we had been together for twelve years before her birth. Now, since his injury, any change in his routine throws him for a loop. Rigid, concrete thinking and a lack of emotional and intellectual flexibility are traits of the brain-injured. Travel is very difficult because I can't anticipate frustrations or long waits or even what could go wrong. I can't protect him, or Kelly and me, from what might happen in a new environment. The Mexico nightmare is only the start of several unsuccessful travel experiences. Once, on what should be a short, easy trip to Boston for a bat mitzvah almost two years after his accident, Alan acts up again and again. Forced to sit in traffic for a few moments, he pounds his fist on the dashboard, swearing. He rants and raves. At the parking garage near the Boston Aquarium he loses our ticket and gets out of the car, kicking the car, the curb, and the machine that is supposed to let us out.

The first evening we're there, we attend a celebratory dinner with the bat mitzvah's family, close friends of ours, a rabbi and her husband who went to law school with Alan. Everyone is delighted to see how well Alan looks, and some people pull me aside to say they can't tell anything ever happened to him. On the way home, I'm driving and Alan is slumped in the passenger seat, exhausted, while Kelly chatters merrily in the backseat. I call Craig and Diane, with whom we're staying, to get last-minute instructions to their apartment building, and I think I can turn left at a certain intersection, but it's illegal. I need only go around the block to correct the mistake, but before I can, a "kablooey" Al pops up and starts screaming: I'm a fucking fucking fucking idiot and don't know the fuck anything and I'm an asshole. He begins smashing the inside of the windshield again, and what follows is my least proud moment as a TBI caregiver.

I go crazy. I'm still holding the cell phone, and I begin beating him about the head (the head!) with it, screaming through clenched teeth, "Alan, I hate you! I will kill you if you keep this up! I cannot live this way. Do you understand? I will *kill* you! I intend to *kill* you!"

"Mom, Mom, stop! He can't help it, he's brain-injured. His brain is making him do it," says Kelly from the backseat as she reaches between us and tries to wrest the phone from her psychotic mother. A nine-year-old forced to be the voice of reason. At least I know she's mastered the patter about brain injury.

Somehow we make it into the parking garage and up to the guest room in the apartment building. I continue to seethe. I've had it. I'm ashamed of behaving like that in front of Kelly but convinced that if I *had* killed Alan right there in the car, I could claim he wasn't my husband at all, just some angry, addled alien inhabiting my husband's former body.

The next morning Alan takes his shower first. When I step out of the shower stall, the mirror over the sink is steamed up and there is writing on it. "Help me. I have TBI," it says, in Alan's new babyish handwriting.

Time management is another brain injury problem. Alan was never great at it before he got whomped on the head, but now he's hopeless. If, say, we're due at a concert at eight p.m., he might think to take a shower at seven forty-five. Send him out to get a half gallon of milk, and he's likely to return two hours later. He's due at work by nine o'clock, yet he decides to take the dog for a walk at eight-thirty. I must nag him and explain time frames all the time. Al attends a support group for the working brain-injured every Thursday at eleven a.m., and every Thursday he leaves *after* eleven to drive there. When I tell him that I know someone in the group has complained about his tardiness, he bridles: "What the fuck do they know? Everyone is late. Besides, they're only a bunch of brain-injured people."

Bill focuses on developing strategies for this time problem at the office. Alan is not supposed to work more than four hours a day in the beginning, yet about ten minutes before he should leave the office he'll often start a new project or attempt a chain of phone calls. Any overtime at work shows up in his fatigue level later. He can't cheat his body the way he used to. A person with TBI cannot "work through" fatigue or get a "second wind." One week, when Bill is away and not monitoring Alan, I note that he has worked more than thirty hours at the bank. That weekend, he sleeps off and on continually, and when he is awake he has frequent fits of anger. Even on the following Monday he has not recovered his energy level. On a normal day with four hours' work, he must still come home and sleep for a few hours before he can regain his emotional and physical equilibrium.

Before his accident, Alan was an antsy, high-strung man. Now he can sometimes be even more frantic while also aimless in his activities around the house. He doesn't sit still until he nearly collapses with fatigue. During the first year of reentry, we have a monthly meeting of Alan's rehabilitation team—Cheryl Boyd and Bill from Community Skills and Crystal Mangir from the Office of Vocational Rehabilitation—at our house. Sometimes Alan can't concentrate at all. In one team meeting report a year and a half after injury, Bill notes Alan's hyperactivity and his tendency to be distracted by things around the house:

> We had lunch during our session and, when we finished, he cleared the plates off the table. Seeing that the dishwasher was still full, he proceeded to empty it entirely and refill it as we tried to continue our discussion. He appeared able to listen to the conversation but did not participate, probably because doing the dishes while engaging in conversation is too cognitively challenging for him. When Ms. Crimmins suggested he wait until later to empty the dishwasher, he responded, in a curt voice, "I'm listening to everything." After he finished, Mr. Forman walked out of the room without saying anything. When she called to him, he explained that he was going to change the CDs. Again, Mr. Forman needed to be cued that that was not a priority and that he

should sit down and join the discussion. He did, but it was obvious that he was easily distracted, had difficulty regulating his behavior, and was unable to attend to simultaneous tasks.

Around this time, Al develops an obsession with laundry. He is constantly washing things, even garments that shouldn't be washed. He buys giant boxes of detergent. The laundry is always in a state of transition—some clothes folded, some not. Most is heaped in piles along the walls, on the floor of our bedroom. Our ancient cat Minnie pees on the piles, and Alan has to start all over again, like Sisyphus at the Laundromat. Sometimes he starts loads in the washing machine and then forgets them so they develop a horrible moldy smell that he can't perceive. He keeps doing laundry no matter what, even when I point out that our cleaning person, Lisa, will do it. Lisa, a wonderful, warm person, tells him that, too, but to no avail. I try to explain that he is not accomplishing anything—in fact, he sometimes destroys clothes—and that he is using up valuable energy he needs for other activities. He says I am making it up, that someone has to do all the laundry. I also find that he has scoured our closets, taking stuff to the dry cleaners' that none of us has worn in years.

About eight or nine months after the accident, an even scarier obsessive-compulsive streak begins to emerge. Compulsive buying and eating are common among the brain-injured. It's ironic since Al has so little energy to spare, but he will spend it on the strangest quests. Kelly plays with a certain cloth Frisbee at another kid's house, and he searches all the toy stores in the city for an entire afternoon until he finds one for her. She mentions that she wants a particular Beanie Baby stuffed toy, and he looks everywhere for it and then sometimes buys a half-dozen in the process. He stops in stores every day and buys bunches of stuff. We're strolling on Walnut Street one evening, and I make the mistake of saying that I love a poster I see in a window. He runs out the next day and buys it for $250. It's odd, because before he was quite frugal. But his premorbid behavior did include a fascination for sales, although he seldom shopped. Alan comes from a house where his mother always had twenty-five bottles of ketchup in the basement, just in case. He liked to buy in bulk even before his brain injury, but now he's obsessed. We kid about that old joke, that God invented goys because someone has to pay retail. If there is anything on sale, he will buy it, no matter the quality. He comes home with stacks and stacks of CDs, terrible recordings, three for ten dollars. One day he walks in the door with a dozen CDs. Bill asks him, "Do you really need so many CDs?" and Al says, "That's not the point. I don't *need* any of them." Some of the CDs have still never been opened.

Strange things appear, such as a crappy used cuckoo clock, which taunts me. Alan mounts it in our family room. The little bird comes out every half hour, chortling "Cuckoo! Cuckoo!"—a comment on our new post-TBI life. Finally, blessedly, it breaks. He buys pairs and pairs of earrings for me, all on sale but nonetheless adding up to hundreds of dollars. I send Alan out for two bottles of wine, and he comes back with three cases.

Auctions are Alan's downfall. (Come to think of it, they were *our* downfall, since we got the Canadian cabin at an auction.) As a trusts and estates lawyer, he sometimes has to attend. When he is just barely back at the bank, he goes to an auction for a wealthy client's charity. He returns with the oddest things, bargains, he says. A portrait of Abraham Lincoln. Ugly pins with rhinestone butterflies. That first year, I'm not that alarmed. He's back to work, if part-time. I'm delighted to see him out and about, acting as a trust officer in a social setting. By the next year, though, our credit card bills have gone through the roof and I've been reading more about the bankruptcy rate among families with brain-injured members. Within that year, I have seen him go into Salvation Army stores in strange cities and buy chipped teapots and piles of old sweatshirts. So when he tells me he has to attend the charity auction again, I figure I will go with him, just to be safe. But at the last moment our baby-sitter cancels. Terror grips me, thinking of him alone and bidding. I ask him to sit down before he leaves. I look right at him: "Alan, you are not to buy anything over twenty dollars. You understand?" He says he does. I get him to promise that he won't. I make him repeat the promise.

At about ten that evening, he comes in with a big shit-eating grin. He thinks I will be really pleased because he got a great bargain. He bought a vacation in a cabin. On a lake. Only nine hundred and fifty dollars. He can't understand why that would upset me.

I spend a lot of time running around undoing what he has done. This is not unusual. I've corresponded with the loved ones of the brain-injured; they've told me of discovering that their father or husband went out and bought an expensive car, a trailer, a vacation. In this case, Alan's client comes to the rescue, buying back the vacation and giving it to a nephew. On another occasion, I get a strained call from the secretary at Kelly's school. There's been a silent auction, and Alan was the high bidder on at least six expensive things. I'm amazed. I had seen him looking at the booklet and said, "Now, Al, don't get any stuff from there. That's not for us."

The secretary is so nice when I begin to cry. "Look, we understand he has a problem. We can just give everything to the next-highest bidder."

"What did he buy?" I choke out. She lists crystal vases, earrings, restaurant meals. In the end, we decide we should let him "win" one of the bids, a sushi dinner. Otherwise he will obsess about why none of his bids was successful.

. . .

I miss the old Al's cynicism, his sarcasm, his incredibly witty, verbal nastiness. His verve now is directed at inanimate objects that get in his way, not at ideas. Aside from his temper tantrums, he is placid, almost blank. He smiles a lot more. He doesn't worry much. "He's lost his edge," says my friend Jon when I try to describe how hopelessly "nice" and child-like Al seems. I doubt very much that the New Alan could come up with some of the Old Al's most cynical routines, such as his insistence that "the chicken is the buffalo of the Jew. Think about it. We eat it. We use its feathers for our beds and pillows. We even use its fat."

The New Alan tells me all the time now that I am the most beautiful woman in the world. It's hard to complain about excessive devotion, but I miss his dark side. I miss the guy who told me when I was pregnant with Kelly that he didn't mind us having a kid, but he was damned if he would ever go to Disney World, "even *if* the kid ever got a terminal illness and that was his last request." I always loved his ironic bitter-ness, and he was one of the few people who could really make me laugh aloud with his unexpected take on things. Now I wince as he chortles over mediocre cartoons. He has the personality of a slightly loony backslapping salesman. If others find him less threatening now, it's because with TBI he has become what he wasn't before, a regular, uncompli-cated guy.

Yet sometimes I can understand why the rest of the world finds Alan's new softness more appealing. He has no defenses. He is an open book and seems very emotionally available to people. One night, a year after his injury, we go out with Valerie and Jon, dear friends of ours who run a café, and a few other neighbors. Valerie has just found out that a rare lung disease is likely to kill her in the next few years. Valerie is French and cultivates a cynical Gallic affect. She drops her news casually in the middle of dinner, so offhand-edly that we think she is kidding. "Oh, yes, I am dying!" she insists merrily, and takes another sip of champagne. The rest of us sit there, shocked and trying not to overreact. Alan, who has no social filters left on his reactions, bursts into loud sobs. Valerie turns to me: "It is not like Alan to be so upset!" Yet I can tell that Al has disarmed her, that his sobs are the only adequate reaction to finding out that someone you love might soon die. Everyone at the table feels this way but cannot express it so immediately. This is what people mean, I think, when they say that brain-injured people, in their child-like openness, are examples of what the rest of us should be.

Still, I miss Alan's eyes. His old eyes. The ones that were connected to his original brain. They had a sparkle that's missing now. "The eyes are the windows of the soul" goes the saying. Is Al's soul different? When I look into his post-TBI eyes, they seem dull, almost zombielike. I keep a set of snapshots of the old Al in my office; each time I take them out, his former gaze captures me once again.

People ask: how much has Alan recovered? They seem to want numbers. Out of 100 percent, how much has he come back?

To satisfy them, I'll say he's come almost all the way back, 95 percent. That sounds acceptable. It makes people happy and comfortable. Wow, he made it back 95 percent! But what does that mean? Nothing. It's as stupid as that old chestnut "We only use ten percent of our brainpower," which no one's ever been able to prove. Someone just started saying it and it sounded good, so they passed it on, and the 10 percent brain theory wended its way into conversational folklore. There is no real way of quantifying the brain. I can't say, in terms of percentages, how much Alan has recovered. What percentage of his brain is used in his work? What's the part that now allows him to drive, to make appointments, to take Kelly to her soccer, basketball, and softball games? Does he get extra points for being able to go to a Philip Glass opera or reread a Pinter play, as he did recently? Are percentage points deducted for irrational or inappropriate behavior, which happens all the time?

A better answer when people ask how much Alan's recovered or if he is now better, is "You never get hit on the head that hard and remain exactly the same. He is different, but he is remarkable. He's high-functioning and able to work part-time again."

Or I can try to educate them about TBI, tell them that brain injury is an event from which one never fully recovers. The aftereffect of a major blow to the head is a lifelong, chronic condition that will have its flare-ups and remissions. And a severe brain injury inevitably causes personality changes. Still, Alan's recovery has been remarkable. I can joke: finally, all of Alan's esoteric learning—the ancient languages, the philosophy, the linguistic theory—has paid off. Because although the evidence is strictly anecdotal, doctors and therapists have told me that smart, well-educated people often do better after brain injury. Why?

No one knows, exactly, why it's good to be smart if you get hit on the head. Yet doctors and therapists reach into a grab bag of similes and metaphors to explain a good outcome such as Alan's, one that leaves the person with TBI high-functioning, or even, in rare cases such as his, able to reenter the workforce.

Your brain is like your body: the better shape it's in, the better exercised at the time of injury, the faster and better it will recover.

Your brain is like a computer, and TBI is more like a reconfiguration than a loss. The more RAM of memory you had up there in the beginning and the more powerful "processor" you were toting around, the better the chances that the system will work reasonably well after it crashes, once the hard drive has been defragmented. Did you have a

Pentium brain or an old 286? Or were you one of the more creative iconoclasts working with a Power Mac?

Your brain is a complex highway system with superhighways of information plus secondary roads and byways. If you've studied and read and thought a lot in your life, even when your superhighways get blocked you have the complete infrastructure to fall back on. Those secondary and tertiary roads, even down to the unpaved ones, can be built up, forced to become major thoroughfares for information and memory.

Yet none of these analogies addresses the mystery of personality. Who are we? Is the spirit of a person, his or her essence, merely an accident of chemicals and neurons? If Alan or anybody else can get hit on the head and become a different person, what does that say about the very nature of being human?

13

The time course of TBI is prolonged and, in some cases, lifelong.

—"Rehabilitation of Persons with
Traumatic Brain Injury," National
Institutes of Health Consensus
Development Conference Statement

This stage, Alan's return to work, is hard for me. I have no control over it, for one thing. I don't know as much about what is happening at the bank compared with Alan's increasing competence in his small, at-home law practice. But I can hope, and I can guess. Bill is wonderful at filling me in by phone, and at the end of each month he produces a written report.

According to Bill's reports, when the task at hand requires old learning, "he has been able to perform his job well. He has completed numerous tasks on his accounts and has been able to explain, without difficulty, what needs to be done by other people. I attended several meetings that Mr. Forman had with customers or co-workers and he participated well and acted professionally." Already, only a month after his return, Alan has started attending some meetings on his own.

The tricky part comes when Alan faces learning new skills, such as the bank's marketing-oriented computer program.

According to Bill, Al has experienced difficulty with new learning in two sessions already. In trying to acquaint himself with the new computer program, Bill writes, Alan "needed to exert much more effort than he reportedly would have had to before his injury. More importantly, his learning was much slower and less complete than would be predicted based on his education and occupation pre-injury."

Change is very difficult for the brain-injured, and learning new skills falls squarely into that category. Plus, Al had the idea, before his injury, that computers were stupid. He's always been stubborn about technology; now that tendency, exacerbated by his TBI, comes back to haunt him. He will do anything not to learn the new client-software program. He acts like a little kid refusing to do his homework. He admits to me that he lies to Bill, telling him he has starting using the software when he hasn't even touched it.

Around this time there's an unwelcome change for Al in our house, too. Kelly turned eight in February, and for years we'd promised that she would get a puppy for her eighth birthday. She's one of those kids who lives for animals. I know it's a bad idea to add another critter to our menagerie, but I don't have the heart to tell her we can't get a dog because her dad is brain-injured. For the last seven months all she's heard is "No, we can't do that because Daddy is tired. No, Dad is taking a nap. Try to stay away from Daddy, because he's very stressed." Am I going to tell her now that she can never have a puppy? I decide she's got to be allowed some trappings of a normal childhood. In the middle of April we drive to the wilds of south Jersey and pick out an adorable gray-and-white Jack Russell terrier pup. Kelly names him Silver.

Al hates the puppy, really hates him. Twice I catch him, when he thinks I'm not looking, giving the poor little thing a swift kick. Kelly and I do most of the walking at first—on the few occasions Alan gets pressed into service, he holds the leash so tight that the tiny dog chokes, and then Al screams at him for choking.

Alan has always loved animals, but his family never had a dog, so he has no "old learning" or attitudes stored away about how to treat a canine. He decides that they are stupid. The dog can't use a litter box like our cats. It bites him when it tries to play. It can't even climb on the fences in the yard or purr.

"Jews don't keep dogs," he says when our friends ask why he doesn't like Silver. He's always swearing at the puppy and calling it an idiot. The stress level of the household escalates—just what a family living with TBI needs. Al and Kelly go down to the park to walk the puppy while I cook dinner, and twenty minutes later she comes home crying: "Daddy hit Silver!" My mother offers to find another home for the dog, but I drag my feet. "Cathy, face it, he's never going to adjust to that dog," she says.

I try to imagine the situation from Kelly's point of view as she tells her sad childhood stories, drunk or stoned, late at night in her college dormitory. There's a terrible accident, followed by years of verbal abuse at the hands of a father who often acts like a bratty thirteen-year-old brother. Then she gets the thing she wants most, a puppy, and her parents take it away from her. A friend of mine whose father died suddenly when he was twelve still obsesses about the added trauma of his mom's giving away his dog because they couldn't afford to keep it anymore.

When does Al stop hating the dog? I don't remember. It takes months, maybe a year, but suddenly his attitude does a complete flip-flop. His brain adjusts to the concept of Silver. "I love that dog," he says, misting up. He says he's loved him all along. He and Silver go on long walks together, where strange things happen—Silver falls into the water at the Tinicum Marsh and into the muddy depths of the Delaware Canal near my mother's house. I always worry that Al's lapses in judgment will be the dog's undoing, that the dog will drown or get run over. Though I make Al promise he'll put Silver on a leash while walking the city streets, I often look out my office window and see the dog off his tether, with Al walking far behind. Al calls him "Mr. Buppy" and includes him in his shopping sprees, coming home with dozens of rawhide bones and other doggie paraphernalia. "A boy and his dog," Alan says, not totally ironically. One day I come home to see Alan stretched out on the couch with Silver's snout nestled in his armpit. "Thank you for getting me this little guy," he says dreamily.

The bank is holding a reception for its officers and trust clients at the Philadelphia Museum of Art. Set up at the main entrance, near the stunning marble staircase, it's an elegant party, with an impressive spread of hors d'oeuvres and gorgeous floral displays. Alan looks fine—his coworkers don't know that he took a long nap this afternoon so that he'd be able to function at the party. I'm very emotional, watching him greet clients and tell them that yes, he is better. I notice how open, how casual he is about his injury. He fumbles a few names and says, "Well, you'll have to forgive me. Ever since I got hit on the head, I forget things sometimes."

One client, the woman whose charity auctions he attends, asks me about the accident, and I realize after a few minutes that I'm giving her much more detail than she needs. She just wants to know that the accident was serious, dramatic, that Alan is a walking miracle.

Al's supervisors are already pressuring him to add more hours. They seem to think that he'll be back up to speed in a few more months, even though Dr. Weinstein at Magee keeps signing statements that it would be medically danger- ous for Alan to work more than twenty hours a week. Bill's job has been to educate Alan's coworkers about brain injury and cognitive fatigue, but they ignore what he says. Bill and Al have several meetings with his bosses about workload and expectations; Bill is concerned because Alan is still carrying a full caseload—more than full, in fact, because the average load is 170 accounts and he is still responsible for about 220. It's as if the bank is trying to bully Al into coming back full-time by refusing to cut the number of clients he has. The situation continues for months, and Alan gets more behind in his work—even though he increases his hours to twenty a week, who could possibly keep up with that many contacts? One time his boss takes him aside and says he should be working more hours: "So you're tired. I get tired at the end of the day, too, you know."

Bill is really angry about the bank's attitude, and so is Crystal Mangir of the OVR. In a meeting, Crystal explains to Alan that his expectation of going back to work full-time is fairly unrealistic for someone with a severe brain injury, especially at this point. "Gee, I always thought I'd go back to work full-time within a few months," he says, even though he and I have talked about how part-time work might be all he'll ever be able to manage. I wonder how this man, who arrives home at one in the afternoon looking as if he's just climbed Mount Everest, imagines he'd be able to survive a full day at trusts and estates work. Sometimes Al can barely climb the stairs to drop into bed, minutes after he gets home. But his self-awareness is not returning. One day, almost a year after the accident, Alan calls me from work. An insurance agent wants to shift Al's life insurance policy to a different company, and he's asked if Alan suffered any blow to his head or any bleeding in his brain during the accident. He says he doesn't know but he'll call his wife.

"Alan, that's *exactly* what happened to you. You had a severe brain injury. There was bleeding and swelling all over your brain."

"Oh, really? Well, I told the guy my wife would know."

Amazingly, his lack of self-awareness doesn't seem to affect his job skills much. He continues to get excellent evaluations. He makes his sales goals. Even some of the non-brain-injured employees haven't been using the new computer system, so it's not an issue yet.

Finally, in June, an edict comes down: Al either has to start working full-time or "consider another situation." Meeting that month, the rehab team focuses on whether it would be better for Al to find another part-time job or try to fight the bank through the Americans with Disabilities Act, which specifies that employers must make "reasonable accommodations" for workers with disabilities. There haven't been many TBI cases tried under the ADA, but we think that a need to work part-time is reasonable. It's not as if the bank hasn't allowed new mothers, even at Alan's level, to work part-time. It's just being rigid, inflexible. The people there say that no one has ever held Alan's job, a vice president–level trust officer position, as a part-time employee. They say they can't imagine how to create such a position. It's a failure of imagination, of concrete thinking— maybe the bank is brain-injured, too.

We briefly consider trying to place Alan in another job, but every time I contemplate the enormous stress that would entail, I think: He can do the work. Let's fight to keep him where he is. For dramatic effect, Crystal Mangir tells us that there's always the choice of capitulating to the bank. "I have one client with a brain injury as severe as Alan's. He works full-time, but that is all he does. He comes home at five o'clock and goes to bed. Is that the kind of life you want, Alan, especially in a house with a young child?"

The pressure for Al to return full-time never lets up. I admit to becoming bitter: if Alan had never returned to work, the bank would have been forced to pay three quarters of his salary in disability benefits for life. Instead, he chose to work hard and come back and make only half his salary. I think about him sending the imaginary faxes when he was just out of his coma. Getting back to work was all he thought about as soon as he could walk and talk again. Eventually, we get Kelly's soccer coach, Harold Goodman, to write the bank asking for an accommodation: he details how and why Alan wants to remain a long-term part-time employee. Harold, a great labor lawyer, writes a moving letter, recapitulating all that Alan has been through and noting how hard he has strived to be a valued employee again.

The letter, sent to First Union's headquarters in North Carolina, gets results. We find out that Alan can stay permanently as a part-time employee. It takes another six months, but the bank eventually reduces the number of his accounts. It even gives him a small raise, based on good evaluations. Then, in the very week when the Pennsylvania Office of Vocational Rehabilitation closes his case, deeming him a success story, Alan is laid off, supposedly in an across-the-board reduction-in-force initiative.

"How do you feel?" Bill Gardner asks me over the phone on the day Alan is fired. Bill is surprised and upset that the bank would pull something like this after all the hard work Alan has put into his reentry. I feel betrayed and very angry. Alan merely seems befuddled. He can't feel hostile about such things, and when I rant and rave about how convenient it was that the bank waited to disguise its obvious discrimination, he says nothing. The only other person laid off in Alan's department is a woman in her seventies. We talk to Harold, who makes some inquiries. He feels that our suspicions are right but that it would take years to fight such a case. Instead, he suggests that he approach the bank and point out that Alan filed a complaint before, that he has a disability, and that this could look like retaliatory action. His goal: to get Alan extra severance pay. In the end, he negotiates four months more pay and extended benefits. A few months after Alan's dismissal, we find out that First Union is hiring trusts and estates officers again.

Alan still knows many lawyers in town, and he easily picks up a temporary job as a maternity replacement in a law firm. Ironically, the woman he replaces is in his old trusts and estates position at Montgomery, McCracken, Walker & Rhoads. We hope, initially, that he might be able to stay on part-time even after she returns, but that doesn't happen and Alan must begin looking for a part-time legal job again.

I can't help but wonder what will happen to Alan in the future. The bank's dismissal was a terrible blow and seemed to mock all of his rehabilitation efforts. He merely wanted to work part-time, and he was performing well. Wasn't it bad enough that the accident effectively stopped the momentum of Alan's career during his prime years? I worry, too, because I know what happens to many TBI survivors in the first five years: they begin a downward trajectory, eventually becoming unemployable. In future years we will have to make decisions about what Alan can and can't do and avail ourselves of whatever services we can to allow him to work to his full potential, which now looks as if it will be part-time employment for the rest of his life.

On the bright side, the New Alan is an outgoing, cheerful guy. He still has marketable skills. People like him, and he is part of a strong community of friends and business acquaintances. He is currently going to networking lunches and calling everyone he can think of to get a job. I smile when I think of how much initiation that takes, with or without a brain injury. I'm proud of him. I like to think that somehow the job situation will stabilize if we remain attentive and Alan's health stays good.

One day, three months after Alan is fired, his Canadian

client Jim DaCosta calls. "What's going on, eh?" he says. "I just got this letter from the bank saying that Alan left to 'pursue other opportunities.'" I relish the chance to let loose my hostilities and tell Jim the whole story of how the bank ultimately treated my husband. It's almost a relief that Alan no longer has the job, so I don't have to lie as I've been doing in my conversations with Jim ever since Alan returned to work, pretending that the bank is an honorable institution.

On the wall of our kitchen, next to a crayon sketch made by Kelly in the second grade, hangs one made by her dad, who went to pick her up one day and decided to try his hand at grade-school art. Kelly's little hippie school doesn't have grades in the beginning—they call the different years Primary Units (P.U.) 1, 2, and 3. Al signs his drawing of an insect "Alan—P.U. 25."

Alan tries very hard to be a good father to Kelly, sometimes to the point of overindulging her. But I console myself by thinking that his excessive attention to her requests and his extravagant, misguided gifts somehow make up for all the nasty things he can't stop himself from saying whenever the cognitive fatigue engulfs him. He enrolls her in all the sports she wants to play, tutors her in the finer points of hitting a baseball or kicking a soccer goal, and attends all her games with gusto. For father and daughter, sports have become a wordless bonding ritual, a sacred place where both can please each other. When Kelly wants to take up horseback riding, I say the lessons are too far away, but Alan makes the commitment to drive her every Tuesday afternoon to the city-run stables near the Wissahickon woods, a half hour from our house.

. . .

Al's new wackiness, when it doesn't aggravate the hell out of me, can be enchanting. He was always fairly romantic, but now he's downright sweet. I come home from a long business trip and he has filled the living room with roses. He leaves mushy cards all around. When I mention that there's a particular novel I've wanted to read, he buys it and brings it home the next day. If I land a big consulting job, he stocks the refrigerator with champagne.

Of course, there's the flip side. He gets it into his head to order three thousand praying mantises from a garden catalog (our urban backyard is about twelve by ten feet). Apple trees arrive in the mail. He finds two garter snakes down at the park and brings them home. One of them escapes in the house, and we never find it. He lets Kelly talk him into "surprising" me with a Christmas tree that is more than fifteen feet tall and six feet wide. It takes two days, three saws, and the help of three friends to get it even to stand up in our living room. Basically, there's never a dull moment.

Brain injury, Alan and I often say, is the gift that keeps on giving.

He's frustrated by his physical clumsiness. I watch him try to put on his coat, snagging his hand again and again on the right sleeve. If he's really tired, he loses his perception of where his body is in space. He stands up in a diner and brushes against a tray, spilling cream all over the floor. One night we're out in a restaurant with friends and Alan leaves the table. A moment later we hear a loud *thwack!* and all the patrons turn their eyes toward the patio, where Alan has just tried to walk through the screen door. ("Did you hear about the man who walked through a screen door and strained himself?" I say, remembering one of my dad's dreadful jokes.)

Only recently have I begun explaining to Alan that he could have a seizure at any time in the future. I don't want to belabor the point, but it's a possibility. People with TBI can be seizure-free for years and then suddenly suffer one. The caregivers on my Internet list often report renewed seizure activity in their loved ones, sometimes decades after the initial injury. I worry about it and watch for the signs all the time. But how would I be able to tell, really, if Alan were having a seizure or a stroke or just exhibiting some of the more extreme TBI symptoms that can flare up at any time? One Saturday night we have a few guests over for dinner, and Al is so tired that he can't follow even the simplest parts of the conversation. He even seems to be having trouble chewing his food. I fear the worst, but after he leaves the room and naps for just fifteen minutes, the symptoms subside.

Alan goes through a period of getting stung by bees. He's allergic, so it's truly awful—his eyes and lips swell up until he looks barely human. One sunny morning I accompany him down to our garden plot. There's a beehive right behind it. I watch as Al walks toward our tomato plants, and there's only one way to put it: he's walking *into* the bees. It's a strange sight. His movements are erratic, just ever so slightly "off," and the bees can't judge exactly how to fly around him. "Fuck fuck fuck!" he yells as a few brush against him. No wonder he's been getting stung repeatedly.

I feel crazy even mentioning this incident to others: The Man Who Walked into Bees. But Sarah understands. "It's like when you're swimming toward a school of fish," she says, "and they know automatically how to part and swim around you. Swarms of insects do that flying through the air, too. I believe you—Al's confounding the bees."

"The sudden loss of smell (anosmia) is not uncommon after sudden blows to the head," says a small entry in *Basic Clinical Neuroanatomy*. The olfactory bulb in Alan's brain must have been damaged: he hasn't been able to smell anything since the accident. It's a greater loss for him than I realize at first. In a pine forest high in the mountains, I comment on the delightful, fresh aroma. "You know I can't fucking smell anything!" he says and begins to cry. Loss of smell has other strange consequences. He's packed spoiled food in Kelly's lunch box, and when Silver rolls in goose crap or dog poop he thinks it's just mud. Also, I must sometimes tell him that *he* smells, since he has waited too long between showers and can't tell.

The New Alan still gets overstimulated very quickly. A year and a half after his injury, we go to New York on an overnight trip. I suddenly feel as though I'm married to a bumpkin, not a man who grew up in Brooklyn and went into Manhattan sometimes several times a week. "There are so many people here," he says as we walk the sidewalks. "I mean, wow. I can't believe how many people, look at them all, and the noise!" He marvels; his comments seem to be on a continuous loop. A horn will go off, a vendor will bustle by, a huge crowd of pedestrians will surge toward us as a light turns green, and he starts once again expounding on how hectic New York is. Yet miraculously, he can still do many things he did before. On Broadway that trip we see a revival of Ionesco's *The Chairs* and the new Mamet play. We go to a lot of theater in Philadelphia, too. If anyone had told me, in the few months following Alan's accident, that he'd be able once again to enjoy a very complicated, verbal play, I would have laughed bitterly.

I love going out with Alan, because, as the brain injury experts put it, "he responds to external cues." In our house he can actually act more brain-injured than in public—at home he just lets it all hang out. But when we're in a restaurant or at a play, he usually acts appropriately. Then I can see glimpses of the Old Alan. These experiences remind me of the dreams I had after my father died, when he would be alive again and I would be hugging him or talking to him eagerly. When I awoke, I'd be depressed that my father really was gone but happy that I could still imagine him in his fullness. I feel the same way about the brief and tantalizing brushes I have with the Ghost of Alan Past.

"Daddy is still the one who finds things," says Kelly, and she's right. I can't believe that Al's ability to locate objects came back even though cognitive therapists predicted it wouldn't. He loses things more than he used to but still far less than I, a person who owns six hairbrushes so that she can be sure to locate one at any given time.

Not all the cognitive deficits have lessened, though. The New Alan will often say anything that pops into his head. He can work to control the disinhibition, but things slip out. Seated at Kelly's class play, he turns to the parent next to him and says loudly, "Gee, there are a lot of Jews in this school. I never knew there were so many Jews." The parent doesn't quite know how to respond. "Al," I whisper. "That's a weird thing to say."

"What? What?" He gets louder. "I'm a Jew. I'm allowed to say it. Look—look at the names in this program. I'm just saying a lot of them are Jews."

To tell the truth, the injury seems to have reactivated Alan's obsession with being Jewish, which he had as a teenager and somewhat when I first met him in his twenties. Nowadays I sometimes call Alan my bar mitzvah boy.

Kelly, who has inherited Al's athletic skills, gets recruited for a special basketball team at the Jewish Y, and Al points out to some unfortunate parent at practice that technically Kelly isn't Jewish, because her mother isn't. Then he discovers that one player has only a Jewish grandmother. "Hey," he says, "what are we playing by here, Hitler's rules?" Kelly and I have become accustomed to cringing.

At Magee someone told me about a TBI patient who

returned fairly successfully to his job as a pharmaceutical executive. Yet once, at a corporate reception, he suddenly broke away from the other guests and ran over to the food table, where he ran his finger down the length of the celebratory cake and licked the icing off his finger.

Gatherings of any sort can get Alan all jazzed up, too. At Jimmy Schank's Easter egg–decorating party the first year after the accident, Al creates several obscene eggs with giant phalluses and pretty realistic pubic hair. Luckily, his disinhibition is hardly noticed at this gathering, where some of the guests are watching a documentary on male strippers in the next room.

Two summers after Al's injury, we attend an elegant cocktail party at the home of friends. I beg him not to wear his totally inappropriate African shorts outfit, a hideous gold-and-aqua print short set. "Inappropriate" has become a big term around our house. I tell him it's a nice party. I ask him to dress like a grown-up. He refuses to change. In the ridiculous ensemble, he looks like that old TV detective, Cannon, on vacation. Then, as we're getting out of the car, the drawstring on the shorts breaks, so he has to hold up his pants with one hand for the entire evening. All the other men are wearing khakis and blazers. As soon as we arrive at the party I ditch him, staying as far away as possible and hitting the gin and tonics fairly steadily. I can hear him laughing hysterically every few moments, and once when I bring myself to look over, his head is tilted to the sky in mirth and his shorts are slipping down.

A man approaches me. "Hey, I love your husband. He laughs at all my jokes."

"Well, I wouldn't get too excited. He's brain-injured. He laughs at everything." I immediately regret saying it.

"Yeah, he told me."

"He did?"

"Yeah. I said to him, 'By the way, why are you wearing pajamas?' and he said, 'Don't you know? I have brain damage.'"

Later this man's wife comes up to me with an interesting story. She says she asked about Alan's accident, and he told her very solemnly that he has been reborn. He used to be Alan, but now he has a new identity. He is now "Al."

Al shows other signs of regaining some self-awareness as he moves along on his TBI journey. One night we're eating out with Joellen in our favorite Vietnamese restaurant. Al goes to the bathroom and comes back.

"Well, that was a brain injury moment," he says, explaining that he'd almost peed in the wastebasket before he realized it wasn't a urinal.

Now that I've become steeped in the literature and jargon and life of the brain injury community, I keep thinking about one sentence from the Episcopal Book of Common Prayer that used to intrigue me as a child: "We are not worthy so much as to gather up the crumbs under thy Table." Of course, this line is addressed to Jesus, but it often comes to mind when contemplating the lives of other brain injury families. I want to say to them, Please forgive me. I don't even deserve to be thought of as a caregiver. I'm not made of the same mettle as you. How can I even pretend to be suffering, how dare I complain, when so many of you are struggling to care for your immobile, incontinent loved ones twenty-four hours a day, seven days a week, and I'm traipsing out to the theater with a husband who can make dinner reservations and take our kid to softball practice? Gee, my credit card bills are high. Boo-hoo.

Alan is an anomaly, an incredibly high-functioning survivor of TBI. We have been lucky. The wide world of the brain-injured includes people who never wake up from coma, people whose TBI has made them blind, those who never speak or walk again, who remain agitated or confused for the rest of their lives. Only one in twenty of the hundreds of thousands of seriously brain-injured people in our country gets the proper rehabilitation for TBI. Their families give up their jobs and social lives to care for them and fight for their medical benefits. Brain injuries, severe and mild, occur in the United States at the rate of two million per year, constituting what medical experts are just beginning to call "a silent epidemic."

At the Sunday-morning brunch at the Brain Injury Association USA's conference in New Orleans in 1998, I begin talking to a cheerful, friendly woman from the Louisiana rice-growing region. Her son sustained a severe brain injury in a car accident his senior year of high school. Just as she is telling me about how, at the age of twenty, her son is bedridden and can only point to letters on a board, Alan runs up behind us at the buffet and taps me on the shoulder. "I've saved you a seat!" he says, and I can see the astonished look on my new friend's face when she finds out that Alan is also a brain injury survivor.

"I think I am much happier now," Al says. "I feel kind of peaceful about myself. I think I used to worry too much, and now I don't worry at all."

He's right. He can back a friend's car into a garage pillar, defend himself by saying, "The fucking pillar was in the way!" and then start humming only a few moments later. The Old Alan would have obsessed about doing something like that. The Old Alan would have been kicking himself. But not now. Alan was always edgy, neurotic. Before the accident he suffered from insomnia and depression. He used to be sick all the time with colds and the flu, and I always suspected it was due to stress. Since the accident he hasn't had a single cold. Now he acts as if he hasn't a care in the world.

In May, ten months after the accident, Alan and I decide to go away for our wedding anniversary. But by the time we work out the dates when Sarah and Joanne can watch Kelly and figure out where we will go, our trip is delayed and our window for getting away coincides with the dreaded anniversary of the accident. I am feeling anxious about the approach of July 1, but I find I can't really talk about it. Later I hear from other caregivers and from trauma experts that it is natural to feel depressed on such significant dates. Since Alan doesn't remember the accident, the date means nothing to him. Kelly also doesn't seem to realize its significance. She's excited about staying with Sarah and Joanne. I figure maybe we can just pretend we're celebrating our wedding anniversary a little late. I still want to get away.

So in late June, Alan and I find ourselves in Key West, one of my favorite places. It's suffocatingly hot, but we have a wonderful air-conditioned suite at the Casa Marina, a 1920s hotel that's been updated. Clark Gable and Carole Lombard once stayed here, and I'm a sucker for that kind of nostalgia. The ocean water is so warm you can go in and out with no thought of a towel.

Of course, the brain injury is always with us. Al admits that he cannot for the life of him figure out how to get around the town, which is strange, since he's been in Key West before and it is a tiny place, squeezed onto the southernmost island in the United States, no wider than ten streets.

Staying here is heaven. Every day we are on the beach until about five and then we go back to our room and make love, falling into a deep sleep afterward. Then we go out again to float in the sea and watch the vivid sunset. We resume an old, silly game we used to play when we were in our twenties: Al carries me around in the water, cradled in his arms like a baby, and then I carry him. It's endlessly amusing and soothing. We go out to dinner at about ten every night. There's little of the stress of real life, so Al seems even higher-functioning than usual.

I'm so relaxed, I almost don't notice that our next-to-last day is the dreaded July 1, the date when our lives took a terrible turn. At about the time last year that Alan was being transferred to the ICU, we're floating in the tepid water, watching the sun sink over the tranquil bay. It feels almost too perfect.

"Just think of me as your third husband," Al says at dinner that night. I laugh. He's never really gotten over the fact that he's my second husband—he hates the idea of my brief, unhappy marriage that ended when I was twenty-one.

"Oh yeah?" I say. "But where did my second husband go?"

A year after Alan's injury, one of our neighbors stops me on the street. Do I feel as if we have our old life back? she asks.

"What we have," I say, "is a reasonable facsimile of our old life."

Around the same time, I find, in a pile of stuff in our basement, a black plastic case containing the audiotapes we took with us on our car trip to Canada. It's the same box of tapes I eventually took to the hospital in Kingston after our Toyota had been fetched from the lake and Alan was still in his coma. I can't resist the compulsion to trip the latch and open it. Eventually I write down the names of all nineteen tapes inside, and over the next few days I listen to them. Rosemary Clooney, Leo Kottke, Patsy Cline, Bobby Short, Sarah Vaughan, Michael Feinstein, the Nat King Cole Trio, Diane Schuur, B.B. King, and many more singers warble in my office, bringing back those afternoons and evenings when it was just me, a comatose Al, and the music in the ICU. I remember that one nurse said she liked to come by to take Alan's vital signs so she could listen to our tape of Ella Fitzgerald and Louis Armstrong singing Cole Porter. Discovering the audio remnants of those terrible days is like finding the black box after a plane crash, all the information still intact.

On the first Christmas after the accident, Honey's daughter Courtney gave us a handsome black-and-white photograph of a smiling Kelly jumping high on a huge trampoline in their backyard in upstate New York. It was taken at about the time Alan woke up in Canada, five days after the accident, when Kelly was staying with Honey's family. In the photo Kelly's hair is flying and her arms are flung high in a carefree swing. We keep the picture in our living room, and I look at it often. I like to think that even so soon after the accident, Kelly could grab a carefree moment. She could still soar into the air, escaping the painful memory of an event that would change everything for all of us.

Kelly will talk about the accident only spontaneously, at odd times, never when I ask her about it directly. On a fine spring day almost three years afterward, as I'm walking her home from school, she tells me that she's been thinking, and she knows who the Mango Princess is.

"You see, Mom," she says, putting her hands on the straps of her backpack and pushing out, "Daddy got hit on the head and he went up to Heaven. And the Mango Princess was there, and she was real nice to him, and she said he should come back to us. And he did come back, and he remembered her, just for a little while."

Acknowledgments

There are many tears in this book, and much laughter. I want to thank everyone who shared these moments with us. It takes a fairly large village to rehabilitate a person with a traumatic brain injury—this book and our current lives would be impossible if not for the kindness and dedication of hundreds of people.

Because of the chaos of the accident and its aftermath, I don't even know the names of some people who helped most. But I'll remember them forever, and if any of you reading this book were our Good Samaritans, please know that I think of you often. This includes the boaters at Bob's Lake who called the ambulances and assisted in getting Alan to shore; those generous souls in the ICU waiting room at Kingston General Hospital in Kingston, Ontario, who made tea and took my phone calls even as they awaited news about their own loved ones; and all the nurses and attendants in the ICU (especially Maureen and Kathy) who talked to me, gave me heated towels, played with our daughter, Kelly, and generally did such an excellent job of caring for Alan while he was in his coma and as he emerged. I didn't know I would ever write a book about Alan's accident, or I would have made sure to take down *all* your names!

The land and air ambulance people in Canada were fabulous, especially the Parham Rescue Squad and the government helicopter team. Thank you for your extraordinary dedication and for keeping my husband alive. Special thanks to Dr. Peter Ellis, Alan's neurosurgeon at Kingston General, who informed us about Alan's condition in a straightforward, caring way, and to all the nurses in the NICU and on the neurological floor. The social workers at Kingston General were enormously helpful in trying to sort out the problems in Alan's transfer from the sane, warm hands of an excellent national health system into the cold clutches of our uncaring HMO back in the United States.

At the Hospital of the University of Pennsylvania (HUP), many people worked to make our time there better, including Alan's neurosurgeon, Dr. Eric Zagar, his rehabilitation physician, Dr. Everett Hill, and many nurses and attendants, especially Megan on the neuro ward. I also owe a debt of gratitude to Dr. David Nicklin, Alan's primary care physician, who helped us through so many problems along the way and nurtured Alan during his recovery.

Dr. Andrew Saykin and Dr. Gwen Sprehn, friends of ours for years and both neuropsychologists, were there for me by phone when I needed them most, especially as Alan emerged from his coma. How wonderful it was to be able to talk to experts who had known Alan before the accident! They helped me anticipate many of the turns in the road ahead.

Dr. Gary Forman, Alan's brother, went above and beyond the call of duty in his dedication, leaving his young family in California to help us during one of the worst weeks ever. I thank his wife, Susan, for letting him go, and Mr. Finkelman and I are grateful for everything he did during that very trying time!

Magee Rehabilitation Hospital in Philadelphia is an extraordinary facility full of dedicated professionals, the epitome of what a healing experience should be. Thank you, everyone there, especially case manager Lisa Gordon, Dr. Dan Weinstein, Dr. John Kline, speech therapist Sue Caspari, occupational therapist Grace Smith, Dr. Barbara Watson, physical therapist Colleen Chancler, Nadine Ball, Brenda Edelman, and Dr. Kelli Williams.

At the Magee day hospital facility, Riverfront, Alan was cared for by many generous people, including Dana Trainor, Nancy Heller, Peggy Fox, Lisa Buonara, Asher Kemp, Gerry Satchel, and Judy Hirschwald.

Although I will probably never meet most of them, the caregivers who participate in the brain injury Internet listserv (CARE-TBI) from all around the country and the world are a daily inspiration to me. As we often say in our postings, only those who live with TBI and its aftereffects can truly know its grinding sorrows and losses, as well as its funny, surreal moments. The members of the list have been a constant source of comfort. Special thanks to Gil Weiner, whom I met through the list, because he has offered extraordinary understanding, information, and friendship. Thanks also to Michelle DeSilets, Peter Gross, and Kathy Boyll, three new friends whose lives have also been touched by TBI, who were there for me during the writing of this book.

What would we have done if we'd never found Crystal Mangir of Pennsylvania's Office of Vocational Rehabilitation? Her dedication to the special needs of brain injury survivors and their families should be a model for all those in the helping professions. Crystal's advice led us to the Community Skills Program, where Alan's rehabilitation team included the very helpful Cheryl Boyd, and Bill Gardner, the counselor who would spend nearly two years helping Alan reenter and succeed in the working world.

William Gardner, Ph.D., was and continues to be an amazing resource for Alan and me. Not many neuropsychologists are forced to work in the midst of laundry baskets, stacks of magazines and books, five antsy cats, and a tiny crazy puppy. Bill retained his equilibrium and sense of purpose as he became a part of our nutty household and later Alan's guide and companion at the office. He also finished his dissertation at the same time, and we commend him for it.

James and Susan DaCosta, who started out as Alan's clients and became fast friends, were wonderfully supportive. Jim even drove our car back from Canada and visited Alan at HUP in Philadelphia. Thank you.

Alan's coworkers at his bank and at the law firms where he had previously worked were great. They came to see him, bearing junk food and refusing to freak out at his disabilities. So often, the brain-injured become isolated and lose friends during hospitalization and rehabilitation. We have been enormously lucky and feel blessed by the community around us.

St. James Shatzer made Al's room the most spectacular on Magee's brain injury unit with his lovely arrangements and other kindnesses. Jimmy Schank brought us entertainment and Indian food. Sandy Masayko fetched groceries and used her keen skills as an occupational therapist to cajole Al toward recovery. Kay Dowgun was a rock of support for me and a loving, calming presence for Alan, always. Kathy Mandelbaum came through time and again with meals and companionship. Rick Johansen helpfully continued Al's athletic rehabilitation at the hoops long after he had left Magee. Marsha and Jeff Gerdes offered extraordinary help to Alan and me and, to Kelly, a home away from home with her dear friend Jennifer Hoffman-Williamson. Harold Goodman provided legal expertise in dealing with Alan's job reentry, and Claudia Goodman extended understanding and good cheer.

The staff at the Lombard Swim Club provides a safe haven for our family and was especially comforting in the time immediately following the accident. Thanks, Brenda, Mack, Carol, Lenny, and so many others. Also, I'd like to thank the people of the Schuylkill River garden plot, who helped out enormously, especially Frank and Ward.

Many friends and relatives performed amazing favors for us in those months of rehabilitation and reentry. Those who offered help, visits, humor, casseroles, information, rides, financial aid, medical advice, baby-sitting, and prayers include Debbie Crimmins, Paul Goerss, Naomi Forman, Robert N. Forman, Marcia Forman Greenberg, Alan Greenberg, Ruth Stein, Craig Leon, David Saja, Steve Huntington, Sue Huntington, Richard Dowgun, Al Filreis, Susan Albertine, Jackie Buhn, Alan Razak, Ali Steele, Jim Steele, Nancy Steele, Bruce Schimmel, Kate Maskar, Carol Stillman, Joan Murphy Stack, Elizabeth Simon, John Hayduk, V. V. Wickenden, Enid Pensack, Sally Schreiber, Isabel Berchtold, Larry Balick, Nancy Adler, Bill Josem, Bernadette McKeon, Stephen Madra, Margaret Tobin, Frank Deming, Tony Farrell, Denise Farrell, Bill Doherty, Alex Thielens, Dorothy Daub, Jay Grossman, Frank Deming, Anne Dalke, Jeff Dalke, Craig McCoy, Norman Albert, Susan Albert, Martin Bodtmann, Lisa McDevitt, Jon Blum, Valerie Blum, Rebecca Lewis, Jonathan Friedlander, Patty Fox, Dan Sargent, Jane Sargent, Chris Abbot, Michael Zasloff, Fred Kaplan, Ivana Willis, Pam McCabe, Gerald Sussman, Judy Wein, Mark Kramer, Susan Harris, Frank Costello, Barbara Blake, the famous Benash, Jeff Bernstein, Jean Stevens, Jeff Abshear, Karol Childs, Ann Sarrantonio, Kathy DiLeonardo, Tom Sarrantonio, Justin Fink, Mary Ellen Jeno, Helen Jessica Jeno, Mark Weiand, Maddy Weiand, Erin Weiand, Taylor Williams, and John Wright. There were many more people, I'm sure, and I blanch at the idea of missing anyone. If I did, please forgive me.

Thanks also to *all* the wonderful staff and teachers at the Philadelphia School, who take such good care of Kelly and have helped our family with the stress of TBI, and especially to Sandy Dean, Maureen Glaccum, Tracy Hagedorn, Diane Pepe, Jane Laties, Jeff Mordan, Joan Kimball, Stephanie Gery, Helene Morlok, Anne DiMezza, Dan Lai, Marcia Kravitz, Michael Zimmerman, Neesa Procaccino, and Anne Clark. I remember also with fondness the kind help of the late Peggy Galson in that first year after the accident. We miss her.

Thank you to everyone who has helped make this story a book, especially those who assuaged my initial reluctance and encouraged the idea from the start, including Diane Kalin, Louise Berliner, Nick Proffitt, Anne Dalin, Steve Ross, Anne Kaier, Jovida Hill, Susan Robertson, Jill Galper, Michael Radyk, Terry Gillen, Sharon Berkowitz, Stephen Fried, Barbara Seaman, Ronnie Polaneczky, and Frank Garrity. I benefited greatly from talking with my friend Robin Warshaw, a wonderful writer and an ongoing source of emotional support. My editor pal Jon Winokur read parts of the manuscript and gave me several great pep talks. I'm also indebted to playwright and friend Tom O'Leary, who has the faith I'll never have and a wicked enough sense of humor to encourage my sick jokes. The spirit of our late friend John Gaggin hovers over many parts of this book, especially the hospital scenes.

Thanks are definitely due Kim Witherspoon, my literary agent, and Jordan Pavlin, my editor, who encouraged me by believing in the universality of our experience. I'm happy to have had the privilege of working with them. I'm grateful as well to Gideon Weil, Joshua Greenhut, Maria Massie, and David Forrer at Witherspoon Associates for all the care and attention they have given this project, and to Bill Contardi at the William Morris Agency. Also, many thanks to Vrinda Condillac.

I must thank the Brain Injury Association USA for its excellent work advocating for those with TBI and for allowing me to attend its national conference in New Orleans in a double role as caregiver and reporter. The students in my creative nonfiction courses at the University of Pennsylvania were also a great resource, encouraging me to use the classroom as a laboratory and sounding board for some of my concerns about nonfiction writing.

Tom Maeder, with whom I've written many books and exhibits, offered his love and usual razor-sharp research skills, going out of his way to give me the jump start I needed on learning everything about TBI. He also worked overtime in our museum-consulting business, Archimedes, while I was finishing the book. I thank him for that and for so many other things.

My good friend and fellow writer Joellen Brown, who has known Alan even longer than I have, encouraged me to transform my raw material into a memoir. With an editor's eye, she read and listened to excerpts as they were being wrenched from my tortured emotions. She's been similarly helpful throughout my career, providing the critical support most writers can only crave. I simply don't know what I would do without her friendship and advice.

The expression "We were all in the same boat" will forever carry profound meaning as I think about Alan and Kelly and the three other wonderful, brave people who went through the accident. To Honey Young, her son, Benjamin, and Sarah Babaian, I can only express deep respect and love for the way they handled themselves during the whole horrible experience. Unlike Alan, they have not been spared the painful memory of that day. They offered unconditional love at a time when they, too, were undergoing physical and psychological trauma. They tied up loose ends, fetched belongings, and took care of Kelly even as I was falling apart. I can never thank them enough for all that they did and continue to do. An accident is a terrible thing to share, yet it has made us closer.

Thanks also to our "sister" who wisely stayed home from that fateful trip—Joanne Babaian, always pitching in to help Kelly feel better.

My mother, Bette Lancaster, never flinched as she watched us confront the horrors of this experience. She's the best friend a daughter could have and, as Alan is fond of saying, the best mother-in-law in the world. She knows intuitively how to provide what a soul needs. It is a gift I envy greatly, and my admiration for her has only grown during these last few difficult years.

I want to thank, extravagantly, Kelly Sylvia Forman Crimmins, who knows that it's not easy to be either the daughter of a writer or the daughter of someone with a traumatic brain injury. The two together are a double whammy that would crush most kids. I'm proud of her strength and sense of humor. Her late grandfather, David Crimmins, would be proud of her too.

Finally, as the dedication of this book indicates, I am deeply indebted to my husband, Alan Forman, for graciously allowing me to tell his story here, no holds barred. All along, he's had to accept my narrative of events he will never remember. I thank him for allowing me the gift of honesty. His courage and dignity are truly amazing and a great part of why so many people have felt drawn to him over the years and now in his new life as a TBI survivor.

A Note About the Author

Cathy Crimmins is the coauthor of the best-selling *Newt Gingrich's Bedtime Stories for Orphans*. She has chronicled the baby boomers' slow and tortuous crawl through life in such books as *When My Parents Were My Age, They Were Old* and *Curse of the Mommy*. Her articles have appeared in *The Village Voice, Redbook, Parents' Digest, Success, Hysteria, Philadelphia Magazine, Funny Times,* and *Glamour* and have been syndicated by the *New York Times* and the *Los Angeles Times*. Crimmins is a creative consultant to science museums around the country and teaches nonfiction writing at the University of Pennsylvania. She lives in Philadelphia with her husband and daughter.

A Note on the Type

This book was set in a type called Baskerville. The face itself is a facsimile reproduction of types cast from the molds made for John Baskerville (1706–1775) from his designs. Baskerville's original face was one of the forerunners of the type style known to printers as "modern face"—a "modern" of the period A.D. 1800.

Composed by Stratford Publishing Services,
Brattleboro, Vermont
Printed and bound by Berryville Graphics,
Berryville, Virginia
Designed by Anthea Lingeman